The British
Political System

The British Political System

Samuel H. Beer
Harvard University

Reprinted from *Patterns of Government*, Third Edition

Random House, New York

First Paperbound Edition

98765432

Copyright © 1958, 1962, 1973, 1974 by Random House, Inc.

Library of Congress Cataloging in Publication Data

Beer, Samuel Hutchison, 1911–
The British political system

"Originally published as Part 2 of the third edition of Patterns of Government: The Major political systems of Europe, edited by Samuel H. Beer and Adam B. Ulam."
Bibliography: p.
I. Great Britain—Politics and government .
I.   Title.
JN175.B43   320.4'42   73–21759
ISBN 0–394–31817–x

Manufactured in the United States of America

Foreword

This volume is a paperbound edition of Part 2 of the third edition of *Patterns of Government: The Major Political Systems of Europe*. The larger work includes sections on Britain, France, Germany, and Soviet Russia and an introductory part on modern political development—all now available as separate paperbacks.

The five parts of *Patterns of Government* are integrated by the common theme of modernization. But each country account is also written so as to be suitable for study either separately or in conjunction with other countries not considered in *Patterns*. In the latter connection one attractive possibility would be a combination that would include the United States; for in each of the country accounts of *Patterns* a comparison with America, seen as a typical modern polity, is never far in the background of the analysis. Whatever one's preference, the present publication of the introduction and the country accounts as separate books provides the necessary flexibility.

A word about the general approach of *Patterns*: After a brief eclipse, history is making a strong comeback in political science, largely under such headings as "modernization" and "development." A period of neglect was healthy, since it obliged political scientists to decide what use they really wanted to make of history. In the third as in the previous editions of *Patterns*, a leading characteristic of the methodology is the use of both theory and history in the study of contemporary politics. The authors hold that patterns of political behavior in the present can be best explained if we have an understanding of how they originated and what traits they displayed in the past. In taking this view, the authors follow the example of some of the leading figures in modern political science, from Montesquieu to Weber, who used history to enlarge the body of empirical political theory and then used that theory to analyze and explain the historical process as it flows from the past through the present into the future.

Each country is examined as an example of a highly developed modern polity. This approach has two implications. First, it means emphasizing certain features the countries have in common. Second, it means treating these common features as the issue of a course of historical development moved by similar forces, passing through similar phases, and culminating in similar problems. But the stress on the common features of modernity does not lead the authors to overlook the crucial differences that distinguish the four systems. Quite the contrary. To show what is common helps them to bring out the differences more sharply. As a specialist in the country he is writing about, each author is accordingly concerned not only with its common modernity, but also with the traits and tensions that are unique to it.

What I have said in general about the country accounts of the new edition of *Patterns* applies to the present volume on Britain. For all its concern with modernization, it is not, I should like to stress, a book of mere generalities. Its pages carry a substantial load of fact. Its level of analysis is not so "scientific" that the reader will have difficulty connecting what is said in it with everyday happenings in political meetings, legislative bodies, or government offices. If he visits Britain, this book will help him recognize and understand the political life he sees, reads about and discusses with the people who live there.

Harvard University   SAMUEL H. BEER

Contents

1 The Modernity of Tradition in Britain 3
 Economic Failure 5
 Bentham and Burke 8
 The Great Age of Reform 9
 Founding the Welfare State 14
 Cabinet Government and Party Government 21
 The Bipolar Conception of Authority 23

2 Cabinet and Prime Minister 26
 Making a Cabinet 29
 Collective Responsibility 33
 The New Structure of Decision Making 36
 Prime Ministerial Government 43

3 Control of the Public Sector 48
 Ministers and Civil Servants 51
 The Question of Expertise 54
 Territorial Decentralization 59
 Functional Decentralization 62

4 Control of the Economy 66
 From Planning to Management 68
 From Management to Planning 71
 The Politics of Inflation 72
 The Treasury 75
 The New System 77

5   The Authority of Parliamen   83
    Party Government and Democracy   84
    Sovereignty and Symbolism   86
    Class Composition   91

6   The Functions of Parliament   95
    The Decline of Parliament   95
    Criticism and Control   99
    Legislation   102
    Finance and Expenditure   107
    Proposed Reforms   109

7   The Power of Parliament   114
    The Continuous Electoral Campaign   115
    Party Organization   116
    Party Discipline   119
    Back-bench Influence   121
    Opposition Influence   127
    The Inner Circle   130
    The House of Lords   131

8   The Foundations of Modern British Parties   135
    Basic Conditions of Mass Politics   135
    Party and Modernity   140
    Party and Development   145
    Party, Pressure Groups, and Class   149
    Party and the Intellectuals   152

9   The Modernization of British Parties   155
    Values and Party Development   155
    Whigs and Tories   159
    Liberals and Radicals   162
    The Radicalization of Liberalism   164
    The Collectivist Period   166
    Conservatives and Collectivism   173
    The Collectivist Consensus   175
    The Relevance of Party Government   178

10 The Continuities of Collectivist Politics   180
    Functional Representation   180
    Party Government   189
    Manifesto and Mandate   197

11 The Challenge to Collectivist Politics   201
    Party Decomposition   202
    Class and Voting   204

The New Volatility   208
Bases of Class Behavior   210
Modernization and Class   214
The Liberal Revival   216
The New Politics of Reform   218
Conclusion   220
Epilogue: Northern Ireland   221

Appendix :   British General Election Results   228

Select Bibliography   231

Index   237

UNITED KINGDOM OF GREAT BRITAIN AND NORTHERN IRELAND

SHETLAND ISLANDS

ATLANTIC OCEAN

OUTER HEBRIDES

ORKNEY ISLANDS

SCOTLAND
Aberdeen

NORTH

Glasgow
Firth of Forth
Edinburgh

SEA

Firth of Clyde

NORTHERN IRELAND
Belfast
ISLE OF MAN

Newcastle

REPUBLIC OF IRELAND

IRISH SEA

ANGLESEY

R. Mersey
Liverpool Manchester
Ship Canal
Sheffield

Leeds   Hull

R. Humber

The Wash

R. Trent

R.

Birmingham

Severn

ENGLAND

WALES

Cardiff
Bristol
Southampton

London

R. Thames

Dover

Plymouth

ISLE OF WIGHT

ENGLISH CHANNEL

FRANCE

SCALE

0 20 40 60 80 100
MILES

	Area in Square Miles	Population
England and Wales	58,649	48,770,086
Scotland	30,411	5,227,706
Northern Ireland	5,499	1,527,593
United Kingdom	94,559	55,525,205

London, Her Majesty's Stationery Office.

The British
Political System

One

The Modernity of Tradition in Britain

Writing shortly before World War I, A. Lawrence Lowell of Harvard could introduce his classic work on British government and politics with this encomium:

> Measured by the standards of duration, absence of violent commotions, maintenance of law and order, general prosperity and contentment of the people, and by the extent of its influence on the institutions and political thought of other lands, the English government has been one of the most remarkable in the world.[1]

Nor were these merits lost on the governed. "The typical Englishman," he observed,

> believes that his government is incomparably the best in the world. It is the thing above all others that he is proud of. He does not, of course, always agree with the course of policy pursued . . . but he is certain that the general form of government is well-nigh perfect . . .[2]

Fifty years later an eminent French observer, although no less Anglophile than Professor Lowell, felt compelled to make a different report. Having observed how the French early in the eighteenth century came to admire

---

[1] A. Lawrence Lowell, *The Government of England.* 2 vols. (New York, 1908), Preface.
[2] *Ibid.,* p. 507.

"the governance of England" and to spread its praises throughout Europe, Bertrand de Jouvenel noted the sharp decline of this appeal in recent years Although, in his view the British had formulated most of the new twentieth-century goals of government, during the past generation they had failed to display their usual leadership in showing how these goals could be best pursued. With understatement so British as to include the characteristic double negative, he concluded: "Surely Britain is not incompetently governed: that is not the point; the point is that its governance is not of such conspicuous excellence as to invite imitation."[3]

This gentle chiding by a courteous foreign friend is only a pale intimation of the storm of savage criticism that the British have directed against themselves during the past decade. Its crescendo was especially marked in 1963 by a special issue of *Encounter,* a decorous, highbrow journal with an international standing. The title of the special issue, "Suicide of a Nation?" did not exaggerate the harshness of its contents. Typically one contributor began:

> Each time I return to England from abroad the country seems a little more run down than when I went away; its streets a little shabbier, its railway carriages and restaurants a little dingier; the editorial pretensions of its newspapers a little emptier, and the vainglorious rhetoric of its politicians a little more fatuous . . .[4]

Through the intervening years this mood of national self-criticism has persisted. In the early seventies a perceptive journalist, reporting "the lacerating self-contempt of the past few years," could say that "Britain is living out a quiet agony."[5]

While the target of these attacks has not been confined to politics and government, they have provided a central focus of criticism. The performance of the polity is felt to be poor on many counts. As a ground of discontent, "loss of empire" has played a much smaller part than many foreigners imagine. Whatever the subconscious, psychological reactions may be, Britons explicitly show few regrets over the end of empire in Africa or the Indian subcontinent. Loss of status as a world power is considered a more serious matter. In 1945 toward the close of Britain's heroic performance in the war against Hitler, Churchill could still appear to meet with Stalin and Roosevelt on a plane of equality, but the situation is very different today. A failure to adjust to her reduced circumstances in a world of the two superpowers has troubled the sense of national purpose. The dissolving Commonwealth has not provided a substitute role, nor has the

---

[3]*Government and Opposition,* 1 (October 1965), 135–136.

[4]Malcolm Muggeridge, "England, Whose England?" *Encounter,* 21 (July 1963), 14.

[5]Patrick O'Donovan, "Who Do We Think We Are?" *The Observer* (London), June 27, 197

continuation of the wartime alliance with the United States. The third option, entering Europe, gave rise to the humiliations of de Gaulle's vetoes and then to the no less painful agonies that accompanied acceptance.

Economic Failure

Dissatisfaction with the performance of the polity, however, has been more sharply focused on economic policy than on foreign or colonial policy. In the view of politicians, experts, and leaders of opinion, the British economic record since World War II has been deeply disappointing and well below what it could have been. In his budget speech of March 30, 1971, the Conservative Chancellor of the Exchequer reflected this judgment, placing the blame—it should be noted—on previous Conservative as well as Labour Governments:

> For many years, under one Government and another, the economic performance of our country has been poor. Over these years we have become accustomed to unfavorable comparisons with other industrial countries—slow growth, recurring balance of payments weakness, faster-than-average inflation, a low rate of investment, a falling share in world exports, and increasingly bad industrial relations . . .
>
> If we are realistic we should recognize that unless there is a change in the trend —a change not only compared with the last five or six years, but with the trend over the last two decades and more—the prospect is that by 1980 our standard of living in this country will have fallen considerably behind that of most of the countries of western Europe.[6]

The economic problem, which centers on the question of more rapid growth, may be a problem without a solution. Conceivably there could be objective conditions that ineluctably condemn the British economy to a performance inferior to that of other advanced countries. If this were true, it would be a mistake to regard the inability of public policy to improve economic performance as an indication of failure in the political system. Political leaders and other students of the question. amateur and professional, however, have largely rejected this argument. Party spokesmen and prospective Prime Ministers have persisted in perceiving the problem as one that could be solved in some sense by political and governmental means.

Certain broad comparative reasons support their belief. In the first place, the British economy turned in a superb record of performance during World War II. This was the Britain that invented radar and the jet engine,

---

[6]814 *H. C. Deb.* 1358–1359 (30 March 1971).

built the Mulberries—huge floating docks used during the Normandy invasion—and, although starting far behind Germany, reached a much higher level of mobilization. In those years Britain excelled in the very spheres of material production in which today she is compared so unfavorably with many other European countries. Her record was a story not of slow-moving traditionalism, but of a highly competent, adaptable, modernizing people who showed supreme ability in that most modern of activities, total war. "You defeated us," said Albert Speer, Hitler's Minister for Armaments, "because you made total war and we did not." The basis of this economic achievement was political, as British leaders attest by their frequent efforts to recapture "the spirit of Dunkirk."

In the second place, the economies with which the British economy compares unfavorably are in the same broad stage of development. We are not comparing Britain with countries in the early stages of industrial "takeoff," but with countries that have been industrializing for more than a hundred years and that have—this is the rub—reached and surpassed the British standard of living. In 1939 at the outbreak of World War II the real product per head in Britain was the highest in the world, except for the United States. Then after the war the other advanced countries moved forward rapidly. Whether the basis is the growth rate of gross national product or the growth rate of gross national product per capita, Britain ranks at the bottom of the list. By 1970 in product per person, Britain had fallen behind not only the United States, Canada, Australia and New Zealand, but also among Western European countries: Sweden, Germany, Switzerland, France, Denmark, Norway, the Netherlands, and Belgium, in that order. By the end of the next decade it seems likely that Britain will also have been surpassed by Finland, Japan, and perhaps even Italy and Austria.

Some critics ridicule the "international G.N.P. race," and, no doubt, a blind effort to increase production, without regard to what is produced, who gets the increment, and what the side effects are, can be self-defeating. On the other hand, without improvements in productivity there is little chance of advances in economic welfare. Where economic growth lags, hospitals and schools do not get built and real wages stagnate. When we recall that Britain was one of the pioneers in constructing the welfare state, it comes as a shock to see how poorly she compares with the other states of Western Europe in this respect. During the postwar period Britain has ranked below both Germany and France in percentage of national income spent on social welfare and, in recent years, below all members of the European community. To be sure, higher welfare expenditures are not identical with a higher standard of living, since they can be more than offset by low wages. In the comparison of Britain with the continental countries, however, this factor does not greatly change the picture. In hourly earnings of manual workers (both male and female) in manufacturing industry Britain does stand above Italy and France, but falls below the other four members of the Common Market—Luxembourg, Germany, the Netherlands, and Belgium, in that order. As we shall see in more detail when we look at the pattern of policy of contemporary Britain, there are urgent needs, public and private, that could utilize a greater output of material goods and services.

Britain's industrial supremacy in the long past, the prodigies of her war economy, and the lead in recent times by countries with variously structured economies support the presumption widely and strongly shared in Britain that if her people went about the matter in the right way, they too could have the high, continuing rate of economic growth required by their public and private needs. To say in what sense the roots of the problem are political and how the failure to take such action is a fault of the political system is best left to the more detailed discussion later. Yet the general direction in which analysis leads will be briefly indicated at this point.

It will not be denied that there are specifically economic causes that contribute to Britain's problem. No doubt her position as a massive importer and exporter puts her in an exposed position in the international economy, which is made still more delicate by the use of sterling as a reserve currency by many other countries. As a result, Britain must often take steps to depress her internal economy in order to protect her balance of payments. Also, looking at her problems in the context of comparative economic development brings out important differences between Britain and other countries. Because she was the first to industrialize, Britain does have, relative to most continental countries, a smaller sector of agriculture and self-employment whose resources can be drawn into more efficient employment in large-scale industry.

Yet we can readily conceive that these problems might have been dealt with satisfactorily if it had not been for other difficulties, which are in essence political. One set of major difficulties was related to the new group politics, which emerged powerfully after the war and to which later chapters will devote a good deal of attention. In the new politics the votes of groups of consumers were pursued by the two major parties in an intense and unrelenting competition in promises of prospective benefits. As a result, consumption, both public and private, was encouraged and the proportion of national product devoted to investment depressed, long-run economic growth being sacrificed for the sake of the immediate benefits of the welfare state and private consumption. The new group politics was also involved in the inability of Governments to control the cost-push element in Britain's chronic inflation, especially in very recent years, the pushing up of wage costs by trade union pressure. Unable to reach agreements that would provide the necessary restraint, Governments of both parties have been forced to resort to severely deflationary measures, with the result that for perhaps one-half of the years since the war the operation of the economy has been deliberately depressed by public policy. Under these conditions of "stop-and-go" economic policy, economic growth could hardly fail to lag.

The failures of economic policy are serious in their own right. They are also felt and perceived as a sign and an example of a general loss of governmental effectiveness. The values of modernity charge the polity with major tasks in controlling the environment external to the political system, of which the economy is only one major sector. Failures of economic policy therefore suggest a loss of capacity to control social change in general and a loss of grip on the nation's destiny. The problem of economic policy raises this larger question of a decline in the power of the polity to adapt, to change, to cope, to solve problems that was displayed by the long success story of Britain in modern times.

Bentham and Burke

As de Jouvenel's comments suggested, British excellence in the art of government is an old story. If, therefore, we are to understand the reasons for that excellence in the past and to perceive what basic changes may have taken place and whether these account for recent deficiencies, an explanation with an appropriate time dimension must be sought. In the vast literature about British government and politics, a familiar approach promises to have the explanatory power that is required. Broadly, this approach points to the integration of both modern and traditional elements in the British polity as the grounds for its achievement. The emphasis—to borrow the title of a superb study of modernization in India—is upon "the modernity of tradition."[7]

The line of analysis is twofold: The branch emphasizing the contribution of modernity may be called the Benthamite hypothesis; that emphasizing the contribution of tradition, the Burkean hypothesis. The former directs attention to precisely those elements which constitute the cultural premises of modernity, rationalism and voluntarism. It finds in the attitudes and structures deriving from these premises the factors explaining both the responsiveness and effectiveness of British government. It is the straightforward modernist view that the liberated intelligence is a sufficient basis for political order and progress. The free marketplace of ideas tends to winnow the sound from the unsound among proposals for public policy. Election of governments gives society the means for making sure sound proposals are registered at the seat of power. The trained intelligence of the bureaucrat in turn refines these proposals so as to solve the problems

---

[7]Lloyd and Susanne Rudolph, *The Modernity of Tradition: Political Development in India* (Chicago, 1967).

originally giving rise to criticism and reform. Indeed, intelligence, whether in or out of government, is the principal and sufficient motor of the whole process of adaptation and improvement. If modernity has faults, the remedy is more modernity.

To this British version of the political theory of the Enlightenment, the Burkean hypothesis represents a skeptical but constructive reaction. In contrast with intelligence, this view points to the role of sentiment in binding men into political communities and supporting the structures by which they concert public action. Tradition is necessary to stabilize men's sense of decency. Regardless of the extent of the suffrage, a viable polity requires strong and able leadership in the form of a governing class. Tradition, hierarchy, community—these are the elements stressed in the Burkean hypothesis. They create lasting behavioral solidarities, from the "little platoons" to the great "establishments," which at once satisfy the human heart and provide a basis for effective governance. Nor is their existence incompatible with reform. On the contrary, Burke was the first British political philosopher to state explicitly and systematically the argument for continuous adaptation of public policy, making the case for reform as a normal means of both conservation and improvement.

The use of this dual approach can be illustrated by two periods of major achievement in British political development. The first is the great age of reform in the early part of the nineteenth century, when Britain fundamentally altered both her political system and her economic policy, setting for the world a pioneering example of peaceful, progressive reform. The second centers on the first half of the present century, when in response to the strains of industrialism and the rise of the working class, a period of social reform was inaugurated that ultimately led to the construction of a welfare state and managed economy—again by peaceful, parliamentary means.

The Great Age of Reform

As the record of Europe in the past and of developing countries today shows, the potential for large-scale collective violence within modernizing countries is very high. One of the particularly critical periods of transition is the onset of industrialization. Even now when the experience of many countries has made it a familiar phase of economic development, industrialization imposes severe strains on a society. All the greater and harder to control were the dangers faced by Britain when, first among nations she, so to speak, blundered into the Industrial Revolution. Again and again during the forty years after Waterloo observers foresaw the imminent outbreak of revolution. In 1817 a Swiss historian and economist visited England and was terrified by the spectacle. He predicted that unless economic development was drastically slowed down, society would pass through a series of crises ending in the destruction of civilization by a mob of angry workers.[8] Writing in 1844 of the horrors of working-class life in England's huge urban centers, the young Friedrich Engels declared that the transformation of England since 1760 had been as great as that between Bourbon France of 1789 and the France of his day. Declaring that "prophecy is nowhere so easy as in England," he foresaw a war of the poor against the rich that would be "the bloodiest ever waged."[9]

Tension centered on the great increase in numbers of two new classes created by economic modernization: the commercial and industrial capitalists and the wage-earning proletariat. While the industrial working class excited fear in conservatives and hope in socialists, it was hardly well enough organized or well enough led to be a serious revolutionary threat by itself. But the industrial working class as the potential followers of middle-class revolutionaries on the model of the French insurrectionists presented a far more formidable threat against the entrenched power of aristocracy.

The issues were political and economic and in both respects touched interests of fundamental importance. The political issue consisted in the fact that the aristocracy and gentry had a virtual monopoly on the formal instruments of authority in the state, the main seat and symbol of this oligarchic system being the unreformed House of Commons. The issue of economic policy arose from the restrictive burdens of the mercantile system, which in the eyes of traders and manufacturers increasingly meant the Corn Laws, the tariff protecting the production of grain and thereby the economic base of the landed classes. The essence of the story is that in the upheaval of 1832 the landed classes voluntarily agreed to share their authority with the commercial and industrial classes in a reformed Parliament, which, fulfilling the gloomy predictions of its opponents, proceeded in the next few years to whittle down and finally repeal the Corn Laws, establishing free trade as a pillar of public policy. In spite of great turmoil and some violence, the transition to a liberal polity suitable for an industrializing society and designed effectively to promote further economic modernization was accomplished.

Britain's free institutions—free, that is, in comparison with the typical regime of the day—could claim a large share of the credit. Overwhelmingly, the initiative for reform came from outside established government circles. A relatively high level of freedom of speech, press, and association was therefore indispensable to the spread of reform ideas throughout the

---

[8]Charles de Sismondi, quoted in Elie Halévy, *England in 1815* (London, 1949), p. 382.

[9]Friedrich Engels, *The Condition of the Working-Class in England in 1844* (London, 1950), p. 296.

society, while a powerful elected legislature, biased as it may have been, provided linkage to the seats of authority. One of the most striking changes in the politics of the early nineteenth century was the vast proliferation of voluntary associations formed for political purposes. Notable examples can be found in the late eighteenth century, such as the various bodies aiming at parliamentary reform. But these earlier associations were failures and during the wars with revolutionary France were brutally suppressed. From the 1820s, however, this new kind of pressure group became a power in British politics. Among them were the political unions agitating for reform before 1832, the London Workingmen's Association, the various Chartist groups, the Short Time Committees for the Ten Hours Bill in the 1840s, and that great Victorian exemplar of the reformist pressure group, the Anti-Corn Law League, which, founded in 1839, triumphed in 1846. While political parties already flourished in Parliament and in the active political community, it was less they than the new pressure groups that were the source of reform in policy.

In the case of free trade and repeal of the Corn Laws, the sequence of events is a classical illustration of how free institutions and the free market-place of ideas are supposed to work. Properly the story begins with Adam Smith, who diagnosed the burdens of economic growth of the old protective system and bequeathed to later generations an inclusive but practical scheme of reform. Practical intellectuals like him, mainly economists, continued to urge the case in books and in the press and before committees of Parliament. In time they were joined by merchants and manufacturers—in 1820 there took place a famous meeting of London merchants at which they declared themselves in favor of free trade—and gradually some M.P.s and even Ministers began to relax their defense of the protective system. The organization of the Anti-Corn Law League was the last phase. It used all the devices that pressure politics has made familiar since that time: mass meetings, petitioning, intensive lobbying of Ministers and legislators, a huge publication effort, intervention in elections to support friends and defeat enemies. Finally, the parties and their leaders began to respond. As might be expected the first were the Liberals. But it was the Conservative Leader Sir Robert Peel, elected to serve "the sacred cause of protection," who, in a reversal of position that set one of the most fruitful precedents of modern politics, led the way to its abolition in 1846. "I will not withhold the homage which is due to the progress of reason and truth," he said, "by denying that my opinions on the subject of protection have undergone a change."[10]

---

[10]83 *H. C. Deb.* 69, Third Series (22 January 1846).

Tocqueville on England

This modernist account, while true, is a little one-dimensional and needs a few Burkean qualifications. It will be helpful to look for guidance to an acute foreign observer. During the nineteenth century the success of Britain in avoiding revolution, enacting progressive reform, and achieving unprecedented prosperity and dominance as a world power was a source of painful, but often penetrating, reflection by thoughtful Frenchmen. Undoubtedly the weightiest of them was Alexis de Tocqueville, whose *Old Regime and the French Revolution* (1856), a study in which he frequently contrasts France and England, has shown the same enduring value as his *Democracy in America* (1835–1840).

If we turn to Tocqueville's analysis, our attention is directed not only to Britain's free institutions, but also to the character of the men who held power under them. In explaining the tragedy of the French Revolution, his recurring theme is the contrast between the upper classes of France and England. In medieval times, he observes, both countries had similar institutions, including a Parliament of estates and a class of nobles. In both, the nobility performed important functions, especially as leaders and rulers in their localities and in the national Parliament. As the two nations moved into modern times, however, their paths diverged. In England the feudal aristocracy maintained its political function, developing into a modern governing class and continuing to exercise its leadership through Parliament and in the countryside. In France, on the other hand, this transformation was not accomplished, the aristocracy being loaded with privileges but deprived of effective authority in great matters of state. The medieval Parliament, in effect, ceased to exist; the last meeting of the Estates-General took place in 1614, while the function of governing under the Bourbon monarchy was vested in a bureaucracy ramifying from Paris. But a bureaucracy owing its authority only to its official status could not perform the essentially political function of a modern governing class. The English aristocracy and gentry, however, retained their contact with other classes, their rule in Parliament, and their political function, shaping the course of public affairs, guiding opinion, and lending authority to new ideas. In turn, they were not confronted with the rage for equality that afflicted France, but, on the contrary, maintained their ancient prestige in a highly deferential nation.

This traditionalist model of British politics lights up important aspects of the great age of reform. While the agitation for the act of 1832 was strongly urged by classes poorly represented in the old Parliament, there was also in Parliament a core of aristocratic advocates of reform that had a continuous history going back half a century. They had kept the cause alive and lent it their prestige through the long years of repression. A youthful member of this earlier aristocratic movement became the Earl Grey, who as

Prime Minister carried the Reform Act of 1832. Moreover, his Cabinet was equally aristocratic and boasted a larger total acreage of land than any preceding body of Ministers. The foreboding aroused by this step toward popular government must not be underestimated. Even to the young Gladstone, as he later recalled, there was "something of the Anti-Christ in the Reform Act of 1832." Yet the measure was shaped and forwarded by a body of men who commanded the very peaks of power and prestige and whose political, economic, and social interests were deeply identified with the established order.

Lord Grey was confident that the reform would renew what he regarded as the "natural alliance" between the Whig party and "the people." While his hopes for a partisan monopoly were dashed, in a larger sense his expectations were overwhelmingly confirmed. The new electorate of middle-class and lower-middle-class voters—far from sending representatives of their own class and economic interests to dominate the new House of Commons—preferred men of landed wealth and members of the aristocracy and the gentry. In the Parliament that finally repealed the Corn Laws, only 17 percent of the members were businessmen. Among those who voted for repeal as well as those who opposed it, the landed classes greatly predominated.

Looking ahead, we may note that the deference that the middle class had shown to the aristocracy was similarly displayed by the working class toward the upper classes as the franchise was gradually broadened in later years. Recording his impressions of British politics in 1908, A. L. Lowell observed that "the upper classes in England rule today, not by means of the political privileges which they retain, but by the sufferance of the great mass of the people and as trustees for its benefit." Moreover, he continued,

> the sentiment of deference or snobbishness becomes, if anything, stronger as the social scale descends. The workingman, when not provoked by an acute grievance to vote for a trade union candidate, prefers a man with a title, and thus the latest extensions of the franchise have rather strengthened than weakened the hold of the governing class upon public life.[11]

Hardly second to its governing class, a further reason often cited for the stability and effectiveness of British government is its pragmatic style of politics, the contrast being drawn with the ideological style of French, German, and other continental polities. Tocqueville's comparative analysis also puts forward an explanation of this crucial characteristic. In his view perhaps the most fateful consequence of the political abdication of the French aristocracy was the resulting vacuum of leadership. In this situation,

---

[11]Lowell, *op. cit.,* II, p. 508.

toward the middle of the eighteenth century, the radical intellectuals of the Enlightenment—the philosophes—took the lead in forming public opinion. Lacking any contact with practical politics as well as the guidance of a true political class, these men of letters believed and taught that a new social and political order could be constructed "by simple elementary rules deriving from the exercise of human reason and natural law."[12] The results were violence, disorder, and ultimately dictatorship.

This same reasoning explains why Britain in contrast with France produced not radical but practical intellectuals, such as the economists who demonstrated the vices of the mercantile system and the Benthamite reformers who conceived most of the great measures of reform that have given the period its fame. Not only did free institutions give them access to the seats of power, but the traditions of the governing class made it open to ideas for change. William Pitt himself, before the crisis of the war with revolutionary France made him into the stern enemy of reform, befriended Adam Smith and was receptive to his ideas.

The free institutions of modernity were indispensable to the British achievement of avoiding revolution, admitting new classes to power in the state, and adjusting public policy to the needs of an expanding economy. Yet these institutions were balanced by strong premodern and aristocratic elements. Or rather they were integrated with these vigorous survivals. The elected Parliament functioned in a social and economic context that assured the dominance of the traditional elites. But these elites themselves harbored modern attitudes that prepared them to accept and even champion ideas of reform.

Indeed it is wrong to contrast even in this dialectic way British free institutions and traditional survivals. For British liberty itself had a twofold character, making it at once modern and traditional. It included the brisk modern liberty of the free marketplace—in thought as in trade—where merit, sharply judged on utilitarian grounds, gained the day, and the contest was open to all. At the same time British liberty meant protection and support for standing in the old ways. Liberty to innovate and to rise in the world survived, because it was modulated by imitation of the past and disdain for excessive mobility.

Founding the Welfare State

The second episode relates to the rise of socialism and the early phases of the welfare state. Resulting from the dual thrust of modernization toward industrialization and participation, these events have been paralleled

---

[12]Alexis de Tocqueville, The Old Regime and the French Revolution (New York, 1955), p. 139.

in all European countries. On one hand, economic development brings into existence the typical class structure of the capitalist economy, confronting managers and owners with a growing urban proletariat. On the other hand, the democratic ethic is propagated in a form that legitimates not only demands for political equality, but also economic equality.

The potential for self-destructive conflict is evident, and late-nineteenth- and twentieth-century history richly documents it. The conflict of classes makes effective government difficult at a time when the growing complexities of a mature economy require even more government intervention. If the conflict centers on the clash of two large class-based parties, it raises the danger that strong ideological positions may so sharply separate the contenders that they will not feel it safe to tolerate the peaceful alternation in power of the democratic method. Or if, as is more usual, the class conflict proliferates into a multiparty system, the task of constructing a stable and steady majority may be virtually impossible. Yet the need to plan and control the economy in its internal and domestic aspects mounts relentlessly, requiring strong government and coherent policy. The interwar history of most European countries, dominated by the rise of highly organized and militant extremes on Left and Right and the massive conflict of communism and fascism within nations and between nations, vividly illustrates the tragic possibilities.

In comparison with France, Germany, and the Soviet Union, Britain handled these problems with outstanding success. This is not to deny that there were ugly moments. The general strike of 1926 brought out more than two and a half million workers for nine days in what was taken to be an effort to coerce the government by direct action. Yet the conflict did not lead to violence and, as the British never fail to remind one, at Plymouth the strikers and policemen whiled away the hours by playing football together. Shortly afterward understandings were reached between employers and unions, which in effect made the strike obsolete as a means of industrial conflict—at any rate until the recent rise of the unofficial walkout.

The culminating success came after World War II. In 1945 the Labour party took power, backed by a huge parliamentary majority and committed to far-reaching social and economic reform. In the succeeding years the essential structures of the welfare state and managed economy were created. Viewed in historical perspective, the political success was impressive. A vast industrial proletariat mobilized by economic modernization had been effectively integrated into the polity, while the needs of this class, transformed into practical governmental programs, had given drive and direction to a comprehensive reconstruction of policy.

There is a simple Benthamite way of telling this story and explaining what happened. Its main explanatory variable is the practical good sense of the British workingman who uses politics to improve his conditions of work and life under advanced industrialism. In the first phase interest centers on the skilled workman whose unions developed rapidly after the middle of the nineteenth century. His purposes in politics were concrete and practical—they were called "the interests of labour"—and related to such things as the discriminatory master and servant law, which concerned the individual workman, or the burdens on trade union activity arising from legislation or judicial decision. The Trades Union Congress (T.U.C.), founded in 1868, and affiliating unions organized on a nationwide basis served as a lobby in relation to the central government. The two big parties, the Liberals and the Conservatives, competing for the votes of the skilled urban workmen enfranchised by the act of 1867, were modestly responsive to these pressures. The period provides a nice illustration of the Benthamite principle of "dislocability," that is, the way in which representative government enables the voter to control the representative by threatening to switch his support in order to defeat—or "dislocate"—him.

A second phase was entered with the rise of the "new unionism" of the 1880s. The unskilled workers that were members of these organizations had greater need for government intervention to protect their interests, and consequently we find the first serious efforts to form an independent party. Yet Lib-Lab collaboration dominated the years until World War I, producing such achievements as the vast political and social reform program of the Liberal government elected in 1906. Finally, however, as Liberal support for further reform faltered, especially in the straitened circumstances of postwar capitalism, the working class was obliged to turn to a more radical alternative. In 1918 the Labour party, founded mainly by trade unions at the turn of the century, officially adopted a socialist ideology and in the following years won increasing support among the working class.

This party was a very different sort of political formation from the small, loose parties, dominated by their parliamentary leaders, that had arisen in the great age of reform. Labour was a modern mass party enrolling millions of members, both directly through individual memberships and indirectly through trade union affiliation. It was strongly cohesive in its behavior out of Parliament as well as within. Above all, it was the source of the program that, item for item, was carried out by the Labour government of 1945–1951. If pressure groups had been the source of ideas in that earlier period, in this instance the source was party. Like the economy itself, the polity had moved from an individualist to a collectivist phase, party government representing the new instrument by which the democratic will was made effective. At the same time, the old disciplines of Cabinet government were strengthened and put in the service of coherent policy making, necessitated by the growing responsibilities for managing the economy.

Behind this success story does lie the practical, good sense of the British workingman. But how do we account for that? "Practical good sense" is

not something we can take for granted, as the comparative study of socialism in various countries immediately reveals.

Schumpeter on England

How to account for British success was precisely the central problem for
Joseph A. Schumpeter, an eminent Austrian economist of the last generation, when he summed up "almost forty years' thought, observation and
reflection on the subject of socialism" in his classic, *Capitalism, Socialism
and Democracy* (1942). He looked at the development of socialism
broadly in the whole European context. But his special concern was with
the contrast between Germany on the one hand and Britain on the other.
The crucial difference was in the ideology and rhetoric of the two socialist
movements. In Germany Marxism with its corrosive doctrine of capitalist
exploitation and its prophecy of ultimate violent revolution supplied the
beliefs, values, and expressive symbolism of the Social Democratic party,
by 1914 the largest socialist party in the world. To be sure, many of the
party's leaders were by then dedicated democrats who, even in imperial
Germany, would have been ready to accept step-by-step reformism. But
these facts were not admitted publicly in official utterance. On the contrary, the party clung to "a Marxist phraseology of unsurpassed virulence,
pretending to fight ruthless exploitation and a state that was the slave of
slave drivers."[13]

One result was to intensify the hostility toward the socialists of the other
parties, already less than eager to share power with them. Hence, when
social reform did come, it came from above, so to speak, as in Bismarck's
social security legislation, and not from a political base that included the
working class. Moreover, after World War I, when the Social Democrats
did finally assume their place as a party of government, rather than revolution, the old patterns of intransigence and alienation were perpetuated by
a massive Communist party. Thus the fateful polarization of politics under
the Weimar Republic, which helped prepare the way for Nazism, had
roots in the spirit and direction given to German socialism by Marxism
many years before.

In contrast, Schumpeter emphasizes, British socialism was Fabian rather
than Marxist, meaning that it took its character from the writings of the
small group of intellectuals who founded the Fabian Society in 1884. While
the Fabians generally accepted the central doctrine of socialism, namely,
the common ownership of the means of production, they also laid great
stress upon step-by-step measures of reform and, most important, upon
the necessity and possibility of achieving their ends by peaceful, democratic means. That the new party of the working class adopted this style

---

[13]Joseph A. Schumpeter, *Capitalism, Socialism and Democracy* (New York, 1942), p. 342.

of politics was not because it had no other choice. In the later years of the nineteenth century in Britain, as in other countries, many varieties of socialism were being offered to the masses. The Social Democratic Federation, founded three years before the Fabians, was distinctively Marxist and for years struggled with little success to win over opinion and gain a following.

The influence of intellectuals is not to be underestimated. In a real sense, whether Fabian or Marxist, they were the teachers of the working class as it emerged into political consciousness and had the power, within limits, to make or mar their students. Yet if we are to understand why the British working class were more inclined to respond to their Fabian than their Marxist teachers, we cannot fail to take into account the long-established, pragmatic, and nonideological style of British political culture. Moreover, these attitudes, supporting the conviction that free institutions could be made to work, had been greatly reinforced by the achievement of the great age of reform itself. The power of these precedents is made clear by Bernard Shaw, one of the original Fabians, in a later comment on what the society set out to do:

> It was in 1885 that the Fabian Society, amid the jeers of the catastrophists, turned its back on the barricades and made up its mind to turn heroic defeat into prosaic success. We set ourselves two definite tasks: first, to provide a parliamentary program for a Prime Minister converted to Socialism as Peel was converted to Free Trade; and second, to make it as easy and matter-of-course for the ordinary respectable Englishman to be a Socialist as to be a Liberal or a Conservative.[14]

In a country exceptionally prone to follow tradition, the tradition of an effective modern polity was an important condition for the continued effectiveness of that polity. Moreover, structures that had shaped the experience producing this tradition continued to function. In what is almost an echo of Tocqueville, Schumpeter attributes primary importance to Britain's governing classes. Discussing what enables democracy to work, he cites as "the first condition . . . the human material of politics —the people who man the party machines, are elected to serve in parliament, rise to cabinet office." If this human material is to be of sufficiently high quality, "the only effective guarantee is in the existence of a social stratum itself a product of a severely selective process, that takes to politics as a matter of course."[15] This stratum should be "neither too exclusive nor too easily accessible for the outsider." It should draw on circles whose members have shown ability in fields of private endeavor but should also endow them with a specifically political tradition giving them a profes-

---

[14]Bernard Shaw (ed.), *Fabian Essays.* Jubilee edn. (London, 1948), p. xxxiii.

[15]Schumpeter, *op. cit.,* pp. 290–291.

sional code and a common fund of views. What this elite contributes to government is emphatically not expertise or specialized knowledge, as with the bureaucrat, but, on the contrary, the prime political ability "to handle men." Nor is this an ability that comes as easily to the modern businessman as to the aristocrat.

England, according to Schumpeter, had such an elite, which "after having proved itself able to avoid an analogon to the French Revolution and to eliminate the dangers threatening from dear bread . . . continued to know how to manage social situations of increasing difficulty, and how to surrender with some grace."[16] Like France in Tocqueville's analysis, however, Germany failed to develop such a political class. Under the empire the government, meaning by that the large and well-trained bureaucracy, took the initiative in matters of social policy. During the Weimar Republic (1919–1933), although politicians, members of Parliament, and Ministers were overwhelmingly honest, reasonable, and conscientious, most of them were otherwise "distinctly below par." In Germany it was still true that "ability and energy spurned the political career. And there was no class or group whose members looked upon politics as their predestined career."[17]

The important consequence of these contrasting conditions was not that in one country concessions were made to working-class demands while in the other they were refused. Indeed, in matters of social security imperial Germany was years ahead of Britain. The important point—paradoxically a tragic fact—is that these benefits came from above, being designed and introduced by the bureaucracy. Not that in Britain the initiative for reform came wholly or even largely from the working class and its organizations. Indeed, the Liberal Government that came to power in 1906 was on many points more innovative and progressive than the Labour party of the day.

The crucial fact was that again, as brought out in Tocqueville's analysis, the British political class maintained contact with the "other classes." While Bismarck did promote real and substantial social reforms, he also attempted to suppress the socialist movement in a twelve-year-long battle, which succeeded only in creating a chasm between the established leadership and a large part of the working class. This was from 1878 to 1890. At about the same time, Disraeli was forging that long-lasting alliance between an upper-class leadership and a lower-class following that was to make the Conservative party dominant in the age of democracy. His government (1874–1880) put through a program of social reform, modest by our standards, but remarkable for its time; and between 1886 and 1900

---

[16] *Ibid.*, p. 321.

[17] *Ibid.*, p. 291.

the Conservatives won a majority of the two-party vote in four successive general elections. This could not have been done without massive support from the working class. After Disraeli's death, the London *Times* remarked: "In the inarticulate mass of the English populace, he discerned the Conservative workingman as the sculptor perceives the angel prisoned in the block of marble."

During the interwar period and on to the present the Conservative party, the party *par excellence* of the governing class, continued the work of Disraeli and Lloyd George in developing social reform to meet the ills of industrialism. Moreover, as the Labour party took the place of the Liberals as the other of the two major parties, more and more young men who were marked by unmistakable signs of the English upper classes—with regard to speech, dress, manners, and education—appeared in Labour's ranks. Indeed, by 1950 Winchester, one of the more distinguished and exclusive "public" schools, had educated all three Ministers who presented the Labour Government's budget of that year, a coincidence of which the Ministers showed that they were mindful by presenting to the school library a specially bound volume of *Hansard* "as a memorial of an unique event never likely to be repeated."

In the political development of European countries two periods of special danger have been the transition from an aristocratic to a liberal polity and the transition from a liberal to a collectivist polity. Sometimes these transitions have brought tragic violence, and sometimes they have been aborted. The previous analysis of the success of Britain in accomplishing the transitions brings out in broad outline how the integration of modernist and traditionalist elements might account for the achievement of British government. We need to be cautious in trying to summarize the reasons. They are deeply embedded in history, and history, because it is concrete, has a way of being very complex. Keeping this caution in mind, we can say that the theme running through the previous analysis has been the union of hierarchy and liberty. Both the Burkean and the Benthamite hypotheses are necessary to the explanation. This does not mean that the separate accomplishments of each factor can be totalled together. The essence is that, contradictory as they may seem, hierarchy and liberty have been interdependent. Whig lords, whose arrogance was beyond compare, were yet the authors and defenders of Whig liberty. British trade unionists threw off the old subordination of their forefathers and fought doggedly for their rights against powerful interests. Yet they also knew how to accept the leadership and authority necessary for successful long-term organization. In British political development, modern and traditional forces have often been opposed. But the more durable truth has been their interdependence. As Benjamin Constant remarked almost 200 years ago: "England is the country where on the one hand the rights of the individual are most carefully safeguarded, and on the other, class distinctions are most respected."[18]

Cabinet Government and Party Government

The role of political elites, while properly given great attention by students of British government, is inseparable from the institutions within which these elites operate. The two principal institutions of the British polity are cabinet government and party government. If we ask how policy is made responsive to the wishes of the political community, the key structure is party government. Based upon the competition of two strongly cohesive, programmatic parties, party government is held to promote responsiveness in two ways. First, because of party unity the voter can hold responsible the candidates of the majority party for what government does when that party is in power. If the party he supports wins a majority, it will act together in the exercise of authority, presenting to the electorate a highly visible object of support or attack. The system makes government responsible by creating a linkage between the casting of a vote and the acts of government such that voters can exercise ultimate control.

Second, party government also makes government responsive in terms of program. Each of the competing formations presents a statement of the politics it proposes to carry out if it wins the majority. This enables the electorate to control not only who will govern, but in broad outline what they will do. Moreover, since the parties are not the mere Tweedledum and Tweedledee of "ins" versus "outs," but represent significantly different approaches to the common purpose, the respective programs will have coherence. This is important for the implementation as well as the making of policy, since the coherence of a government's program means that the massive, far-flung, interdependent activities of the modern state will be directed toward compatible and mutually supporting goals. In contrast a government that, as in the United States, is based on a system of parties with loose cohesion and without unifying principles will tend to produce a series of "casual majorities," whose objectives may be inconsistent with one another and shaped by no deliberately thought-out view of policy as a whole.

Two-party competition, unity among partisans in the legislature and executive, programs based on distinctive political outlooks—these are the main ingredients of the doctrine of party government. Its consequences are not only to make government democratically responsive, but also to create

---

[18]Quoted in *Encounter*, 21 (July 1963), p. 19.

the conditions of policy making and execution highly favorable to effective problem solving. The party program converted into a mandate by victory at the polls provides a coherent basis for policy making, while the steady support of partisans ensures government leaders of the legislative power necessary to carry out their mandate and—perhaps even more important —assures them of the continuous and prolonged support indispensable if policy is to be reflectively matured and adapted to the environment over a period of time. Finally, all along the line from the formation of policy through its implementation, a steady partisan majority guided by a coherent program gives leaders the base from which to resist the distorting demands of pressure groups.

So stated, party government could conceivably be adapted to various constitutional structures, whether presidential or parliamentary. Its main principles have seemed sufficiently transferable to generate a long and lively controversy among American political scientists as to whether party government should (and could) be brought to these shores. But party government obviously fits best with the constitutional structures of its country of origin. From the constitutional viewpoint, the key element in the British solution to reconciling democracy and effectiveness is cabinet government.

In contrast with presidential government, cabinet government means that the heads of the executive departments and the chief figure among them, the Prime Minister, sit in the legislature and are responsible to it in the sense that they must not only account for their actions to the legislature, but also resign from office if the legislature insists. This norm of the parliamentary responsibility of Ministers has, however, characterized British government at times in the past when, in comparison with recent generations, the Cabinet and Prime Minister had far less influence over Parliament and could depend upon it with far less confidence for support in legislation and expressions of confidence. The development of the cohesive, strongly led political party in the collectivist era has probably had as much effect upon this aspect of the British constitution as the constitution has had upon the shape and structure of party.

Nevertheless, cabinet government obviously adds to the efficacy of party government. It avoids the temptations of conflict and the opportunities of deadlock present when the chief executive and the legislature are elected separately, as under the American system. The leader whose party wins a majority becomes Prime Minister and in turn chooses from among his principal lieutenants in the parliamentary party the members of his Cabinet. This body is the chief executive, and although it is plural rather than unitary, the primacy of the Prime Minister and the norm of collective responsibility as well as the common acceptance of party program and principles provide the solidarity necessary for coherent government. Moreover, including in the deliberations of this chief executive persons who are also in charge of the various departments of state means that the knowledge and experience of the administrator are directly worked into policy making.

Such is the conventional model of party and cabinet government that is commonly used to explain the success of the British polity in combining responsive and effective government. It is an impressive case supported by long experience. If recent years have seriously disrupted the record of performance, we must inquire whether this familiar analysis of how the system works is still correct or whether changes, both internal and external to the political system, have finally rendered it out of date. The questions deriving from these premises will constitute a framework for the later chapters concerned with particular sectors of the British system. The discussion of parties, Parliament, the Cabinet, Civil Service, and policy will focus on the working of party government and cabinet government today.

The Bipolar Conception of Authority

The institutions of party government and cabinet government, like the interrelationships of followers and elites, also illustrate the modernity of tradition. Cabinet government, with its norms defining the authority of the Prime Minister and the responsibility of Ministers, is an institution that has grown up in fairly recent times to meet the needs of democratic Britain in the age of the welfare state and the managed economy. Yet in crucial respects this highly modern structure depends upon attitudes deriving from a medieval past. In a brilliant essay L. S. Amery, a Conservative politician and thinker of the past generation, has expounded the dual nature of the British conception of authority.[19] This conception he distinguishes from the Continental view of representative government, which derives from the French Revolution and which makes political power a delegation from the individual citizen through the legislature to an executive dependent on the legislature. In contrast, the British constitution, today as in the distant past, has two basic elements: an initiating, directing, energizing element— nowadays the Cabinet—and a checking, criticizing element—nowadays the House of Commons and especially the Opposition. Given this notion of authority, it follows that "Parliament is not, and never has been, a legislature, in the sense of a body specially and primarily empowered to make laws." The function of legislation is mainly exercised by Ministers, while the principal task of Parliament is to secure full discussion and ventilation of all matters as a condition of giving its assent to what the Government does. "Our system," he concludes, "is one of democracy

---

[19]L. S. Amery, *Thoughts on the Constitution* (London, 1947).

but of democracy by consent and not by delegation, of government of the people, for the people, with, but not by, the people."[20]

The bipolar structure that Amery traces back to the Middle Ages and makes the central feature of the British constitution does not mean that Britain is not democratic. It means rather that British democracy has grown up within a certain framework of authority to which it has been obliged —perhaps at the sacrifice of some consistency—to accommodate itself. The idea of the mandate expresses the belief that Governments are responsible to the people for their major acts and policies. As the suffrage has been broadened and particularly since the Reform Act of 1867, this idea has been taken more and more seriously. In 1903, for example, Joseph Chamberlain raised the tariff question so that at the next general election the public might give a "mandate" on it. In 1923 Stanley Baldwin, the Conservative Prime Minister, dissolved Parliament, not because of an adverse vote of confidence or a defeat on policy, but solely, he alleged, because he felt he could not undertake tariff reform (then a very important issue) without obtaining an expression of popular will on the matter. The principle of the mandate is certainly a part of British political culture, and, what is more, is frequently acted upon.

But mandate theory has never fully replaced the idea of independent authority. Even in the heyday of mandate theory some very important policy decisions were made without mandate, and without in the least outraging anyone's constitutional feelings. Thus Baldwin, who felt he could not reform the tariff without a specific mandate, gave women equal suffrage without the slightest suspicion of one. Much more important, it seems to be generally recognized that the Government ought sometimes to ignore its lack of a mandate or even to act counter to a mandate, if doing so would be definitely in the national interest—a loose principle, which may cover a multitude of independent actions. The case most frequently cited to make this point is the famous "Baldwin Confession" about Britain's failure to rearm against the Nazi threat before 1935. Baldwin argued that until 1935 every government had been given a mandate for disarmament and collective security under the League of Nations and that the country's mind on the issue had been revealed emphatically at general elections and by-elections. Hence he felt that rearmament could not legitimately have been undertaken until 1935, when some sort of mandate for it was given. The position taken against this argument by Baldwin's opponents was that the Government—having had, as it claimed, a clear apprehension of the military danger and the futility of the League of Nations—should have acted in the best interests of the nation anyway; that in fact it was its *duty*, as the Government of the country and His Majesty's Ministers, to do so,

---

[20] *Ibid.*, pp. 11–12, 20.

regardless of any electoral consequences. It may be true that one or the other conception of the authority of government is invoked only when it is politically convenient to invoke it, but the great point is that both conceptions can be used for political convenience. Both conceptions have solid roots in British political culture.

Speaking always with an acute sense of relativity—that is, with regard to what is humanly possible and with regard to what other countries have accomplished—we may say that the story of British government in modern times is a story of high achievement. With all due qualifications, the record of effectiveness and responsiveness has been remarkably good. It is precisely this long record of achievement that makes the disappointments and failures of recent years disturbing to the British and intellectually challenging to the political scientist.

Has the balance between tradition and modernity been thrown off in some undesirable way? Has modernity run to excess, introducing deficiencies that in the past were more likely to trouble the unstable countries of the continent? Or is it the other way around? Has Britain lost her old ability to adapt traditional elements to developing modernity? Or, finally, have the old formulas at last become obsolete, whether we think of the complementary elements of party government and cabinet government or of the older, persisting structures that underlie these contemporary mechanisms? That is to say, has a phase of political development been reached that makes out of date the modernity of tradition? These spacious doubts and broad perspectives will inform the more particular problems and hypotheses that will be considered in the following chapters.

Two

Cabinet and Prime Minister

As increase in scale entails greater specialization, the expansion of policy of a modern polity normally leads to a growth in the number of departments and other agencies of state power. This raises the classic problem of how to achieve coherence in policy. Coherence means at least avoiding overlapping and conflict. This is no mean feat when one considers the capacity of government programs unintentionally to produce problems for one another—their "hidden policies." But coherence means more than just absence of conflict. It also means there is some positive drive uniting these numerous and far-flung activities—not necessarily some simple goal, such as "victory" in wartime, but rather a system of priorities that marshals energy and purpose to some fronts and withdraws them from others. Moreover, this unity has a temporal dimension. Programs change, of course; however, they do not simply zigzag in response to arbitrary thrusts on the rudder, but show continuity, as perseverance in tackling a problem is maintained and innovation builds on previous achievement.

Coherence, a bland and abstract word, may not seem to deserve being put forward as a major criterion of public policy. Yet the loss of coherence describes some of the more tragic and characteristic failures of the highly developed modern state. Fragmentation in the polity and in the processes of policy making leads to a loss of control over the nation's destiny and the dominance of the blind forces of technique. If politics is to be a process of social choice, the first requisite is that the instruments of governance should themselves be subject to control.

According to the conventional model, cabinet government has virtues that are highly relevant to this complex of problems. Because the Cabinet includes the men in charge of the principal branches of the executive, the system is said to produce positive and coherent action. By their common membership in the Cabinet, Ministers are enabled and obliged to make the action of their respective departments compatible and mutually supportive. Thanks to their party majority in the legislature, they are freed of the inconsistencies that the casual majorities of a leaderless legislature will impose on public policy.

The source of these virtues is, in the first place, the fusion of powers. In contrast to the separation of legislative and executive powers found in the American system, the Cabinet joins these powers in one body. This fusion does not consist merely in the fact that the executive actions of the individual departments and of the government as a whole are directed by a body of men who are also members of the legislature. The important point is that these men, while exercising the whole panoply of executive powers, also in effect command the legislative power, including that crucial power of any polity, the power to tax and spend. The men exercising these powers can be deprived of them, but this does not lead to the recapture of these powers by the legislature; the same massive authority is simply given to a new set of men. Cabinets come and go, but the Cabinet continues.

Not only does the Cabinet exercise a fusion of executive and legislative powers, but it also gains from the dual nature of the British conception of authority. The decisions of the Cabinet enjoy legitimacy—that is, they are accepted and obeyed—in large part because they are regarded as expressing the wishes of the voters through the mechanisms of party government. But there is no denying that the Cabinet is also conceived as having a wide sphere of independent authority. This further support of its powers derives from Britain's monarchic past. Any Cabinet acts within a complex of constraints and supports, serving to mark out the sphere within which it can in fact freely make decisions. One crucial support for a wider sphere of decision making is the ancient expectation among members of Parliament and Britons generally that "the Queen's Government must be carried on."

In the eighteenth century "the executive authority of the King was put in commission and it was arranged that the commissioners should be members of the legislative body to whom they are responsible."[1] But this was not just an event of the eighteenth century. The conception of cabinet authority that originated in this way continues to be a living force in British government and politics. Not least, it impresses the members of the Cabi-

---

[1] Sir Courtenay Ilbert, quoted in Patrick Gordon Walker, *The Cabinet* (London, 1970), p. 14.

net themselves. An ex-member recently described how Ministers, while gathering at Number 10 Downing Street for a Cabinet, laugh and joke and call one another by their first names, as one would expect of political colleagues. But once they enter the Cabinet room and the meeting starts, "the whole atmosphere changes." Members now address their remarks only to the Prime Minister, and even the oldest of friends refer to one another in the third person and by their ministerial titles. For "here is no longer a set of individual men, but the collective sovereign power of the state."[2] The Cabinet is "not just a meeting of persons but a continuing body, that has for centuries been the seat of ultimate authority."[3]

From a decision-making structure so admirably fashioned it should not be strange if the output in policy and administration were coherent, decisive, and relevant. Yet a closer look at cabinet government today suggests that it is not working as the conventional accounts say it does but, on the contrary, suffers from such fragmentation in structure, incoherence in action, and immobility in responding to problems as to remind one of the less happy moments of those political systems burdened with a separation of powers or a multiparty system. A Minister in the Wilson Government contends that "the major problem of government today" is "how to make informed collective decisions at the cabinet level on economic and financial strategy." He concludes that the failure to solve this problem has relegated the Cabinet to "the margin of politics."[4] A common complaint among civil servants and outside observers is that British government is greatly overcentralized. As a result of the overload on central government generally and on the Cabinet in particular, many important decisions, they claim, are made quickly and badly, or properly, but with vast delay; while, as many observers have remarked, pressure groups have gained far wider opportunities than in the past. Hence, because of internal pressures forcing decisions away from the center and external pressures drawing them toward the periphery, what looks like a tightly centralized and neatly coordinated system is tending to become polycentric, pluralistic, and unintentionally dispersed.

What may seem an opposite view is also heard. This is that cabinet government has developed into prime ministerial government. A leading member of the Wilson Government has compared the present position of the Prime Minister with that of the American President and concluded that a Prime Minister may well exert "greater power than a President."[5] A

[2]Patrick Gordon Walker, *Encounter,* 6 (April 1956), 19.

[3]Walker, *The Cabinet, op. cit.,* p. 106.

[4]Harold Lever (former Financial Secretary to the Treasury), in *The New Statesman,* 80 (30 October 1970), 552.

[5]R. H. S. Crossman (former Secretary of State for Social Services), *The Myths of Cabinet Government* (Cambridge, Mass., 1972), p. 6.

professorial authority writes: "Now the country is governed by the prime minister."[6] There is no such simple answer to the question of who governs Britain. But, like the talk about prime ministerial government, the second statement does at least suggest that the Prime Minister has been gaining in authority in relation to the Cabinet. This is quite compatible, however, with a general fragmentation of cabinet authority. If the collective function of the Cabinet were to decline, it would be natural for the Prime Minister to loom as a relatively greater figure, but this would not necessarily halt the general trend toward less coordination of decision and more dispersion of authority.

Bearing in mind the conventional model of cabinet government sketched in the previous pages, as well as current criticisms of this model, we may now take a more detailed look at how a Cabinet is constituted and how it works.

Making a Cabinet

The first step in constituting a Cabinet is the appointment of a Prime Minister. This act is performed by the Sovereign, but is so hedged by conventions of the Constitution and by political circumstance as to leave her virtually no freedom of choice. The basic convention is that the Sovereign must appoint whatever leader is capable of commanding the support of a majority in the House of Commons. The occasion to act may occur when a general election has reversed the positions of the two main parties in the House. In such a case the Queen's function is simply to ask the known leader of the successful party to form a Government. If this leader were to die or become incapacitated, each party would undoubtedly avail itself of its established procedure for the election of a leader—which the Conservatives have had only since 1965—making obvious and inevitable the Queen's choice.

It must be mentioned that a Cabinet could also be brought down by a defeat in the House of Commons. Such defeats are unknown in this day of two-party dominance and tight party unity. But the basic rule of parliamentary government still obtains; namely, the Cabinet must retain the support of a majority of the House, and the rise of a third party or a decline in party cohesion could again, as in the past, subject a Government to defeat in the House of Commons. In case of such a defeat, under the conventions of British government a Government would have two courses open to it. The Prime Minister might dissolve Parliament and appeal to the

---

[6]John P. Mackintosh, *The British Cabinet,* 2nd ed. (London, 1968), p. 529.

electorate by means of a new election, or he might decide to resign. If he chose to resign in the midst of party confusion, conceivably the Queen could be confronted with a choice among several leaders of Opposition parties, each of whom had a chance of forming a Government. Presumably, the convention that the Sovereign must not get involved in politics would lead her to seek and follow the advice of the outgoing Prime Minister and other party leaders.

The first task of the Prime Minister is to choose his Cabinet and Government. The Cabinet formed by Edward Heath after the Conservatives won the election of June 18, 1970, consisted of seventeen members. It included the heads of the old and important departments such as the Home Office, Foreign Office, and Treasury, as well as the heads of the so-called super-ministries formed in recent years by the amalgamation of several departments. Bearing the title of Secretary of State, the latter were in charge of such huge agencies as Defence, Social Services, Trade and Industry, and the Environment. The Cabinet also included members without departments, such as the Leader of the House of Commons and the Minister in charge of Britain's negotiations with the Common Market. In addition to the Cabinet, the Government included some sixty-nine other members. A few were Ministers at the head of a department, but not in the Cabinet. A new category consisted of Ministers subordinate to the heads of the superministries, but with the status of a department head. Below them ranked the Ministers of State, who also assisted the heads of larger and more important departments in positions of considerable responsibility. Other assistants to Ministers were the parliamentary secretaries and under-secretaries, who technically are not Ministers of the Crown, since they are not appointed by the Queen. Also included in the Government were the whips, whose main function is to help the Prime Minister ride herd on his supporters in the House and who are usually given appointments without significant departmental duties. Finally, occupying a kind of twilight zone between members of the Government and ordinary backbenchers were the thirty to forty parliamentary private secretaries (P.P.S.s). Serving principally as a means of contact between a senior Minister and the backbenchers of his party, the P.P.S. should not be confused with the Minister's private secretary, a civil servant whose sphere is in the department. Although neither a Minister nor a member of the Government, the P.P.S. is subject to a more stringent discipline than the ordinary backbencher and is likely to lose his post if he so much as abstains in a vote.

Altogether, counting members of the Government and P.P.S.s, the members of the two Houses who are attached to the fortunes of the Prime Minister and his Cabinet by holding a post, official or unofficial, will probably number well over a hundred. Overwhelmingly they are in the House of Commons, constituting a substantial fraction of the majority of its 630 members. There is a power of patronage here that a Prime Minister confronted with an obstreperous party will find useful. In 1964 Harold Wilson raised the number of Ministers alone to ninety-eight, almost 50 percent over what it had been under Churchill and Macmillan.

As the scope of policy expands and the bureaucracy grows in size and complexity, there is pressure to increase the size of the Cabinet. Yet there seems to be a kind of upper limit fixed perhaps by the simple physical fact that only a certain number of people can do business around a table. Although the Cabinet numbered twenty-three by World War I, this was still its average size under the Conservative Douglas-Home and the Labourite Harold Wilson. As for a lower limit, in both world wars the size of the Cabinet has been drastically reduced to half a dozen or so. This has led many observers and even some politicians to advocate similarly small Cabinets for peacetime. If the vast, important, and highly complex business of total war can be carried out more effectively under a Cabinet of half a dozen, surely the work of peacetime government would benefit from a similar change. The trouble with this recommendation is that while the activity of a wartime government is vast and complex, its goals are immensely simplified. One word describes them, "victory," and from it a system of fairly clear priorities can be derived. Indeed, so settled were the means and ends of British government during the latter part of the war, that the Cabinet hardly met, leaving the implementation of the agreed policies almost entirely to Churchill. In peacetime the multiplicity of demands of a politically mobilized society reasserts itself, requiring that the departments representing these demands be given direct access to the authoritative decision maker. To satisfy this pressure in view of the increasing differentiation of the pattern of power is difficult. At one time just after World War II, the increase in the number of departments seemed to mean that more and more of them would not be represented directly in the Cabinet. Amalgamations leading to the creation of superministries, however, have reversed this trend, and the Cabinets of Wilson and Heath have included all ministries except three or four less important ones.

Although constitutional convention gives the Prime Minister complete discretion in deciding who the members of his Cabinet will be, his actual power is greatly circumscribed by political realities. Every Prime Minister has certain eminent party colleagues whose appointment to the Cabinet is a foregone conclusion. In the nature of the two-party system, each party has wings of opinion whose leaders must be included in the interest of harmony. It is therefore inevitable that a Cabinet will include men who want the Prime Minister's job, and given their existence, the Prime Minister will normally prefer to have them inside, blanketed by collective responsibilities, rather than outside, raising a storn on the back benches and in the country Regional forces play little part in determining Cabinet rem bership. Major exceptions to this are Scotland and Wales, which, with the rise of intense Celtic nationalism, have been directly represented in recent Cabinets by their respective secretaries of state. Nor are the factors bearing on a Prime Minister's choice purely political. Sheer managerial ability can raise a man to Cabinet level, although its presence or absence is probably more important during the reorganization of a Cabinet than at the time of its formation. Competence of this order undoubtedly had a great deal to do with the exceptionally long tenure—six years—of Denis Healey as Minister of Defence under Wilson.

These constraints, then, political and otherwise, shape the "shadow Cabinet" of the Prime Minister during the time when he is Leader of the Opposition. Yet the comparison of this leadership group when the party is out of power with its successor when the party takes office, suggests the substantial freedom of choice possessed by the man who is, in Churchill's phrase, "Number One." The feelings of those who await his decision is another good measure of this freedom. "It is like the zoo at feeding time," said Lord Salisbury. "It's been terrible: I have had people in here weeping and even fainting," remarked Ramsay MacDonald in 1929. In 1945, Attlee at the last moment switched Ernest Bevin, whom he had slated for the Treasury, with Hugh Dalton, whom he had led to expect the Foreign Office. Similarly, in 1964 Wilson switched Richard Crossman, who had been shadow Minister of Education, with Michael Stewart, who had been the front-bench spokesman on housing. Moreover, what the Prime Minister can give, he can take away. Once his Cabinet has been tested by a period in office, he has even more freedom in shuffling its members or, indeed, in getting rid of them altogether. An illustration of the extreme to which a Prime Minister can go, which, even though not typical, has continued to impress Cabinet members, was the purge of July 1962, when Macmillan suddenly dismissed seven members of his Cabinet, including the Minister of Defence and Chancellor of the Exchequer.

Under the long-established conventions of Cabinet government, a party leader, when summoned by the sovereign to form a Government, makes his own decision on whether to accept. Having accepted, he selects the members of the Cabinet, which as a body speaks for the whole Government. He may shift members of the Cabinet from one office to another or dismiss them, which in a sense is merely a consequence of the fact that his own resignation brings the Government to an end. The decision to resign, or that crucial political decision of whether and when to dissolve Parliament and have an election, is his sole decision. Such is the field of his authority. Needless to say, the actual exercise of his authority is subject to multiple constraints. But as a factor in the determination of power—the ability to impose one's will on a situation—these norms of British political culture all tend toward magnifying the office, not only in its constitution but also, as we shall see, in its operation.

Collective Responsibility

A major convention of British Cabinet government is the rule of collective responsibility. In the words of a recent Cabinet Minister, collective responsibility means "that every member must accept and if necessary defend Cabinet decisions even if he opposed and still dislikes them," unless, of course, he chooses to resign.[7] It means that and a good deal more. Not only are members of the Cabinet bound in vote and speech to defend the authoritative decisions of the Cabinet system, but so also are all members of the Government and, though not so tightly, their parliamentary private secretaries. Moreover, the decisions to which they are bound are not only those of the full Cabinet. The decisions of Cabinet committees now have the same validity as decisions of the Cabinet proper. With the expansion of policy Cabinet committees have increased in number and grown in authority. From the occasional ad hoc committee of the mid-nineteenth century there has developed an array of standing committees, which in the postwar years has sometimes numbered well over a dozen, along with such ad hoc committees as may be found useful. At one time all decisions of a Cabinet committee had to go to the full Cabinet for approval. Beginning in World War II, their decisions were accepted as binding, unless a member of the committee chose to appeal the decision to the full Cabinet. In 1967 Wilson took the further momentous step of excluding appeals unless the chairman of the committee gave his assent. Although this new rule could not take away the right of a Cabinet member to bring a matter before the Cabinet, it greatly reduced appeals.

There are other decisions that, although not made by the Cabinet, have similar consequences. Some arise when the Prime Minister intervenes in a particular field, either by himself or in consultation with the Minister concerned and perhaps a few others. In September 1938 the Prime Minister, Neville Chamberlain, without prior Cabinet approval, sent a telegram to Hitler to arrange a meeting and later signed the Munich agreement before informing the Cabinet. Except for one Minister who resigned, the Cabinet accepted these acts—and defended them in a four-day debate. In November 1967 the decision to devalue the pound was taken by the Prime Minister and Chancellor of the Exchequer, but was immediately reported to the Cabinet for its approval.

Not only the Prime Minister but ordinary Ministers can effectively commit the Government, a fact that may be of great importance when fields such as economic, financial, or defense policy are concerned. There is an old convention of the Constitution that Ministers are individually responsible to the House for the actions of their departments. This still holds when

---

[7]Walker, *The Cabinet, op. cit.,* p. 30.

it comes to answering questions and expounding and defending department policy. But party discipline today is such that individual Ministers are no longer forced out by adverse votes, as they once were; they can count on the Government's rallying its majority to the defense of their decisions, even if the decisions were actually made in the depths of the bureaucracy, quite innocent of ministerial knowledge or influence. Just as politics dictates support, politics can also lead to the withdrawal of support. A case in point is the resignation of Sir Samuel Hoare over the Hoare-Laval plan in 1935. With the Cabinet's knowledge and approval Hoare, the Foreign Secretary, made an agreement with Laval, then the French Premier, approving a partition of Ethiopia as a means of appeasing Mussolini. When word of the agreement was leaked, a storm of wrathful protest swept Britain. The Cabinet bowed, repudiated the agreement, and dropped Hoare from office.

With the consequences of collective responsibility so far-reaching, it is crucial that the decisions entailing it be properly made. Collective decision making must be such as to make collective responsibility tolerable. A major question for any departmental Minister is, What questions should go to the Cabinet, or to a committee, possibly as the first step on the way to the Cabinet? There are no precise rules governing this matter. It is a political question for politicians to answer. Whatever might harm the Government politically is a general rule. Such harm might arise from parliamentary or public controversy. Hence the Cabinet has considered not only whether to apply for admission to the Common Market, but also the location of a third airport for London.

Disputes between Ministers and departments are another source of questions for collective decision, in which cases the Cabinet acts as a court of appeals. The major category naturally consists of conflicts between the spending departments and the Treasury, which has the task of preparing the estimates of expenditure for submission to Parliament. At one time the initial responsibility for determining the overall limit on expenditure and the ceilings for programs and departments was put on the Minister in charge of the Treasury, the Chancellor of the Exchequer. When a spending department refused to accept its allocation, the matter would go to the Cabinet for decision. A major battle might ensue, as in 1951 when Aneurin Bevan, Minister of Britain's newly established National Health Service and Leader of the left wing of the Labour party, clashed with Hugh Gaitskell, Chancellor of the Exchequer and the rising star of the moderates. At issue was the provision for the Health Service, which Gaitskell sought to restrain in a time of heavy inflationary pressure. Failing to carry the Cabinet, Bevan chose to resign rather than accept the collective decision. "The Chancellor of the Exchequer," he said, when explaining his resignation to the House, "is putting a financial ceiling on the Health Service."[8]

In these conflicts the Chancellor fought from a strong position, since he was the man responsible for finding the money by taxation and other means to cover expenditure. Yet his position was tactically weak, since the spending Ministers were tempted to gang up on him in pursuit of their respective departmental interests. Recently the control of expenditure was moved further into the committee system. While no rigid scheme was established, the new arrangement was to have the sum total of expenditure determined by the small and powerful Cabinet committee concerned with economic policy and chaired by the Prime Minister. Thereafter the task of allocating the total among departments might be assigned to an ad hoc committee or committees. The effect was to confront each Minister with his responsibility for overall expenditure as well as for his department's needs, and so to prevail upon him to adopt a government-wide, as well as a departmental, point of view. As two officials closely connected with the origination of this reform wrote, "each minister would be forced to balance the claims of his own department against what would have to be foregone by all the others."[9]

Cabinet Ministers wear two hats. Each is at once the head of a department and a part of the chief executive that stands above departments. Under a unitary executive such as the American presidential system, the two roles are physically separated in such a manner that department heads in conflict appeal to their superior, the President, for a decision. It is of the essence of a plural executive such as the British Cabinet that the two roles are combined. The danger of the plural executive is precisely its pluralism, which tempts individual Ministers to forget their government-wide responsibilities. If, however, Ministers can be brought fully to recognize both responsibilities, a degree of coordination in administration and coherence in policy may be reached that is superior to that of the unitary executive system. For now the chief executive is not confronted with the problem of departmental Ministers he must watch and control. On the contrary, the chief executive consists of those Ministers who, under the British system, bring a full knowledge of departmental actions and intentions to executive decision making. The high quality of such decisions—their coherence and comprehensiveness—is presumably also a justification for the far-reaching burdens of collective responsibility.

These arrangements do have some curious consequences. They may at times oblige a Minister to declare his support for, and expound the virtues

---

[8]487 *H. C. Deb.* 41 (23 April 1951).

[9]Lord Plowden and Sir Robert Hall, "The Supremacy of Politics," *The Political Quarterly,* 39 (October–December 1968), 369.

of, a policy that in fact he detests and shortly before has been tearing to pieces in Cabinet. This is not, however, considered to be lying to the House, but simply a consequence of the convention of collective responsibility. That convention also logically implies secrecy about disagreements in Cabinet, since revelations of such disagreements would mean that Ministers were not presenting a united front. Strict observance of the rule of secrecy would be politically intolerable for ambitious men who often have a strong and opinionated following in party and the public. Ministers therefore find ways of quietly letting their true position in Cabinet be known to the press.

Since collective responsibility is a convention binding only among members of a Government and not between a Government and Parliament, it can be relaxed by any Government. This happened in 1932, when the National Government allowed certain of its members to speak and vote against its tariff proposals in order to avoid their resignation. This Government, however, consisting of Conservatives, Liberals, and a few Labourites, was one of the rare cases in British history of a true coalition government. Its behavior was reminiscent of the practice of coalition governments formed under parliamentary systems where there are many parties. Under the French Third Republic, for instance, although there was a constitutional rule of collective responsibility, sometimes a Minister in speaking and voting might disagree with the position taken by the Cabinet. This occurred when dissension within the Cabinet became so sharp that certain Ministers insisted on the right to vote against a government bill and were allowed by the Prime Minister and a majority of their colleagues to do so without incurring the obligation of resigning from the Ministry. Likewise, in Britain before the rise of cohesive political parties, the rule of collective responsibility was followed only slackly. In George III's time Ministers spoke and sometimes even voted against policies adopted by the Cabinet. Party has clearly played an outstanding role in the development of this aspect of the British Constitution.

The New Structure of Decision Making

How to maintain the conditions for coherent policy making is an acute problem for every modern government in this day of the welfare state and managed economy. It is not a problem that admits of ideal solutions in any country. Yet it is also obvious that a system of executive decision making that originated in the eighteenth century and reached its classic form in the nineteenth should not survive the twentieth without major adaptations.

One of these has been the development of the Cabinet secretariat. Before World War I no records of Cabinet proceedings were kept, and

Ministers were not permitted even to take notes on Cabinet discussions. The only exception was the Prime Minister, who wrote a personal letter to the monarch reporting decisions and the discussion leading to them. The results are vividly suggested in a famous note from the private secretary of a Cabinet Minister to the private secretary of the Prime Minister in 1882:

> Harcourt and Chamberlain have both been here this morning, and *at* my Chief about yesterday's Cabinet proceedings. They cannot agree about what occurred. There must have been some decisions, as Bright's resignation shows. My Chief has told me to ask you what the devil *was* decided, for he be damned if he knows.

Action was first taken with regard to defense policy. The Committee of Imperial Defence, the first of the standing committees of the Cabinet, was created in 1903. It had only one permanent member, the Prime Minister, but the persons usually attending included the political heads of the defense departments along with the commander in chief from the military bureaucracy, while the heads of the military intelligence departments served as joint secretaries and a clerk from the Foreign Office kept minutes. As the committee's work grew and subcommittees proliferated, the committee acquired a sizable secretariat to prepare the agenda, keep minutes, and perform liaison work with other departments—notably the Foreign Office—that were interested in defense policy. In 1916, under the pressure of war, Lloyd George, shortly after becoming Prime Minister, took over this secretariat and put it at the service of the Cabinet and all Cabinet committees. By 1969 the total staff numbered 108, of whom about 45 directly serviced the Cabinet and its committees. The head of the Cabinet office, known as the Secretary of the Cabinet, like the other members of the staff, is a permanent official and ranks as one of the three top civil servants, the other two being the permanent secretaries of the Treasury and of the recently established Civil Service Department.

The bland-sounding tasks of the Cabinet secretariat in fact constitute an important element in the network of power relations within the British executive. The innocent task of preparing the Cabinet agenda can mean keeping one Minister waiting for decisions while another is given ready access, a good reason why the agenda is drawn up under the direction of the Prime Minister. The secretariat sees to it that all items of Cabinet business are properly supported by memoranda and that the memoranda are circulated to the proper people at the proper time. It makes sure that non-Cabinet Ministers whose departments are involved in an item of Cabinet business are present at the relevant discussion. Perhaps its principal function relates to the minutes, which are based on notes taken—in longhand—by the secretary of the Cabinet and two assistants. A minute (or conclusion as it is often called) summarizes the documents on which the decision has been made, sets out the gist of the pertinent statements of fact and of the general arguments urged, and concludes with a statement of the decision taken, summed up orally by the Prime Minister. After a meeting the minutes are promptly sent to departments. They are important not merely as a record, but above all as instructions telling departments what to do. These minutes from the Cabinet and Cabinet committees provide, in the words of an ex-Minister, "the whole of the civil service with their marching orders day by day." They are the means by which the government machine is set in motion and controlled. Moreover, they keep Ministers and officials constantly and accurately informed as to what department has come out on top in the current Cabinet battles, information that cannot fail to influence the outcome of emerging conflicts at the ministerial or official level.

The constant communication of this sort of information to the decision-making centers of the government is of the utmost importance to the smooth and rapid working of the Whitehall machine, as it is to any modern bureaucracy. At any given moment throughout the British administration many issues involving different departments are coming up for decision, and the knowledge of the latest Cabinet decision on policy will help direct these issues toward solution. Inseparable from this information relating to substance, however, is the further information relating to the balance of power within the Cabinet. Accurate knowledge as to how this balance is tipping, and especially as to which side the Prime Minister is taking, can save a great deal of time by discouraging subordinates from making vain efforts to appeal decisions that are bound to fail. Finally, in addition to these tasks of preparing for meetings of the Cabinet and Cabinet committees and of recording and circulating their decisions, the secretariat has the vital function of follow-up. It does this by periodically checking with departments to ensure that the authoritative decisions have been carried out.

While the secretariat consists of officials and so is subject to the authority of successive Cabinets, the system has some unexpected features. One is that while the Prime Minister orally sums up the Cabinet conclusion, the secretary actually formulates the minute that communicates this decision to departments. This minute is not subject to approval, that is, change, by the Cabinet. Nor can the Prime Minister alone order it to be changed. A well-authenticated story has it that Ramsay MacDonald once tried to get the Secretary of the Cabinet to make an addition to a minute. The official replied, "I can't do that, prime minister, unless I have a minute in writing instructing me to correct the minutes." MacDonald did not press the matter further.[10]

---

[10]R. H. S. Crossman, Godkin Lectures (Harvard University, 1970).

A consequence of the alternation of parties in power is that no Cabinet may see any minutes or other papers of a previous Cabinet of the other party. The purpose is to protect the confidentiality of discussions among Ministers and to prevent any partisan exploitation of them. For similar reasons, at Number 10 Downing Street, the papers collected by the small office that directly serves the Prime Minister will be bundled away for safekeeping when a general election changes the party in power. Likewise, no incoming Minister of a different party may see departmental papers "indicating the views expressed by their predecessors of a different party."[11] This protects the confidentiality of Ministers' exchanges with other Ministers, civil servants, and outside bodies, including foreign governments. While Ministers will not have full access to the previous history of a policy, they will, of course, know what policies were decided on, their civil servants helping them and the new Government to maintain whatever continuity may be required. Such arrangements are consequences of ministerial control and party government. They also mean that such entities as the Cabinet secretariat are, in the words of an ex-Minister, "a power in their own right."

Along with the growth of the secretariat, the growth of the Cabinet committee system has paralleled the expansion of policy in the twentieth century. In 1929, apart from the Committee of Imperial Defence and a small number of ad hoc committees formed from time to time for special purposes, only one standing committee of the Cabinet was in operation, the Home Affairs Committee, charged with considering items of domestic legislation. Even at this late date in Britain's modern political development most business was transacted in full Cabinet. In contrast, after World War II, the Labour Government of 1945–1951 used as many as fifteen standing committees. While the changing problems of public policy mean that old committees will die and new committees will be created, something in the nature of a basic framework seems to be establishing itself. Among the dozen or so used by the Wilson Government the principal standing committees were:

1. The Overseas Policy and Defence Committee, presided over by the Prime Minister.
2. A small Economic Policy Committee, also chaired by the Prime Minister and concerned with strategic decisions.
3. A large Economic Policy Committee, chaired by the Chancellor of the Exchequer and including all the departments concerned with economic problems.
4. The Social Services Committee, chaired by the Secretary of State for these matters.

---

[11]800 *H. C. Deb.* 293 (28 April 1970).

5. The Home Affairs Committee, dealing with matters of domestic policy not under the previous committee.

6. The Public Expenditure Scrutiny Committee, which had the function of reviewing departmental estimates and allocating expenditure among the various departments.

7. The Legislation Committee, which supervised the drafting of bills, making sure they corresponded with Cabinet decisions, and dealt with that crucial and sensitive matter of rationing parliamentary time among departments and Ministers by deciding the order in which bills would be introduced into the House.

Under Wilson, the Prime Minister also met with a small group of his senior colleagues—the Management Committee or Inner Cabinet, most of whom were also committee chairmen—to discuss upcoming business and their strategy for dealing with it in Parliament and elsewhere.

In the normal course of political development the growth in scale and complexity means that the mass of government business increases and the number of departments multiplies. At the same time the problem of coordination becomes more difficult as departments are excluded from the Cabinet and the Cabinet itself is overburdened by the increase in business. Cabinet committees help to relieve the pressure on the Cabinet and to coordinate departments with closely related concerns. In a further step aiming at better coordination, several related departments in a number of cases have been amalgamated into a superministry. In the early 1950s an attempt was made to set up coordinating Ministers—"overlords"—without combining the departments they were to supervise. This did not work, since the overlord was not given the ultimate authority over, and responsibility for, the respective departments, a fact that was brought home when Parliament asked who was to answer to it for the departments. The necessity for amalgamation was finally accepted and has led to the establishment of superministries, each with a single responsible Minister at its head, but with a number of other Ministers assisting him—in the case of the huge Ministry of Technology, making a total of seven Ministers for that one department in the Wilson Government.

Under the Wilson Government the superministries included, in addition to Defence, Social Services, responsible for the work of the two former Departments of Health and Social Security, and Technology, which, as the central point of contact between government and industry, took over many or most functions of the former Department of Scientific and Industrial Research, the Atomic Energy Authority, the Ministry of Aviation, the Ministry of Power, the Board of Trade, and the Department of Economic Affairs. The Heath Government went on to create a new Ministry of Environment—concerned with housing, transport, land use, pollution, public buildings, local government, and regional policy—and to combine a somewhat reduced Ministry of Technology with the Board of Trade to constitute a new superministry of Trade and Industry. Some may think that the Treasury should be included under this heading of superministry, especially in view of the extension of its functions since the war from the traditional financial concerns to major tasks of economic policy. As the traditional coordinating department in the whole system, however, it is a staff agency with few operating responsibilities, but with a unique and powerful position in relation to other departments.

The superministries, as is intended, make possible the direct representation in the Cabinet of nearly all fields of policy—but not without problems. The Secretary of State is assisted by Ministers subordinate to him who will have a closer acquaintance with various aspects of the whole field of departmental policy. As the head of the department, however, it is he who, under the doctrines of both individual and collective responsibility, must represent the department and speak for it in Cabinet. Much as he may need help, he can bring along one of his more knowledgeable subordinates to a Cabinet meeting only with permission, which is sometimes refused.

Another aspect of the emerging pattern is the fact that the superministries tend to parallel the major Cabinet committees. In the case of the Social Services Committee, for instance, the Secretary of State for that group of fields makes a strong chairman. Needless to say, such arrangements, while strengthening coordination among groups of departments, may also fragment Cabinet authority by creating centers of power that are harder to control than their constituent parts were in their original state of dispersion and autonomy. The ability of a department to commit the whole Government becomes far more serious when it is a superministry operating out of such a complex of power.

Another significant development is the tendency to establish committees of officials parallel to Cabinet committees. Such a committee consists of civil servants from the same departments represented on the ministerial committee. Its job is to prepare issues and decisions, raising questions for action by Ministers and itself moving toward decisions in the light of existing policy. There is nothing new in the interdepartmental committee. It is inevitable where departments have a mutual concern, which may well involve conflict, that their representatives should meet and discuss a question before sending it up to Ministers. From disagreements that first emerge at this level arise many of the questions that constitute the Cabinet agenda.

Also at the official level the views and wishes of interest groups may gain access and be taken into consideration. There is nothing illicit or novel about this. Consultation between government departments and outside groups—such as trade unions, trade associations, professional organizations, and large enterprises (including those in the nationalized sector)—is an established feature of the process of identifying problems of public policy and canvassing possible solutions. Indeed, as later discussion will bring out (see Chapters 4 and 10), the National Economic Development Council (N.E.D.C.), established in 1962—which had members drawn from Government, business, the nationalized industries, and the trade unions, along with the similarly constituted score or so of little "neddies" for particular industries—institutionalized and systematized this practice of consultation for the broad purpose of achieving better economic growth.

While consultation with interests is inevitable in Britain, as in any other developed modern state, it may also add to the centrifugal forces acting on policy making. For example, land use is a subject of acute concern to interests in both the public and private sector: farmers, real estate developers, and expanding manufacturing concerns, as well as government departments interested in sites for public housing, new airports, superhighways, and so on. Before any such question can go to Ministers, there must be prolonged discussion at the official level. Yet once parties at this level reach agreement, which is necessarily intricate and weighted with compromise, it is very hard for Ministers at any level to reject such an agreed solution, let alone attempt to fabricate a new one on their own. Some close observers concluded, after watching administrative developments of the early postwar years, that by far the most important development was this tendency of the interdependent decision-making process at the lower levels in effect to commit the higher ministerial authorities. The corporatist tendencies of the modern state promoted by its ever widening intervention in the economy create major problems for coherence in policy making.

The dual role of Cabinet Ministers helps counteract centrifugal tendencies. Similarly, their officials, insofar as they try faithfully to represent their respective Ministers, will be restrained in their assertion of purely departmental or sectional interests. Moreover, the mechanics of the developing Cabinet office provide an infrastructure that can be used to guide the crucial decisions toward the center. The official committee paralleling the Cabinet committee may very well have as its chairman a civil servant from the Cabinet secretariat, whose resources for assessing the problems before the committee and whose influence on its deliberations may be strengthened by his having a staff of his own drawn from the Cabinet office. Thus in the Cabinet office are included not only the secretaries of the Cabinet committees to which the official committees are correlated, but also some of the chairmen of official committees with their staffs.

The British Cabinet, under conditions of party government, provides the essentials of an effective coordinating body—a representation of the elements to be coordinated along with a mechanism and an incentive to unify them. As policy has developed and the public sector has grown creating new centrifugal tendencies, new agencies were created to strengthen the unifying forces: Cabinet secretariat, superministries, Cabinet and official committees, the new Civil Service Department. Even when these were effective, however, they have left the main initiative in policy making to the several departments. To make the Cabinet itself the initiating body is theoretically possible. This would entail giving it the resources to survey and evaluate the whole complex of government policies and to compare them with other possible lines of action with a skill and judgment equal to that of the departmental bureaucracies. This is a tall order, but the Heath Government has moved in this direction. It brought in teams of outsiders, mainly from business, to provide a new overview of policy, showing the strategic relations between different policies and helping Ministers make decisions about priorities. A small Central Policy Review Staff (C.P.R.S.), composed of civil servants and of experts brought from outside, was also added to the Cabinet office. Its task was to look at problems and ideas that were not any one department's specific responsibility, to provide the Cabinet with evaluations of departmental proposals free of the compromise that interdepartmental committees tend to produce, and especially to work with the previously mentioned groups engaged in shaping a system of priorities. Its potentialities can be better assessed after we have examined the scope and structure of the public sector. (See Chapter 4.)

Prime Ministerial Government

However we may assess the Cabinet system as a structure of policy making, it is clear that it has changed a great deal since the nineteenth century and indeed since the interwar years. The Cabinet has adapted to the collectivist age. In large part this has taken place in a step-by-step adaptation to a series of particular and immediate problems, each considered in isolation and on its own terms rather than in the context of some grand plan. This is the way in which governmental structures normally do develop and to which the British, with their pride in empiricism and muddling through, are especially devoted. The virtues of not trying to do too much at one time by way of a grand plan are obvious. The danger is that a series of uncoordinated steps, each quite sensible in itself, can set up a feedback of unanticipated consequences that is overwhelmingly negative. The paradigm of this process of governmental counterproductivity is that proliferation of specialized agencies in the highly developed modern polity which, although each new creation probably heightens effectiveness in one field, raises complexity to such a pitch that the government machine as a whole tends to go out of control. The central structures of policy making suffer grievously from this tendency in Britain, as in all modern states.

There are various ways in which attempts are made to offset these tendencies. One is to reduce the total level of governmental activity, that is, to reverse the trend of modernity toward a constant expansion of policy. The Conservative Government that came to power in Britain in June 1970 was pledged to such an effort. The order of possibility open to modern governments along this line was suggested by the new Chancellor of the Exchequer when he said he proposed to reduce the *increase* of government expenditure from its existing 3.5 percent per year to 2.8 percent per year. New government structures can be created and old ones can be strengthened to cope with fragmentation. In Britain the Treasury has traditionally functioned as a coordinating department, and it will be appropriate to discuss how its powers have developed when we consider problems of administration and planning.

Another line of attack is planned decentralization, which removes from central authority those categories of decision that can be taken by functional or regional units and so makes it possible for the central authority to deal with the questions that are properly its concern. This is a need that many civil servants and even Ministers have recognized for a long time and that, especially in recent years, has inspired various changes in the machinery of government. Planned decentralization makes no sense unless it is matched with arrangements to make sure that the crucial issues are brought to the attention of the central authority and that this central authority has the facilities for dealing with them. This obvious necessity has been responsible for one of the most interesting and controversial developments of the Cabinet system—the presumed increase in the authority and function of the Prime Minister.

As we have seen, the old established conventions of cabinet government regarding the constitution and resignation of a Cabinet, the appointment and dismissal of Ministers, and the dissolution of Parliament and calling of an election, give a Prime Minister wide opportunities for influencing the decisions of his colleagues, individually and collectively. They are important not so much in their exercise as in their potentiality for exercise. One is reminded of the old "fleet in being" theory, that British battleships kept the peace not by what their guns did, but by the widespread knowledge of what they could do. The norms of prime ministerial authority with regard to certain grand, but only occasional, decisions have numerous offspring in the form of more specific controls. Such, for instance, are the powers of the Prime Minister regarding Cabinet committees. As he constitutes and names the Cabinet, so also does he determine what Cabinet committees, standing and ad hoc, are to be set up and who are to be the members, including the crucial figure of chairman, with his power over appeals. If a matter is to be referred to a committee, the Prime Minister says to what committee. Similarly, he determines the agenda for the Cabinet itself, and his oral summations give the government machine its principal marching orders. That the Prime Minister says and does these things and that Ministers expect him to do them cannot fail greatly to improve his chances of winning such conflicts as may arise between him and one or several of them. One cannot fail to be reminded of the powers that

Speakers have sometimes had in American legislatures, both state and national—for example, to appoint committees, name committee chairmen, and assign bills—and how they have sometimes used these powers in building formidable empires of influence.

Moreover, and this is the crucial point, when we consider the question of an increase in the Prime Minister's influence, while these controls or powers may be considered merely the logical projection of his traditional constitutional authority, they have emerged with, and relate to, a whole new system of collective decision making, as described in the previous pages. This new structure would seem to give that old authority not only a new appearance, but also a new reality. Under the classic Cabinet system the Prime Minister was obliged to win any important matter by fighting it out in full Cabinet where his opponents would be able to appeal to their colleagues in the name of the public good, party principle, personal ambition, and other familiar grounds of political motivation. Conceivably, under the new system the Prime Minister, anticipating resistance in the Cabinet, could send the matter to a committee. If he were prudent, he might even send it to an ad hoc committee with a membership selected by him especially for this purpose and with a chairman who would discourage appeals that, in any case, if pressed, would reach the Cabinet only by way of the Prime Minister. Following this procedure—to continue the speculation—the Prime Minister could presumably expect a favorable decision to go out to the government machine without the risk at any point of formal confrontation with its opponents.

What is lacking from these ominous portraits of "prime ministerial government" can be summed up in one word—politics. No one can doubt that the conceptions of legitimacy that are the basis of the British Constitution endow any Prime Minister with substantial authority. In little, his relations with his colleagues reproduce that primordial political situation, the confrontation of "chief" and "administrative staff." His prime ministerial authority enables him within limits to control and use their powers as political leaders and administrators. Within the power relationships of the Cabinet, this authority is a constant, changing only slowly over time. Yet, as we have seen, the lines of power set up by authority are supplemented (and sometimes diverted) by other, often more volatile variables. Thus what a Prime Minister can "get away with"—to use an expression that British insiders themselves sometimes use—will also be determined by his position in the party and in the country. Indeed, these variables also include highly personal relationships with colleagues, depending upon friendship and family, as well as capacities for psychological domination and subordination. In trying to get his way, a Prime Minister cannot fail to recognize, allow for, and use such factors. For example, just as his colleagues know that if he resigns the whole Cabinet comes to an end, he knows that if they—or the politically more eminent among them—resign, his premiership will be gravely discredited. Neither of these things needs to happen to make their possibility a continual influence on Cabinet interaction. Moreover, it is not just this extreme possibility that constrains the Prime Minister but also lesser and more realistic dangers. Cabinet dissension can spread to the back benches of the party, making Parliament harder to handle, and indeed to the Civil Service, creating problems of administrative control.

A closer look at a crucial series of decisions in foreign policy will illustrate this analysis. In October 1956 British troops in cooperation with French troops attempted to seize control of the Suez canal, nominally in order to protect this international waterway against the dangers of war created by an attack on Egypt launched by Israel, actually in order to deprive Egypt of control of the canal and promote the installation of a more friendly government there. When the United States prevented the British from obtaining the international financial assistance needed to get them through the crisis, the British were obliged to declare a cease-fire and ultimately to withdraw without achieving their purposes, nominal or real. This ill-fated operation was an intensely personal policy of the then Prime Minister, Sir Anthony Eden. Before World War II he had been one of the chief opponents of appeasement of the fascist dictators, and he again saw the old pattern of aggression when Nasser in breach of solemn agreements seized control of the canal with strong Soviet support. A certain edge was added to Eden's reaction by the fact that it was he who, only two years before and against the opposition of a substantial faction in the Conservative party, had made arrangements with Nasser regarding the canal highly favorable to Egypt.

Indeed, so personal was the policy that for some years after the affair, it was thought that Eden had carried out the whole thing on his own authority and without the knowledge or consent of his Cabinet. While Eden moved much planning and decision making to a small committee of more eminent Ministers and often acted on his own, he did keep the Cabinet informed and won acceptance of the fundamental decisions, only three Ministers out of a total of some eighteen dissenting from the plan for an invasion. The very fact that this was a highly personal policy, however, weakened Eden's position when the Americans behaved in so unexpected a manner. His colleagues had accepted his proposal for the use of force, but not the disastrous financial and economic situation that suddenly loomed as a consequence. This issue being raised, the Minister concerned, Harold Macmillan, Chancellor of the Exchequer, reversed his position of support for the policy and brought a majority of the Cabinet to his side. A Prime Minister with a stronger political and personal position might have been able to disregard that majority or to rally it for a prolongation of the use of force. Eden, however, was confronted not only with dissension in the Cabinet, but also with the prospect of its spreading. Two Ministers had already resigned. Some senior foreign service officers were on the verge of resignation, an almost unprecedented step. Revulsion among back-benchers threatened abstentions in parliamentary votes. Eden felt obliged to acquiesce. As a leading student of executive power remarks, "his plight speaks to the exercise of power in a collegium."[12]

We cannot expect that the British Prime Minister will have the kind of power over his Cabinet that an American President has over his. It is of the essence of the British Cabinet that a substantial number of its members will be men with strong political bases in Parliament, the party, and the country. An American Cabinet, on the other hand, rarely contains—at any rate in recent years—many men of major political stature. The political figures whom the President must continually take into account are to be found rather in the Congress, especially among the chairmen of its powerful committees.

Nevertheless, the Prime Minister like the President can provide an energizing, directing, and coordinating center for government. In operating within the new structure based on superministries and Cabinet committees, his old authority gives important powers of control. Moreover, the developing machinery on the official level centers in his office. At Number 10 he has a small office of only a half-dozen or so top civil servants but of growing importance. He is also directly in charge of the new Civil Service Department, whose major concern is questions of machinery of government. Moreover, the Cabinet office, while serving the Cabinet as a whole, is primarily at the disposal of the Prime Minister. With its network of officials undergirding the Cabinet committees, it can keep the Prime Minister informed of what is going on. Specifically, for instance, its permanent head, when briefing the Prime Minister on the agenda, can tell him just how a certain proposal originated and what has been said for and against it. The new central policy review staff will probably further strengthen the Prime Minister. While it will make available to all Cabinet members an assessment of proposals that is independent of departmental evaluations, it will operate directly under the Prime Minister, the government figure who overwhelmingly has the greatest interest in the impact and success of government policy as a whole. It is highly unlikely, however, that such mechanisms can change the essential collegiality of the Cabinet system.

---

[12]Richard E. Neustadt, *Alliance Politics* (New York, 1970), p. 95.

Three

Control of
the Public Sector

To draw a line between the polity and the rest of society is becoming more and more difficult in Britain, as in other advanced countries. Only a few decades ago it might have seemed plausible to draw that line where the bureaucracy—that is, the men and women directly employed in public administration—confronted the rest of the populace. But today the bureaucracy, huge as it has become, is only a small segment of the "public sector." Moreover, the public sector itself is intimately and purposively connected with the private sector by linkages that transmit its influence into the rest of the society, especially the economy. Export industries, for instance, while nominally part of the private sector, are shaped and conditioned by government programs in the service of broad policies to protect the balance of payments. Under British law workingmen are free to bargain collectively with their employers over wages and conditions. In fact, governments exert vast efforts to make these bargains come out in a way not too unfavorable to the general health of the economy. The so-called private sector is continually expected to carry out public purposes.

The main problem of public administration is how to make this huge machine with its multiple and many-jointed linkages an effective instrument for carrying out government policy. Whether it is effective will depend not only on the capacities of persons and structures, but also upon the policies that the central authorities have charged them with carrying out. If these policies arouse hostility, evasion, or resistance, or indeed if they fail to elicit the willing cooperation of the groups affected, the machine will not work. What people can be prevailed upon to accept from government is a major determinant of government's effectiveness. Their consent must be won. If, for instance, trade unions resolutely refuse to accept controls over the price of labor, the machinery set up to exercise this control in the service of planning will break down. The main problem of public administration thus merges with a principal question of public policy. For in a modern democratic state such as Britain a central question of conflict over public policy has been how far and in what ways state power shall be extended over the lives of individuals and groups. The general trend toward centralization and the expansion of policy has meant that more and more areas of free private activity have been included in and subjected to the pattern of power.

The main forces of modernization—democracy and science—might seem to make this trend inevitable. Yet the extent and manner of government control in Britain, as elsewhere, has been a main issue of political conflict. Moreover, the main shifts in approach have not been determined solely by the outcome of general elections. The extension or retraction of government control has been affected not only by how people have voted, but also by how they have reacted directly to attempts to control their behavior. Not only the realities of getting elected, but also the realities of governing have determined the fluctuating boundaries of the pattern of power, and the main shifts in government attitudes toward economic control have occurred not at elections but between them. As we shall see in this chapter, the problems of public administration lead straight into the central problems of politics.

Conventionally, the public sector is constituted by the central government, the local authorities, and the public corporations. The latter consist largely of the nationalized industries: the airlines, railroads, coal mines, and gas, electricity, steel, and atomic energy industries. One index of the size and influence of the public sector is monetary. In 1968 expenditure, current and capital, for the public sector came to a little over £19 billion. This amounted to 52 percent of a G.N.P. of nearly £39 billion. The impact of the public sector on investment and, so, on economic growth is suggested by the fact that it accounted for nearly 50 percent of gross domestic capital formation. In terms of employment the public sector included 25 percent of the total work force, some 6.3 million in comparison with 19 million in the private sector. Of these 6.3 million the central government accounted for 1.9 million, the local authorities for 2.3 million, and the public corporations for 2 million. In the higher-skill categories the share of the public sector increased, including about half of all university graduates and a third of all qualified scientists and technologists.

It is the departments of the central government, with their growing armies of clerical, technical, and administrative employees, that attract most attention as the embodiment of modern bureaucracy. Table 3.1

Table 3.1 Growth of the United Kingdom Civil Service (Nonindustrial Staff)

1797	16,267	1914	280,900
1832	27,000	1939	399,600
1871	53,874	1950	664,200
1901	116,413	1960	634,600
1911	172,352	1969	889,500

DATA SOURCES: W. J. M. Mackenzie and J. W. Grove, *Central Administration in Britain* (London, 1957), p. 7; and *Annual Abstract of Statistics* (London: H.M.S.O., 1970).

shows their increase in numbers since the eighteenth century.

This expansion in scale was accompanied by an increase in specialization, reflected in the creation of new departments. Tracing back the departments that independently or as parts of amalgamations were still operating in 1970, one finds that the following had already come into existence by the end of the eighteenth century: Admiralty, Treasury, Post Office, Foreign Office, Home Office, Board of Trade, and War Office. During the nineteenth century the Colonial Office, Scottish Office, and Departments of Agriculture and Fisheries, Education, and Works were set up. In the twentieth century the pace quickened, with the following departments created up to the outbreak of World War II: Labour, Air, Pensions and National Insurance, Health, Transport and Civil Aviation, and Commonwealth Relations. Since the start of World War II the following were established: Supply, Fuel and Power, Housing and Local Government, Education and Science, Land and Natural Resources, Overseas Development, Welsh Affairs, and, in an attempt to cope with this very proliferation of specialized departments, the superministries of Defence, Trade and Industry, Health and Social Services, and Environment.

Beyond this central bureaucracy are the other agencies of the public sector, especially included under local government and the public corporations. And merging with the public sector is a set of organizations, groups, and relationships that, whether technically public or private, are in fact indispensable to the implementation of public policy. A recent government report remarks that

> the complex intermingling of the public and private sectors [has led to] a proliferation of para-state organisations: public corporations, nationalised industries, negotiating bodies with varying degrees of public and private participation, public participation in private enterprises, voluntary bodies financed from public funds. Between the operations of the public and private sectors there is often no clear boundary.[1]

---

[1]Fulton Committee, *Report on the Civil Service,* Vol I (London: H.M.S.O., 1968), Cmnd. 3638, p. 10.

Ministers and Civil Servants

To control and give direction to this huge machine means in the first place making it responsive to the policy-making center—that is, the Cabinet and Ministers—and in the second place imparting to it the capacity to carry out these policies effectively.

The first problem is a special case of the general problem of how to establish democratic control over the instrumentalities of state power at a time when policy is becoming ever more complex and technical. Even if one assumes that popular control over Ministers can be ensured by the mechanisms of party government, one must still question whether a set of politicians with limited expertise and many distractions can effectively control the top bureaucrats who make a career of government service. In Britain the thing to fear, it must be emphasized, is not purposeful bureaucratic sabotage. During the 1930s there were observers who predicted such a conflict even in Britain if and when a socialist government—that is, the Labour party—came to power.[2] As a deduction from simple-minded Marxist premises, the argument was plausible. The upper ranks of the Civil Service are—as they were then—recruited substantially from the upper

Table 3.2 Social Composition of the British Civil Service Administrative Class, 1967 (in Percent)

Father's Occupation	
Higher Professional or Managerial	21
Intermediate Professional or Managerial	46
Skilled Worker	23
Semiskilled and Unskilled Worker	6
Other	3
	100

Education: Type of Secondary School Attended	Year of Entry into Service			
	Before 1940	1940–1950	1951–1960	After 1960
L. E. A. Grammar	30	29	33	29
Direct Grant	20	17	21	18
Public School or Fee-paying School	50	50	46	50
Other	0	4	0	3

DATA SOURCE: Fulton Committee, *Report on the Civil Service,* Vol. 3, Part 1 (London: H.M.S.O.), pp. 54, 73, and 85.

---

[2]See, for example, J. Donald Kingsley, *Representative Bureaucracy: An Interpretation of the British Civil Service* (Yellow Springs, Ohio, 1944); and Harold Laski, *Parliamentary Government in England* (New York, 1939).

and middle ranks of British society, as Table 3.2 makes clear. If the working classes and the upper classes believed their respective interests were fundamentally in conflict, it would no doubt follow that a bureaucracy composed of upper-class personnel would try to sabotage a working-class program. In fact, when the news came through in 1945 that Labour had won, the mood among higher civil servants was euphoric, and with their socialist Ministers they set about putting through a program of reform comparing in magnitude with those other great instances of peaceful revolution, 1832 and 1906. In their recollections no Ministers have been more eulogistic of the Civil Service: "Unequalled in all the world," declared Clement Attlee, the former Labour Prime Minister and a man noted for understatement.

To say that civil servants are loyal to the Government of the day, however, does not mean that they are merely passive tools of ministerial initiative. They have ideas about what ought and ought not to be done, and they are expected to present these ideas to their ministerial chiefs. That they have a role in making policy as well as executing policy is made clear in any of the classic formulations of their function. One of these formulations was presented by Sir Warren Fisher, a notable head of the Civil Service during the interwar years. He said:

> Determination of policy is the function of ministers, and once a policy is determined it is the unquestioned and unquestionable business of the civil servant to strive to carry out that policy with precisely the same good will whether he agrees with it or not. That is axiomatic and will never be in dispute. At the same time it is the traditional duty of civil servants, while decisions are being formulated, to make available to their chiefs all the information and experience at their disposal and to do this without fear or favor, irrespective of whether the advice thus tendered may accord or not with the Minister's initial views.[3]

As Fisher made clear, the norm is that civil servants are expected to criticize Ministers' proposals and to present and argue for their own, but once the Minister has decided, the civil servant must do his best faithfully to develop the ministerial program and see that it is effectively carried out by the department. All this, moreover, is not only convention, but, on the whole, the truth about ministerial-bureaucratic relations and is not disputed in serious discussions of the topic. A more critical hypothesis—suspicion, if you like—undercuts this analysis. It raises the possibility that although the civil servant is typically an honest and obedient subordinate, the Minister may simply not know enough to initiate proposals or to criticize authoritatively what the civil servant puts forward. If so, there

---

[3]Royal Commission on the Civil Service, 1929–1931. Evidence.

would be no conflict, no duplicity, no sabotage, yet a largely one-way flow of influence from bureaucrat to politician.

Certain elements in the situation make this outcome likely. The background of the typical Minister hardly gives him a profound grasp of the problems of his department. Even if he was front-bench spokesman in the relevant field when in Opposition, the absence of a full system of specialized legislative committees before which bureaucrats appear prevents him from getting a close and intimate look at what the department is doing. As a Minister he is very probably moved from department to department, the average tenure being about two years. Such mobility is no doubt helpful in keeping the Minister's mind fresh and in satisfying his political ambition as he climbs the ladder of success, but it also severely limits his experience in any particular field. Also, as the head of a department he is diverted by other duties. A recent study concluded that in the Wilson Government, the average Minister's work week came to sixty-one hours, of which he spent fifteen on departmental business, seventeen at the House, and twenty-nine in other activities. If we think in terms of conflict, this distribution of time puts a quarter-time Minister against a full-time bureaucrat. Finally, there is the fact that the Prime Minister in picking members of the Government is confined almost entirely to members of Parliament—a very narrow base for recruitment—and, moreover, is sometimes obliged to give preference to political and party popularity regardless of competence.

On the other hand, Ministers have powerful means by which to convert their immense formal authority into effective control. In the first place, they are free to call on expert aid from outside. The party research department and officials of interest groups are available to them in office as they were in Opposition. Increasingly important are professionally trained people, especially from the academic world. When the Labour Government took power in 1964, Ministers brought in a score or so of temporary officials —one Labour Minister christened them "the irregulars"—to a great extent in deliberate imitation of the Kennedy administration. The larger frustrations of that Government impeded extensive social or economic reform. Yet the use of "irregulars" received the blessing of a major report on reform of the Civil Service, and the new Conservative Government similarly brought in outside advisers from the business and professional world for the purpose of policy analysis and review.

Even more important than help from outside experts is the party mandate. In Britain, as elsewhere, party manifestoes contain their fair share of fuzzy compromises and nonoperational rhetoric. But usually there will also be a series of quite definite and intelligible pledges tucked away amidst the pompous prose. These may constitute tacit promises to an interest group or specific reforms worked out by party intellectuals and presumably reflecting party principles or ideology. In either case the brief proposal of the manifesto will probably be backed up by a position paper, perhaps published as a party pamphlet, and watched over by a group of outsiders specially concerned with its enactment. With this kind of support the Minister is in a position of incontestable superiority, as civil servants universally recognize, whatever their views of the feasibility or merits of such proposals. R. H. S. Crossman, a long-time leader of the left wing of the party and a redoubtable Minister in the Wilson Government, reported his experience in these words:

> The truth is the British civil service accepts the two party system completely. Indeed, in certain ways it's almost embarrassing. When you arrive in government after winning an election, there they are. They say, "Minister, we have been working on your manifesto; we have all the plans ready for implementing all your legislative proposals." I am well aware that as of today [this was shortly before the election of 1970] my ministry has a section which is busily studying the Conservative manifesto, preparing for the unfortunate possibility of a turn-over.[4]

The respect was mutual. After Crossman had left office a senior civil servant said of his term in office: "It was the most productive two years in the history of this ministry. It was absolute murder for the civil servants; tears, nervous breakdowns. But things *happened.*"

The Question of Expertise

Beyond the question of whether Cabinet and Ministers can control and direct the upper level of the bureaucracy lies the far more complex and important question of the effectiveness of the bureaucracy and related agencies as instruments of state power. This raises problems relating to quality of personnel, as well as aspects of structure, in particular, types of decentralization and means of coordination.

A recent report on the Civil Service by a committee under the chairmanship of Lord Fulton severely criticized it and proposed a series of reforms, many of which are now being carried out. These proposals are worth considering in some detail, as illustrating modernization and its problems. The proposals advocated not merely greater specialization, but especially specialization based upon scientific knowledge. Concerning itself mainly with the upper levels of the bureaucracy, the Fulton Committee sought greatly to enhance the position and authority of the technically and scientifically trained person.

At the time of the report, in 1968, the Civil Service was divided into a

---

[4]R. H. S. Crossman, Godkin Lectures (Harvard University, 1970).

number of classes. Those of interest to us were the generalist and the specialist classes. The former, recruited on the basis of general education and personal qualities, consisted of several levels. At the top was the Administrative class, numbering 2,700 men and women, to which about one hundred new members between the ages of twenty and twenty-four were recruited each year, usually straight from the university. Two methods were used. Method I, the older, was based on written examinations testing general intelligence and academic competence in typical university subjects ranging from Arabic to Zoology. Method II, the extended interview, came out of a system developed during World War II to select army officers and was based largely on close observation of candidates over a period of two days going through exercises that were similar to the work that a successful candidate would perform in the public service. The Administrative class consisted of six grades: assistant principal, principal, assistant secretary, undersecretary, deputy secretary, and permanent secretary. It was the elite of the system, its members enjoying the highest pay scale and virtually monopolizing the top administrative posts from assistant secretary on up. Other general classes that should be mentioned were the Executive class, numbering 83,000 and usually recruited from young people just finishing secondary school, and the Clerical and Clerical Assistant classes, numbering 191,000, who performed the routine work of the departments.

In contrast to these general classes were the Professional classes and Scientific and Technical staffs. Numbering 132,300, these groups were recruited from people outside the Service who had already obtained some special qualification relevant to their work—for example, doctors, lawyers, scientists, architects, economists, engineers, surveyors, and supporting workers. Some of these professional and scientific civil servants, needless to say, were persons of exceptional attainments. Yet under the existing procedures governing appointments, they could not be moved to the top administrative posts unless they were first promoted to the Administrative class. This transfer rarely took place. In 1968 thirty-three out of thirty-six posts of permanent secretary were held by members of the Administrative class.

Probably the major reform proposed by the committee was the abolition of the system of Civil Service classes in favor of a system of grades modeled on the American practice. Such a unified grading scheme was put into effect for the Administrative, Executive, and Clerical classes in 1971. If and when the scheme is extended to professional and scientific workers, not only will the discriminatory titles, conditions, and pay be eliminated, but also the opportunity will be opened up for scientists and other professionally trained people to move more easily into the higher administrative positions.

The rationale for this reform as stated by the committee is wholly modernist. In its view the old system expressed an old fashioned faith in the "generalist" as against the "specialist" for the task of administration. "The ideal administrator," the committee wrote, "is still too often seen as the gifted layman who, moving frequently from job to job within the Service, can take a practical view of any problem, irrespective of its subject-matter, in the light of his knowledge and experience of the government machine."[5] But, according to the committee, this will no longer do as the inspiration for recruitment, training, and promotion when the tasks of government involve highly technical operations, especially in the realm of economic and financial policy. In the committee's view these upper posts must be manned by people who have not simply a general grasp of administration, but who have professional knowledge of the subject matter of the department they are administering.

The scientific and technocratic spirit in these proposals is plain. They are also an attack upon traditionalism in British society as well as in the government Service. For the structure of classes in the Civil Service faithfully reflected the class structure of British society. The system of recruitment was geared to the educational system, which at once determines and reflects class structure. From the time more than a hundred years ago, when the Service was put on a merit basis, it was expected and certainly hoped that its upper reaches would attract the graduates of the old and elite universities, Oxford and Cambridge. Nor has Oxbridge relaxed its strangle hold on those posts, in the period 1957–1963, for example, producing 85.5 percent of the successful candidates for the Administrative class in contrast with only 14.5 percent from other universities.

Moreover, and this is closer to our concerns, although Oxford and Cambridge have greatly broadened the social sources of their student body in recent decades, the social origins of those entering the Administrative class have remained fairly narrow. (See Table 3.2.) In spite of efforts to correct the imbalance, as the Fulton Committee reported, "direct recruitment to the Administrative Class has not produced the widening of its social and educational base that might have been expected."[6]

The upper classes of British society have traditionally defended their privileges on the grounds that they perform an important political function. In Schumpeter's words they constituted that "social stratum" who "after having proved itself able to avoid an analogon to the French Revolution and to eliminate the dangers from dear bread . . . continued to know how

---

[5]Fulton Committee, *op. cit.,* p. 11.

[6]*Ibid.,* p. 12.

to manage social situations of increasing difficulty, and how to surrender with some grace." The Administrative class of the Civil Service has continued to draw substantially on this social stratum. Moreover, its function has not been conceived as essentially technical. Its central concern is "the formation of policy"; it is the "policy-making" class of the Service. In the late nineteenth century the political leadership of the country maintained contact with the "other classes" as the era of social reform and collectivist policy was inaugurated. But the party and parliamentary leaders who carried out these reforms depended upon the close cooperation of their advisers in the newly reformed Civil Service. Oxford and Cambridge turned out a disproportionate share of both British Cabinets and the Administrative class, so that men who had been contemporaries at the universities often later bridged the gap between Westminster and Whitehall.

It is sometimes said that the task of the Minister is to tell the civil servant what the voters will not stand. This saying, although too negative, gets across the point that an important part of the politician's job is to reflect pressures from the people. The top civil servants also feel pressure from the people, in the people's capacity not as voters, but as citizens bearing the burdens and receiving the benefits of the modern state. The people, as individuals, as members of groups, as highly organized bodies in business and social life, can make their demands known through politicians. But they also continually make known their will as the objects of, and often the partners in, bureaucratic action. Their consent and cooperation must be secured if the vast and complex policies of the modern state are to be carried out effectively. The bureaucrat himself is the principal object of these reactions, the management of which is a crucial kind of politics. His task is to make policy effective, but since he does not have unlimited coercion at his command, he can achieve this only by making policy in some degree also responsive. He does not address himself publicly to the demands coming up through Parliament, pressure groups, and parties. But the assistant secretary who spends long hours trying to wear down a little further the hostility of trade unionists to an incomes policy or to warm up businessmen to the point of cooperation with an export drive is, nonetheless, deeply immersed in politics.

Policy making has a large and growing scientific and technical component, but it is not itself an act of applied science. Neither Ministers nor top civil servants can perform their respective functions by deduction from a body of empirically based, systematically organized, and experimentally tested propositions. The element of political judgment in the advice of the administrator takes a good mind—broad, lucid, and flexible—but it has not yet been reduced to a scientific basis. Today, as at the origins of the Civil Service in the nineteenth century, its defenders insist upon this distinctively political character of the tasks of its higher ranks. As one authority has written:

> They must temper their appreciation of technical beauty with a keen sense of their public relations. In short the Administrative Grade and its hierarchical form is necessary precisely because the work of a ministry demands a sense of public policy as well as a grasp of techniques.[7]

None of this should be taken to mean that the role of science and technology in British government has not increased and will not continue to increase. Britain, the home of Sir Isaac Newton, is by no means inhospi-

Table 3.3 Nobel Prizes by Country and Field, 1945–1970

	Physics	Chemistry	Medicine/ Physiology	Three Fields
Great Britain	5	12	8	25
France	2	0	2	4
Germany	2	4	3	9
United States	16	11	22	49
Soviet Union	4	1	1	6

DATA SOURCE: The World Almanac, 1971.

table to science, as one can see from her fantastic comparative achievement in winning Nobel prizes. (See Table 3.3.) Nor are British government and business insensitive to the importance of science to economic progress. In relation to her G.N.P. Britain spends more on research and development than either France or Germany and much more than the United States. Scientists share membership on the majority of the vast network of advisory committees that are attached to government departments. Of the top British scientists constituting the members of the Royal Society, 20 percent held full-time or part-time appointments in government or quasi-government bodies in 1970. Within the Civil Service itself, the impact of science is increasingly evident. Of the sixty or so top civil servants engaged in administration in the huge Ministry of Technology in 1968, twenty-two were scientists.

It is this last statistic that is most interesting as suggesting a possible future. People can grant that the "generalist" with his essentially political talents performs a different function from the "specialist," yet disagree about how generalists are to be produced. In the past the generalists have been trained very largely in the subjects that constituted in Britain the principal means of a liberal education—classics, history, and mathematics. But science—meaning by this both natural and social science—can also

---

[7]S. E. Finer, *A Primer of Public Administration* (London, 1950), p. 120.

be the vehicle of a liberal education. This at any rate is the view taken by the modernist. If he is right, the shift from the traditional to the more scientific subjects that is to be expected in an increasingly technological future need not mean that the administrative generalist will disappear from the Civil Service.

Territorial Decentralization

The capacity of a bureaucratic system can be enhanced by improvements in personnel or by changes in structure. Many acute observers will say that the problem of ineffectiveness in British government results far less from the allegedly irrelevant education of civil servants and inadequate use of scientists than from overcentralization and the consequent excessive load of business on the higher Civil Service. One senior civil servant recently made these private remarks:

> I don't myself think there is any great substance in the oft-repeated stories about inadequate use of scientists and other "experts" (other than experts in government!) in our civil service system. The fashion of criticism changes, and the Fulton Report calls for economists and sociologists to unlock the door to wise decision-making.
>
> We obviously shan't have a smaller public sector in future; but I think we can readily develop ways of managing it better—basically a question of deciding which are the things which have to be decided politically and centrally, and which are the things which can be decided regionally or locally or by independ ent public boards or agencies.

In Britain as in the United States, amid constant praise of the virtues of local government, centralization has gone forward at an increasing rate, especially in this century. In the late sixties, however, the proposals to local government or regional bodies for planned decentralization seemed to take a more serious form. They reflected primarily the desire of central managers, both bureaucrats and Ministers, to shed some of their overload of administration. But there was also a political side. An upsurge of national feeling in Scotland and Wales—Ireland is an older and more complex story —was expressed in demands for more autonomy for these areas of the Celtic fringe. Some observers also say they detect a rise of regional feeling generally in Britain. To this extent there is political support and stimulus for these efforts of administrative reorganization, and we see a corresponding response in the promises of the political parties.

Since the British Constitution, unlike the American or German, is unitary and not federal, local governments have only the powers allowed to them by the central government. For England and Wales (the Scottish system is slightly different), the scheme laid down in a series of great reorganizing

acts of the late nineteenth century still prevailed in 1971. The areas consisted of two basic sorts. There were sixty-one administrative counties,
sometimes coinciding with the boundaries of the ancient shires and ranging in size from massive Lancashire with 2 million inhabitants to diminutive
Rutland with only 26,000. The other basic type was the county borough,
of which there were eighty-three. These consisted of all the largest cities
except London and in a geographic sense were often embraced by the
larger territory of an administrative county, although they constituted a
separate jurisdiction. This meant that the surrounding area of a big city
might be separately governed from the city itself, a separation of town from
country that tended to rule out metropolitan government. London, however, the exception from the general scheme, did have metropolitan government, its 7.5 million people being governed by thirty-two borough
councils and by the Greater London Council. The administrative counties
were further subdivided into noncounty boroughs, urban districts, and
rural districts, the latter including thousands of parishes of medieval origin,
which had such splendid duties as the maintenance of public footpaths.

As in relations between an American state and its local governments, the
central government may and often does use the local governments as
agents for carrying out central government policies. This is not the case
with all central government programs; many are carried out directly.
Whitehall departments, for instance, have local offices that directly administer such matters as tax collection, pensions, national insurance, national
assistance (welfare), and employment exchanges. Needless to say, the
nationalized industries also have their own local agencies for performing
their functions and bringing their services to the public. The traditional
method of executing central policies, however, was to use the established
local authorities. Since these are legally the creatures of the central government, they can in theory be put under any obligation the sovereign Parliament chooses to put them under. In fact, central departments have been
given far-reaching powers of direction and control, as reflected, for instance, in the words of the Education Act of 1944, which gave the Minister
the duty to "secure the effective execution by local authorities under his
control and direction of the national policy." All local borrowing must
have central approval. Many proposed local programs can be put into
effect only with appropriate departmental approval. But the legal power
of direction has been supplemented and sweetened by a system of grants-
in-aid. These normally involve the payment by the central government of
part of the cost of a program and in return impose certain standards upon
its form and execution. Originating in 1835, central grants to local government have grown immensely in this century and constitute a convenient
measure of the pace and degree of centralization.

As Table 3.4 shows, while the absolute amount spent by local government has increased immensely, its relative importance has shrunk steadily.

Table 3.4 Local Government Expenditure 1890–1968

	1890	1905	1935	1955	1968
Local Government Expenditure at Current Prices in £ Millions	50	123	428	1536	4649
Local Govt. Expenditure As Percent of Total Government Expenditure	—	51	38	25	24
Central Grants As Percent of Local Government Current Expenditure	25	32	46	54	58
Central Grants As Percent of Local Government Expenditure, Current and Capital	22	25	40	39	38

DATA SOURCES: Peacock and Wiseman, *The Growth of Public Expenditure in England,* pp. 197, 200, 208; Central Statistical Office, *Annual Abstract of Statistics* (H.M.S.O., 1970).

Local government expenditure has fallen from a half to a quarter of total government expenditure, and of this quarter something like half is supplied by and is under the control of Whitehall. It is a very different world from that of the nineteenth century, when many observers, such as the German scholars Gneist and Redlich, regarded the strength of British local government, in contrast with the centralization of France, as the secret of British liberty. Yet this method of using local authorities to carry out national policies does avoid day-to-day administrative interference and control. With regard to the police, for instance, although the central government sets standards and inspects to see that they are applied, no central department can ring up and give orders to the head of the police force in a local area, as the Ministry of the Interior can do in France.

Recent proposals for reform will not sound unfamiliar to an American. In order to relieve local authorities from their sole dependence on property taxes (called "rates"), it has been urged that they be authorized to impose new forms of taxation such as a local income tax, sales tax, or motor license fee. Also attempts have been made to bridge the gap between the big towns and their surrounding areas with regard to those functions requiring integrated planning and administration. Under the Local Government Act passed in 1972, the Heath Government greatly reduced the number of local authorities, reorganizing them on the basis of two new types. A type of large jurisdiction, called simply a "county," of which there are fifty-three in England and Wales, includes all areas—whether town or country—within its geographic boundaries. A second type of authority, the "district," often consisting of a large town, such as an old county borough, is only a second-tier unit within the larger jurisdiction. Each is governed by an elected council. The new authorities will begin functioning in 1974. The counties will provide the large-scale government services such as strategic planning, transportation, roads, education, social services, police and fire services, while the districts will be responsible for more localized services, such as development control, housing, and garbage collection. In addition to London exceptions to this scheme would include six metropolitan counties around Birmingham, Sheffield, Manchester, Liverpool, Leeds, and Newcastle-upon-Tyne. There is still need for wider arrangements to provide for regional planning.

The idea of regionalism has been gaining ground since the interwar years, when central departments first began to interpose an intermediate level between Whitehall and their local offices and when special agencies were set up to deal with the economically depressed areas. The regional offices of central departments have become strong and well-established units of government. Less success attended the Wilson Government's establishment of eight districts for England, each with an appointive council of laymen and board of civil servants to assist with economic planning. There were uneasy relations, however, between these agencies and the local authorities, which had long seen a possible threat in regional bodies. Tension also arose with central departments, which largely rejected or ignored their recommendations, and the only effective districts were those with special responsibilities in relation to depressed areas. Also, while the boards and councils could initially deal with local interests by negotiation and concession, there was a tendency for these interests soon to demand some real power.

The fact that not much has been done to bring about territorial decentralization, however, does not mean that the question is closed. In 1969 a Royal Commission on the Constitution was appointed to consider "what changes may be needed in the central institutions of Government in relation to the several countries, nations and regions of the United Kingdom." In the campaign of 1970 the Conservative party committed itself even more strongly and explicitly than the Labour party to what its manifesto called "a genuine devolution of power from the central government."

Functional Decentralization

More successful have been the efforts toward functional decentralization. These have brought about the "hiving off"—a favorite word in Whitehall currently—of parts of departments in the form of independent boards or agencies. Far more than Americans, the British in the past have tended to keep government activities within existing departments. To revisit Whitehall these days is to have a mild sense of being in Washington, as more and more agencies appear alongside the old monoliths.

These public bodies, which on the one hand are not parts of a department, yet on the other hand are not purely private, embrace a wide variety of types. Although many have emerged recently, not all are new. Public boards of a commercial character—that is, ones that engage in substantial trading operations—are well recognized. They consist of certain of the great nationalized industries, such as the two airway corporations, B.O.A.C. and B.E.A.; Cable and Wireless, Ltd.; the National Coal Board; the Electricity Council and the Central Electricity Generating Board, as well as the various area boards; the Gas Council and its area boards; and in the case of transport various bodies, including the British Railways Board and the London Transport Board. Also included under commercial boards are the British Airport Authority, the Atomic Energy Authority, the Herring Industry Board, and the Whitefish Authority; the Sugar Board; and, since it was recently converted from a department to a public corporation, the Post Office. Beyond these are a number of regulatory bodies, advisory boards, and finance corporations of which no exhaustive list, let alone authoritative classification, has yet been compiled.

In essence the idea of hiving off is to remove certain activities of the managed economy from the direct control and responsibility of Ministers, each separate operation being given—by statute if necessary—a specific objective with appropriate powers and then being allowed to carry on its own affairs free from political interference. This was precisely the idea that initially inspired the form of organization given the nationalized industries. While nationalization was inherently an act of state centralization, it was agreed by nationalizing Governments, whether Conservative or Labour, that as far as possible the new state enterprises would be given autonomy and removed from ministerial control. A generation's experience with them has brought out the possibilities and problems of the independent agency under the British system.

The National Coal Board will serve as an example. The Board is a public corporation, which means that while it has the commercial powers of a private corporation for the purposes defined in its charter, its members are appointed by the Minister of Trade and Industry, who has certain supervisory powers. When the 1,500 collieries of Britain were nationalized in 1947, their ownership was vested in the board, which manages them through forty-eight areas and eight divisions and half-a-dozen specialized departments, much as a board of directors would run a very large business. A major purpose of the structure was to give the board substantial independence in the business management of production and marketing. According to Herbert Morrison, a Labour Minister who was one of the principal architects of the public corporation, the problem was to get "the best of both possible worlds, the world of vigorous industrial enterprise without the restrictions imposed by Civil Service methods and Treasury control, and the world of public service and accountability."[8] The industry was

---

[8]Herbert Morrison, *Government and Parliament: A Survey from Inside* (London, 1954), p. 251.

charged with covering its costs, which would make it independent of public funds and so of the detailed controls over expenditure exercised over regular departments by the Treasury. The Minister was given certain specified powers, such as powers of approval of schemes for capital development, powers of appointment and dismissal of the board, and powers to investigate and obtain information. He was also given authority to issue "directions of a general nature" in matters that appeared to him "to affect the national interest." Few such general directions have been issued, but the existence of this authority in the background has made it possible for the Minister usually to get his way without formal action.

The importance of the industry makes it inevitable and desirable that the Minister accept responsibility for what one occupant of the post called the "general success or failure of the enterprise."[9] But to uphold the distinction between "general success and failure" and particular actions of the board or its subordinate parts is not easy amidst the pressures and temptations of politics. The Minister may try to accept responsibility only for general policy and not for day-to-day administration, yet Opposition M.P.s will fudge that distinction as much as possible in their desire to score points. Moreover, the same political forces that move them will tempt the Minister to interfere at the levels of both policy and administration. It is entirely understandable and legitimate that he and the board should jointly determine the target for coal production and the prices to be charged for coal. To raise the price of coal, however, can add to the unpopularity of a Government. To close a pit, although necessary for greater efficiency, may threaten a loss of votes in a local election. The basis of these pressures is the enfranchised and mobilized electorate. While the wisdom of efficient administration advises decentralization, the pressures of democracy tend to push decision making back to the central authority.

It would be far easier to control and confine these political forces if the line could be firmly and unmistakably drawn between what must be decided centrally and what can be left to the independent board. The original acts setting up the public corporations defined this line only in such broad terms as "the national interest." Several decades of effort to give precision to the respective spheres of Minister and board have not been wholly successful. A solution would consist in finding a formula for each nationalized industry or similar activity that clearly stated the objectives of the operation and, if possible, also the criteria it was to follow in pursuing those objectives. The whole process would then be self-operating, and the Minister would need to intervene only to see that the formula was being observed. Along this line annual financial targets have been established for the nationalized industries in order to clarify the old vague requirement to

---

[9]Hugh Gaitskell, quoted in Mackenzie and Grove, *Central Administration in Britain* (London, 1957), p. 435.

cover costs "taking one year with another" and in order to use the prospects of a deficit or profit as guides and incentives to managers. Attempts have also been made to reduce to rule the criteria for judging proposed capital investment and the method for setting prices. Thus far, however, several decades of experience with public corporations have failed to give precision to the respective spheres of Minister and board, and the tendency in Britain, as in other countries, is for Ministers to intervene in the affairs of nationalized industries frequently and without a wholly satisfactory rationale. The problem is twofold: to draw a firm and feasible line between the activities of center and locality and then to stick to it in the face of the powerful cent.alizing forces of egalitarianism and democracy.

Again, however, in recent years some political forces supplementing administrative decentralization have grown stronger. These are not only political but indeed ideological, reflecting as they do the disillusionment of some sectors of opinion with the new efforts of economic planning and control that were made in the sixties. In Britain, as in France, this disillusionment has strengthened the advocates of "a return to the market." In their proposals hiving off is not only a method for improving the efficacy of the agencies of state power. On the contrary, one should say. For these reformers see hiving off as a means of reducing state activity by moving certain activities out of government control and subjecting them to regulation by the market. One kind of proposal is to separate off certain activities that can and should support themselves largely or entirely by fees charged for their goods and services—for instance, the Stationery Office, the British equivalent of the U.S. Government Printing Office. Other agencies, such as the Royal Mint, which coins money for many governments other than the British, could be given trading funds and held responsible for using them efficiently. More controversial are proposals to hive off parts of nationalized industries that promise to be commercially viable and return them to private ownership. The Heath Government, for instance, has proposed that Thomas Cooks', the old and famous travel company, which was nationalized along with the railroads, be hived off and returned to private management.

This resurgence of faith in the market, particularly marked in the Conservative party, springs from the recent failures of central economic planning. This is not the first time that the realities of governing have revealed limits to the effort of modern government in Britain to control the economic environment.

Four

Control of
the Economy

Economic planning is a typical effort of the modern state. Its sources are various. In a real sense it can be regarded as the accidental product of the welfare state. If we think of the latter as the response of the democratic polity to the increasing demands for wider and more varied services, we can see how in due time the activities of the state will comprise a major segment of the economy. Public expenditure mounts to a quarter, a third, and even a half of the national product, with taxation in its many forms increasing similarly. In such a situation, whatever the intentions of the state toward the free market, its own activities have an overwhelming influence upon general equilibria, specific lines of production, and the prosperity of particular regions. Having these great and growing effects, the state can hardly avoid trying to calculate and control them. Not to try to plan in some degree and form would simply be a refusal to recognize reality. Thus the managed economy grows naturally out of the welfare state.

A more conventional view finds a principal source of state intervention in the inadequacies of the market. At one time the rationale of intervention was simply to make up for isolated deficiencies of the market system: to impose on industry safety regulations that the average worker would not have the economic power or perhaps the sophistication to insist upon, and to make minimum provision for incapacitation resulting from illness or old age. In Britain interventions of this sort never ceased, even at the height of laissez faire. The collectivist period properly begins when government assumes a responsibility for certain dimensions of the economy as a whole.

Attempts to prevent inflation on the part of the body charged with determining the value of money go back a long way, but not until the great depression of the thirties did government in Britain begin to acknowledge that it could do something beyond balancing the budget to remedy deflation. The great Keynesian breakthrough in economic theory legitimized, broadened, and directed these efforts, as the increasing programs of the welfare state gave governments the fiscal means for carrying them out. The government now fully recognized that the market system had general as well as isolated deficiencies. This recognition was marked by the commitment to full employment assumed by all parties during World War II and expressed in the famous white paper (Command 6527) issued by the Coalition government in 1944.

As a country that imports half of its food and two-thirds of its raw materials and depends upon sales abroad to pay for these imports, Britain is even less able to trust the market to govern her relations with the international economy. During the great depression of the thirties, she broke with her historic commitment to free trade and took the first steps to control her external economic relations. During the postwar years the balance of payments with the rest of the world has been an urgent and continuing problem; periodic external crises, often rooted in internal inflationary pressures, have been the occasions for some of the more characteristic efforts at economic control.

A further phase in collectivist policy was the assumption of responsibility for economic growth, which Britain, like other advanced countries, undertook in the early postwar years. To the short-run goals of full employment, price stability, and external balance, this new task added the long-run goal of constantly increasing productivity and thus, presumably, constantly raising the standard of living. In terms of the larger purposes of political modernity, this new goal constitutes no real innovation. Laissez faire itself, as a prescription for government policy, had been directed toward it, as Adam Smith made clear when he wrote on how to increase the wealth of nations. The thrust of modernity toward the mastery of nature that was expressed in industrialization inspires the international G.N.P. race among the advanced nations today. In the pursuit of long-run economic development, as in the attempt to achieve short-run equilibria, planning is a natural stage in the unfolding of the modern spirit. Both science and democracy point in this direction.

From the viewpoint of the basic forces of modernization, planning must seem inevitable. The empirical and historical record, however, has been marked at times by efforts to withdraw from planning. In planning, as in centralization generally, there have been cycles of tightening and loosening, as spasms of *dirigisme* have been followed by spells of neoliberalism. The history of planning in Britain since the war is clearly divided into such phases. Indeed, the vocabulary used to describe these efforts changes from phase to phase. The term "economic management" itself came into vogue in Britain in the fifties, as a substitute for "economic planning," which, after the frustrations of the Labour government, was felt to imply a degree of central control that was neither feasible nor desirable.

From Planning to Management

As economic policy has shifted back and forth between planning and management, the instruments used to achieve the ends of policy have changed correspondingly. The tighter kind of control attempted during the phases of planning has involved the creation of new ministerial and bureaucratic structures to coordinate and direct the effort. Usually the new instrument proposed is a separate Department of Economic Affairs (D.E.A.). During the phases of economic management, on the other hand, the traditional department of coordination, the Treasury, is largely relied upon for central direction. As planning rises, the Treasury declines; as planning and control are again relaxed, the Treasury moves back into its position of dominance. This is not to say that the Treasury is ever effectively excluded from the major decisions on economic policy. Some would argue that its attitudes are so antipathetic and its structures so dysfunctional to planning that its presence at the center of British government has been the chief reason why planning has had so little success. A more likely hypothesis is that economic control is severely limited by basic traits of the British polity and economy and that over time the Treasury, as an instrument of central coordination, has adjusted to, and psychologically internalized, these limits. The inadequacies of the Treasury—and they are very real—reflect the realities of the economic and political context.

Britain's achievements in economic mobilization during the war raised high hopes for economic progress after the war, and, while many controls were removed, the basic scheme of planning under the new Labour Government that came to power in 1945 was derived from the wartime model. The Treasury was brought back from the obscurity of wartime, when for a time it had not even been represented in the Cabinet. During this first phase of economic policy, which lasted until the late forties, it still occupied a secondary role in planning; and the principal instrument was not the financial budget, but a manpower budget laying down the main lines of control over the economy by means of its allocation of that ultimate scarce resource, labor.

If the British workers and their unions had been willing to accept government control over where they worked, how much they were paid, or both, Labour's postwar system of physical planning would probably have been a success. To be sure, there were other pluralistic forces besides labor that put a drag on the efforts of planners to control quantitatively the various sectors of the economy. Within the government the independence of departments reasserted itself, darkening the prospects of a chain of command from central planners to departmental executors. Business and professional groups used their very considerable leverage against government control. Yet the labor force—because of its size, its human character, and its high degree of organization—remained the most important and difficult factor to control. This has been well understood by economists. "Planned production," one socialist authority had written, "implies either compulsory industrial direction or a planned wage structure."[1] The policy of industrial conscription and labor direction that had been accepted by British workers during the war was out of the question now. During the crisis years of the Labour government, the unions demonstrated, as they have continued to demonstrate, that they would under no conditions accept a wages policy. As a result the "targets" of the manpower budget were missed again and again by huge margins. Increasingly the Government was obliged to resort to the financial budget and the use of Keynesian techniques to affect economic behavior through manipulation of the market, rather than by direct control. By the end of the Attlee regime in 1951, economic planning had given way to economic management.

While the unions would not accept a wages policy, the Government did win their consent to restraint in pushing wage claims during the brief but crucial period from 1948 to 1950. This agreement resulted from a long and complex bargaining process between the Government, organized labor, and organized capital. In response to union demands the Government imposed a capital levy on wealth and continued heavy subsidies to reduce the price of basic foods. It also secured agreement from the peak business organizations that they would limit dividends. In return the unions agreed not to press for wage increases except under a few specified conditions. This important piece of policy making was accomplished outside the parliamentary system, and no statute or other legal document marked its consummation. The essential process was informal bargaining between representatives of Government and representatives of the organized producers groups in the two main economic sectors—capital and labor. Moreover, it worked. Wage rates, which had been rising rapidly, increased hardly at all until the pressures on prices from the devaluation of 1949 made it impossible for the unions any longer to hold the line and the T.U.C. in September 1950 rejected the policy.

As the postwar years wore on, it was realized that contrary to earlier beliefs, the thing to fear was not the old plague of mass unemployment, but the new affliction of chronic inflation. To cope with this, Governments resorted to fiscal and, later, monetary policy. They also found themselves

---

[1]Barbara Wootton, *Freedom Under Planning* (Chapel Hill, N.C., 1945), p. 118.

obliged, as in 1948, to deal directly—and one might say, politically—with the big, organized producers groups of the economy in an effort to hold back wage and price increases. This effort became known as an "incomes policy." The problem with which it tried to deal, the restraint of inflation, was a problem for both economic management and economic planning. To a large extent, this problem was responsible for shifts of government policy from management to planning and back again, as governments of both parties tried in vain to find a successful solution.

The second phase of economic policy extended from the late forties to the early sixties. This was a period of economic management. (To show the convergence in party positions, the term "Butskellism" was coined to describe this phase by combining the names of the two leading economic spokesmen, the Conservative R. A. Butler and the Labourite Hugh Gaitskell.) Thanks to a favorable change in the terms of trade—that is, a fall in the prices of agricultural products and raw materials relative to prices of manufactured products—the balance of payments was deceptively healthy for some years. But the old problem soon arose again. Like Labour before it, the Conservative party attempted to strike a bargain with labor and capital to hold back the cost-based factors of inflation. Failing to come to an agreement with the unions, the Government was confronted with the alternative of disinflation, which meant using fiscal and monetary policy to reduce aggregate demand and thereby creating some degree of unemployment. This was a hard choice for the Conservatives. Under the leadership of their progressive wing, they did not attack the welfare state, as Labour had expected, but added to it. Along with the protection of this large social expenditure, the party had also committed itself to the new meaning of full employment—in effect, an unemployment rate of 1 percent or so in contrast with the 4 percent rate that the fathers of the idea had anticipated. With fear and trembling, politically speaking, the Macmillan Government disinflated, at the expense of 2.8 percent unemployment in January 1959—the highest rate since the war. But prices did level out, and the Government went into the election year of 1959 with a strong expansionist policy, which it was expected would not only bring back full employment, but also coexist with price stability as economic growth went forward.

Full employment was restored, and the Conservatives won their third general election in a row, a feat without parallel in this century. But prices far from being quiescent soon began to mount again, and as her prices went up in the world market, Britain by 1961 was again confronted with a serious balance-of-payments crisis. Several years of restrictive fiscal policy and, so, of slow growth had bought only a brief respite, followed by renewed crisis. The tools of economic management forged in the late forties and early fifties now seemed less than adequate for either the short-run task of economic equilibrium or the long-run task of economic development. It is not strange that the more austere and direct methods of economic planning should once again look attractive.

From Management to Planning

This new line of thought, rising out of British experience, was strengthened when Britons looked abroad. In France, which had just thrown off the old loose ways of the Fourth Republic for the new discipline of the Gaullist regime, long experience with the Monnet plan, a highly *étatist* system of economic control, seemed to be showing abundant results. Between 1950 and 1960 average G.N.P. per capita had risen 3.5 percent in France, but only 2.1 percent in Britain. The lesson was humiliating for the British, and it seemed clear that they, too, should adopt the more *dirigiste* methods of the French planning system.

Like the earlier move from planning to management, this shift to a new phase of planning was not mediated by the mechanisms of party government. It was the Conservatives under Macmillan, a planner in sentiment even in the interwar years, who inaugurated the new phase. Moreover, as often happens among the highly integrated elites of British society, there was a general shift of opinion in the same direction. Like Ministers, civil servants reacted to both the failure of the old looser methods and the promise of the French model. Even more interesting and important, leading business circles, especially in manufacturing, agreed that it was time for government to move toward a more tightly coordinated and positively directed economic effort. This marked a crucial change in the attitudes of organized business. Even after the war British industry had continued to be torn between its old principle of independence of government and the new possibilities for exercising influence on government at the cost of closer association with it. Finally, in the early sixties a decision was made in favor of the latter alternative, a decision reflected in the vigorous advocacy by the Federation of British Industries of economic planning for growth based on the French model. Indeed, it was industry's acceptance of its new responsibilities in the N.E.D.C., set up by the Conservatives in 1962, that led to the amalgamation of the three main peak organizations into one comprehensive organization, the Confederation of British Industry. Nor was this new commitment merely organizational. Individual firms cooperated heartily in providing the massive information needed for the new national plans.

The unions refused to have anything to do with the National Incomes Commission (N.I.C.), a body set up by the Conservatives to give some kind of guidance with regard to prices and wages. (Indeed, its utterances were called "guiding lights.") But organized labor did send its representatives to N.E.D.C. and to the little Neddies for specific industries, which were set up in later years, ultimately reaching a total of twenty-one. N.E.D.C. was not part of the Treasury Department, but, like N.I.C., was created by the then Chancellor of the Exchequer, Selwyn Lloyd, who was N.E.D.C. chairman and the responsible Minister. Bringing in both sides of industry as well as independent members and Ministers, the N.E.D.C. also had a small but impressive staff of economists and professionally trained people and was the center from which the Conservatives launched their effort to increase economic growth.

This was essentially a feasibility study for a period of five years, based on the assumption that national income would grow 4 percent per year and identifying some of the problems, such as the necessary level of exports and the tolerable level of imports, that would arise during the period.

Labour, which took office in 1964, built on these foundations and ambitiously extended the commitment to economic planning and control. Although, as one would expect from their ideological position, they showed greater willingness to intervene in the economy, their system still remained only "indicative," that is, it relied on "pointing out desirable ends rather than on giving orders to achieve them." A new Department of Economic Affairs was established under George Brown, a top party leader, who became the chairman of the N.E.D.C. Using the N.E.D.C. as well as its own staff, the new department produced in September 1965 the comprehensive National Plan whose purpose was "to develop a coordinated, internally consistent set of projections of how the economy might develop to 1970 and thereby create expectations that would induce private economic decisions to conform to the projections."[2] Within six months inflation had brought on a new crisis in the balance of payments. The restrictive fiscal policy undertaken in consequence made certain that the estimate of 3.4 percent annual growth in productivity per capita, on which the plan was based, would not be realized. This offspring of the new phase of economic policy, produced with such great exertion by government and industry under two Governments, was born dead.

The Politics of Inflation

During Labour's remaining four years in office economic policy was devoted to a fruitless struggle with the problem that wrecked its brief and ambitious effort to plan the economy. As its failure became evident, Labour dropped the word "planning" from its rhetoric and prepared the way for the reduction in government control that the Conservatives inaugurated

---

[2] *The National Plan* (London: H.M.S.O.), Cmnd. 2764.

when they took office in 1970. The central problem was inflation, and the history of the National Board for Prices and Incomes (N.B.P.I.), one of the most remarkable creations of the Labour Government, illustrates the nature of the problem and its intractability. When Labour took office, Ministers, officials, and the incoming "irregulars" fully understood the vital need to get an operative, not merely rhetorical, agreement with the big producers groups regarding prices and wages. While the unions had refused to come to terms with the Conservatives, it seemed logical to many that Labour—with its social-democratic ideology, its organizational connection with the unions, and its long personal association with union leaders—would be able to achieve agreement, once again, so to speak, as it had done in the late forties.

For two years Parliament played a secondary role, while the Government tried to achieve its ends by voluntary means. The first stage was a "Declaration of Intent," published in December 1964, in which trade unions and employers associations agreed in principle to keep incomes in line. A few months later, the N.B.P.I. was established with a professional staff and including persons drawn from both sides of industry as well as independent members. Its main task was to look into proposed increases in prices and wages and advise the Government as to whether they were in "the national interest." In connection with activities of the N.B.P.I., the Government had the power to require early warning of proposed increases, the power to forbid such increases for a period of time, and the power to order a complete freeze. During the years 1966–1967 these efforts did reduce increases in weekly wage rates by a small but significant amount—perhaps one percentage point in a rate of 6 or 7 percent per year. But the pound could not be protected, and the devaluation of November 1967 added to the pressure on prices whose rise in turn set off a surge of wage increases. By the end of 1968 the Government had virtually given up its effort to use the N.B.P.I. to restrain inflation, and the year 1970 saw a wage explosion that by the autumn had wages rising at an annual rate of 20.8 percent and prices at a rate of 10.4 percent. It remained only for the Conservatives to abolish the board—which is not to say that it will not be resurrected by them under a new name.

Conventionally, the two main types of inflation are identified as demand-pull and cost-push. Either may result in prices rising more than productivity. In the age of full employment and the welfare state aggregate demand fed by government expenditure has often added to the inflationary problem in Britain. It may well be that Labour was slow to take the necessary measures of fiscal disinflation consequential upon devaluation. In any case, by 1970 the austerities of the new Chancellor of the Exchequer, Roy Jenkins, had deflated demand to new levels. Unemployment rose to 2.4 percent by June, and in succeeding months the Conservative Government felt obliged to keep it at these high figures. Yet the price rise continued. Its impetus now was clearly cost-push, especially the wage explosion, which resulted largely from the ability of the well-organized unions to push up wages even under these circumstances. Labour as well as the Conservative Government admitted this fundamental fact by attempting to put a rein on union power through statutory reform. Yet it is hardly the whole truth to think of the unions as organizational giants overpowering the representatives of the national interest. One of the peculiarities of the situation is that these giants often are not masters in their own houses.

One reason for the failure of the incomes policy consists in certain structural weaknesses on the side of both trade unions and employers' associations. These weaknesses throw light on the stage of modernization reached by the British polity. Today government management of the economy in advanced countries entails making bargains. If these bargains are to be kept, there must be coherent and authoritative leadership within these organizations. Yet British producer groups have long been criticized for their lack of cohesion as compared with similar groups in such countries as Sweden.

Concentration is high among unions; some 70 percent of trade union membership in 1967 was accounted for by eighteen huge organizations. (See Chapter 10.) This would seem to indicate the kind of large-scale centralized organization needed to carry out effectively the union side of an incomes-policy bargain. At the same time, however, full employment has created countervailing tendencies, shifting much significant collective bargaining from the national to the plant level. Even when national organizations did accommodate their agreements with regard to wage rates to the criteria of the incomes policy, "earnings drift" at the plant level continued to swell the forces of cost inflation. In addition to full employment this tendency was bolstered by attitudes that go deep in British culture. First among them is "a proletarian spirit that seems conservative even by the standards of a traditionalist society," as an American observer has put it. Its principal consequence was wide support for restrictive labor practices and dogged resistance to practices increasing productivity. Also, in his opinion, "a tradition of paternalism" shared responsibility for the resulting underutilization of labor. This leads management to feel, in the words of one employer, that its "first responsibility is to provide work for these chaps—to keep the shop occupied."[3] Thus, in economic as in political behavior the ancient heritage of class consciousness showed its power.

Earnings were still substantially influenced by the terms of wage settlements on the national level, hence the importance of attempting to influence the negotiations leading to them through an incomes policy. Yet the

---

[3]Lloyd Ulman in Richard E. Caves, et al., Britain's Economic Prospects (Washington, D. C., 1968), pp. 332, 335.

trend to decentralization, which is reflected in earnings drift, meant a real loss of authority for the national unions. In the field of trade unions, at any rate, the present stage of modernization has meant a weakening rather than a strengthening of bureaucracy and large-scale organization. Even less than in the past are the British unions appropriate instruments to control and direct one of the major regulators of the economic system—the price of labor. The Wilson Government, finding that it could control the price of labor neither by persuasion, nor by bargaining, nor by legal coercion, was obliged to give up its ambitious hopes for economic planning. The National Plan was pushed aside, and the term "planning" virtually disappeared from party propaganda. The Department of Economic Affairs lingered on until 1969, when it was finally abolished; its economic planning section was transferred to the Treasury, which again became incontestably the major instrument for control of the economy.

The Treasury

Government in Britain intervenes in the economy on a wide scale, as do governments in other modern polities. In spite of the powerful impulsion given to such intervention by the forces of modernity, there seem to be major limits beyond which such intervention is not effective. These barriers, which have appeared when twice since the war attempts to control the economy have been forced into retreat, are deeply rooted in fundamental systemic traits of the British economy and polity. The Treasury, as the traditional coordinating department of British government, reflects in structure and attitude these characteristics.

The unique function of the Treasury as the principal coordinating department is suggested by its small size in comparison with the size of other departments. In 1971 its total personnel numbered 2,369, of whom some 150 had responsibility for policy. The Chancellor of the Exchequer is the Minister responsible for the Board of Inland Revenue and the Board of Customs and Excise. Each board has a large staff and important functions, and each is itself an independent department, not part of the Treasury and not subject to its officials. The Treasury is a central coordinating agency, not an operating department. When it acts, it acts through other agencies and departments. Its style in conducting these relationships tells one as much about the British political system in general as about the Treasury in particular.

For a department often reputed to be stuffy, the Treasury has adapted with remarkable alacrity to the new and ever-changing demands of the collectivist age. In particular, it has in a series of major adaptations taken on the central responsibilities for steering the economy. Yet the manner in which it carries out these new tasks of economic coordination is in keeping with its much older functions of financial coordination. These functions consisted first in controlling departmental expenditures and second in deciding how the money would be found to meet them. The latter was regarded as the exclusive responsibility of the Chancellor in the sense that, after such consultations as he chose to make, he decided what the pattern of taxation would be for the next year and revealed his decision to the Cabinet only a day or two before presenting it in his budget speech in the House.

In controlling expenditure, however, the Treasury was in constant touch with other departments. Its powers were formidable. Perhaps the most important, and certainly the most characteristic, was the requirement of prior approval. This meant that another department could undertake no activity involving expenditure in the near or distant future unless that activity had the Treasury's approval. Normally, even the planning of such an activity would not be pushed very far unless the Treasury had been consulted. This requirement of prior approval was separate from the annual review of the estimates of expenditure that the other departments submitted to the Treasury for scrutiny and approval before their presentation to Parliament, much in the manner of the review conducted by the Bureau of the Budget in the United States. The exercise of control through the requirement of prior approval meant that the Treasury was in constant, day-to-day and week-to-week contact with the spending departments and was brought into their forward planning of particular expenditures at a very early stage. As the size and complexity of public expenditure increased, this power was relaxed in detail and greater delegations of discretion were made to other departments. Yet in spite of the Treasury's great and growing concern with the total expenditure of a department, it still does not surrender its interest in individual items—for the inexorably logical reason that one cannot decide on the merits of a total figure without having a look at its parts.

Prior approval had a coordinating effect, insofar as Treasury decisions expressed the priorities expressed in Government policy. But Government policy is continually being made and modified, especially by Ministers bringing bright ideas to the Cabinet. To prevent the Treasury from being bypassed in this manner, a rule of Cabinet procedure gives the Chancellor the right to keep financial problems off the Cabinet agenda until the Treasury has had an opportunity to see and criticize them. A further and similar protection is provided by the ancient rule of the House of Commons that only Ministers can bring financial proposals before it. In contrast with American practice, this prevents legislators from presenting to the House the temptation of spending money in isolation from the responsibility for raising it. While this rule does further safeguard the right of prior approval, the comparative expenditure in the two countries does not suggest that it is any guarantee of more cautious finance.

Even this brief recital of some of the powers of the Treasury suggests the special character and style of Treasury control in its classic form. In the first place this power is negative, as indicated by the witticism attributed to Churchill that the Treasury was an "inverted Macawber—always waiting for something to turn down." The Treasury did not take the initiative—dictating to departments what they should undertake in order to fulfill government policy—but rather shaped the initiative already taken by them suggesting alternatives when possible, but essentially trusting to departments to supply innovation and expertise.

Moreover, when we glance at the ministerial superstructure conditioning the official substructure, it is plain that even this negative power must be qualified by the realities of a plural executive and its collective decision making. Aggressive ministerial spenders were not, and could not be, prevented from taking their plans to the Cabinet; and once there they might well, as sometimes happened, defeat a reluctant Chancellor. In turn these realities of Cabinet government were anticipated by the behavior of civil servants in such a way that Treasury officials—while hardly deferential—worked with departments by persuasion rather than coercion, trying to "win acceptance of policy" rather than simply to "enforce policy." The officials with whom they dealt were not subordinates but equals, perhaps themselves permanent heads of "great departments of state" and serving Ministers who, like the Chancellor, shared the sovereign authority of the Cabinet.

This reality of British government was nicely reflected in the experience of the Department of Economic Affairs under the Wilson Government. In the conception of its first chief, George Brown, the D.E.A. was a major overlord department in charge of all aspects of economic policy; the other economic departments, including the Treasury, were merely executive agencies to carry out decisions made at the center. Things did not work out this way—nor could they have, given the fact that Wilson appointed as Chancellor, James Callaghan, a major Labour party leader. The politics of the British kind of democratic leadership and the structure of the plural executive do not permit the strict hierarchical control entailed by economic planning as contemplated by some of the fathers of the D.E.A.

The New System

A main problem in establishing control over the pattern of power is to distinguish matters that must be centrally decided from those that should be left to functional or territorial authorities. This means making sure that the important matters do come before the central authority and, at the same time, that unimportant matters do not paralyze it. But how decide what is important or unimportant? How reduce this crucial distinction to some kind of operational rule or procedure? Without some rule there is a tendency for each case itself to require a central decision on whether it should be decided centrally.

One answer to the question of what ought to be decided centrally is that it depends on how much money is involved; the greater the expenditure, the more deserving it is of central scrutiny. The rule is crude and by no means excludes the need for sensitive political judgment. Actions of government entailing little or no expenditure may be very important and politically controversial—for instance, a deportation case coming before the Home Secretary, proposed legislation relating to the death penalty or homosexuality, or declarations of praise or blame with regard to foreign affairs. Still, as a rough and ready indicator of the degree of importance to be assigned to a proposed activity of government—and this is especially true in these days of the welfare state—the quantum of expenditure is the best available basis. Above all, it is operational. Looking at the proposed programs of various departments, we see a miscellany of qualitatively and physically different activities, whose relative importance is not immediately evident. No one, however, needs to be told that £100 million is a great deal more than £5 million.

As the agency whose ministerial chief's special responsibility was raising money, the Treasury also acquired the function of providing the funds for the spending departments. This latter function meant that it continually knew how much money, and in particular how much more money, departments were proposing to spend. Therefore it inevitably became the main agency through which the central authority impressed upon department activities its sense of priorities, of what was important and unimportant.

Under some systems of government control of the economy, money is a poor indicator of importance. During World War II, for instance, the main economic decisions were made in the course of framing the manpower budget, under which the total labor force was allocated among the chief industries and the fighting services; budgets were provided for critical materials, indicating what industries were to get them; and an important program was established, setting out the physical volume of various types of imports. Under this system the physical quantities of men and matériel, rather than their costs, were the key indicators, and the Treasury sank in importance accordingly. Such a system of physical planning, however, has not yet proved practicable in peacetime. As we have seen, Britain has twice been thrown back on an approach to economic control based not upon superseding the market, but upon manipulating it through the public use of, and control over, money. The Keynesian revolution in economics and the enormous development of quantitative techniques provided the foundation for this type of economic management. The old Treasury and the new economics met and merged, the Treasury becoming the main agency not only for coordinating government activities, but also for coordinating the British economic system. This was not inevitable, but depended upon two facts: First, the Treasury dealt with money, and money was the substantial means by which the new form of control was exercised; and, second, the Treasury's style of coordination was appropriate to the needs of economic management.

Within the broad limits conditioning its style of coordination, the Treasury has developed major new capacities for dealing with economic problems. In one respect it has lost certain of its previous functions. One of the peculiarities of the British system of public administration had been that control over the Civil Service was exercised by the Treasury. This control included responsibility for overall efficiency of the public service, development of management services, settlement of pay and conditions of service, and grading of staff. In 1968 these responsibilities were given to a new Civil Service Department, which, directly under the Prime Minister, now has important coordinating functions in unified central management of the services. Otherwise, the organization of the Treasury falls into three groups. The public sector group consists of a number of divisions, each concerned with control of expenditure by several departments with related fields of policy, as well as a small division concerned with taxation. The finance group is concerned with borrowing and lending, the balance of payments, and foreign exchange. The economic management group deals with major questions of overall economic policy. It is this latter group that constitutes the major addition in structure and personnel. From the prewar years, when the Treasury was quite innocent of professional economic advice, it has developed a considerable capacity, absorbing in turn the economic section set up in the Cabinet office during the war, the central economic planning staff established under Cripps' short-lived Ministry of Economic Affairs, and, more recently, the economic planning division of the defunct Department of Economic Affairs. Indeed, it has itself become Ministry of Economic Affairs as well as a Finance Ministry.

The use of the old financial powers in the service of the new economic responsibilities is a main feature of the control of public expenditure, as it must be at a time when total public-sector spending exceeds half the G.N.P. Today, as in the past, the Treasury seeks balance among the various expenditures in the public sector. Conceptually, the standard of balance means that expenditures should be so allocated that the last pound spent on each activity produces the same amount of public good. It makes marginal amounts relevant to the decision: Is an extra £5 million on one program more worthwhile, or less worthwhile, than £5 million on another? Measurement of public good is so difficult that it is left to politicians and voters. But their judgment can be assisted by techniques of cost-benefit analysis, and the Treasury has taken many pains to develop these techniques. They are especially relevant where the purpose of the programs is largely economic, as, for instance, in a choice between further expenditure on roads or railways. A very large part of public expenditure, however, is more social than economic, including health and welfare, housing and community services, children's services, benefits and assistance, law and order. The modern democratic polity generates great pressure toward increasing such expenditures, and the welfare state includes an array of groups of consumers of welfare state benefits to whom parties and governments are acutely sensitive. Calculation of the social and human costs and benefits of such programs in comparison with their economic costs and benefits has not yet been put on an objective basis. This makes them even more highly political than the more economic programs and gives them a strong impulse toward indefinite expansion.

The tendency of overall expenditure to get out of hand in the democratic welfare state has led to what is undoubtedly the major innovation in Treasury control. This is the new system of establishing ceilings on total public expenditure and on departmental expenditures, as the premises for further decisions on the particular programs constituting these totals. The establishment of a total for public expenditure is a crucial step in economic policy making. It means deciding how the resources of the economy will be divided between public consumption and investment, on the one hand, and private consumption and investment on the other. This confrontation of prospective public expenditure against prospective national resources is the heart of the matter. Ultimately, decisions of such magnitude must be made by Ministers, presumably by the economic committees of the Cabinet and the Cabinet itself. But with its superb professional capacity, the Treasury can develop the alternatives. Each year, and looking ahead for a period of five years, it acts with an interdepartmental committee of officials, the Public Expenditure Survey Committee, to prepare the submissions for ministerial decision. Since the fall of 1970, moreover, the Cabinet and Prime Minister seemed to have in the new Central Policy Review Staff (C.P.R.S.) the resource for criticizing these submissions.

This global or deductive approach to expenditure cannot be exclusive. As already remarked, a decision cannot be made on a total expenditure without scrutinizing its components. A decision cannot be made on the total to go to public as compared with private uses unless there is some idea of what is to be achieved in each of these spheres, vast as they may be. Similarly for the allocation among departments: Their totals cannot be determined without an assessment of the items composing them. This means that, along with the new approach, the old inductive approach to the control of expenditure continues. But now, it is hoped, the old procedures are rationalized by the new discipline introduced by the economic perspective. Under the new procedure the big issues of public expenditure and the economy are looked at as a whole, over a period of years, and in relation to prospective resources.

Moreover, the way in which the components of these totals are conceived for budgeting purposes is being radically revised. Within the Treasury and bureaucracy generally, efforts are now being made to set down proposed expenditures in terms of objectives. This budgeting procedure is called "output budgeting," or "management by objectives" (M.B.O.). Its purpose is to set forth not merely what the items of expenditure will be, but also what blocks of work will be accomplished. In the old-fashioned budget many items of expenditure are scattered under different headings —personnel, materials, and so forth—while under the new system these are brought together so that they can all be seen in relation to the objective —for example, the school, hospital, or road that is to be built. The idea of such a budget is simple; its actual formulation is very difficult. But insofar as it can be done, it enables a government to decide what its main objectives are to be and how much it wishes to spend on each—for example, how much money to combat poverty in comparison with how much to clean up the environment. Such subtotals must necessarily be determined in order to provide a rational basis for the basic economic decision of how much to take for the public sector from the total national resources.

This description of the many advances in the system of economic management may sound like high praise for the Treasury. Indeed it is. One of the Treasury's severest critics of a few years ago recently remarked of its performance since World War II: "The relevant comparison is not with some absolute standard, but with institutions carrying out similar functions in other countries. On this basis the British Treasury was ahead of most other finance ministries."[4] Among these he specifically included the German, French, and American ministries.

Yet the position and role of the Treasury, like the British style of economic control, is by no means fixed. Much criticism is still directed at the way in which the annual decisions regarding taxation and other revenue-raising measures are taken. As they have been for the past hundred years, these decisions are still taken by the Chancellor of the Exchequer, who reveals them to the Cabinet only a day or two before putting them to the House of Commons in his budget speech. While he consults with other Ministers regarding specific problems affecting their responsibilities, he discusses the budget as a whole only with the Prime Minister. In effect, these crucial decisions of financial and economic strategy are pretty well excluded from the collective decision-making processes of the Cabinet system.

In this light we may again look at the potentialities of the Central Policy Review Staff set up in the fall of 1970 (see Chapter 2). On the whole, as we have seen, the initiative in policy making in British government comes

---

[4]Samuel Brittan, *Steering the Economy: the Role of the Treasury* (London, 1969), p. 313.

from Ministers and departments, and the total figure for public expenditure arises from many departmental and subdepartmental proposals. The new methods of surveying public expenditure have attempted to impose upon these components the discipline of a ceiling derived from current decisions on economic policy. In determining this ceiling and related allocations, decision makers and their officials must view the economy as a whole.

At present the agency relied upon to provide the analysis and the policy initiative is the Treasury. But its resources are at the service of only one Minister, not the Cabinet as a whole. The true executive, therefore, while always retaining its formal authority, lacks the resources for authoritatively assessing what is proposed to it and for developing realistic alternatives. One purpose of the C.P.R.S. was to right this imbalance. Conceivably, it could become not simply a device for coordinating departmental initiatives, but rather a means of positive central direction. The total of public expenditure cannot be greatly changed from year to year; one official's estimate was that projected levels can be reduced by no more than 2½ percent per year.[5] Yet the huge public sector constitutes a *masse de manoeuvre* which, if properly directed, over time could have a profound effect upon the economy. To establish control from such a perspective must be the rational administrator's fondest dream. This shift in the character of policy making would also mean a change in the locus of policy making. Positive direction from the center would severely qualify the traditional, uneasy equality among departments and their corps of officials. The superministries have attempted this with regard to groups of departments; perhaps the same could be done for all units of government. Standing at the top would be the Cabinet, or perhaps, if we follow the speculations of some observers, the Prime Minister in a new position of eminence.

To mention these possibilities against the background of the structure and spirit of British government is to suggest how radical and remote they are.

---

[5] Sir William Armstrong (permanent head of the Civil Service Department), in *First Report from the Select Committee on Procedure*. With proceedings, etc. (London: H.M.S.O., 1969), p. 33.

Five

The Authority
of Parliament

Two ruling forces of modernity are the drive for efficiency and the passion for equality. Previous chapters have been concerned with the first of these: the effort to make the machinery of state power more effective. Modern attitudes view this machinery as a means to an end, not an end in itself, and continually press to improve its service to public policy. Cost-benefit analysis—although the first bright hopes for it have become a bit tarnished —is a recent achievement of this effort toward greater effectiveness of the machinery of state power. Yet as the record of government efforts to control the British economy demonstrates, that effectiveness cannot be achieved without regard for responsiveness. As producers, whose cooperation must be won, the governed in a democracy condition in great degree what their governors can accomplish. When the British people chose, they made the severe and strictly controlled system of physical planning of World War II work admirably. Their consent had been won. The British people willed that war and victory in it with a unanimity and intensity that was expressed as meaningfully in their readiness to bear its heavy burdens as in any referendum or general election. Similarly, today, if the performance of government fails to satisfy Britons, the reasons certainly will not be found only in failures of economic science, public administration, or other branches of technical knowledge and their application. The state of the public will is far more important: how the various wishes of the public are formed, what the public expects from government, and what its members will and will not endure.

Party Government and Democracy

In the conventional view, British government displays a high degree of democratic responsiveness, and the mechanism by which this is achieved is party government (see Chapter 1). The doctrine of party government, it must be noted, is only one among many versions of basic democratic theory. As we have seen in our discussion of political modernization, the liberal period in Britain produced versions of popular government that would be hard to reconcile with party government as it is known and practiced in Britain in recent times. Nineteenth-century Liberals and Radicals were highly individualistic in their approach to politics as well as economics. In their view the basic unit of representation was not a class or community, but the individual, rational man. The importance of "conscience" was much in the minds of these offspring of liberalism and religious dissent. On their premises party discipline and strong party organization could not easily be justified. The highest respect was reserved for the independent politician in the sense not of one who was outside party but of one who was in party solely because of conscientious opinion. So while parties did develop in this period and party organization began slowly to be built up throughout the country, in the legislature cross-voting was common and party cohesion very low. The middle period of the nineteenth century was, in the words of one historian, "the golden age of the independent M.P."

In contrast, the political culture of the collectivist period attributes to party a quite different function and a far higher claim to solidarity. Independent voting in the name of conscience is looked on with a much more critical eye. Clement Attlee, the former Labour Prime Minister, reflects this change:

> In my experience a good deal of so-called independence owes more to a desire for notoriety than to conscience. There are some people who delight in a "holier than thou" attitude. I recall an old Labour M.P., Tom Shaw, saying to me, "When I was young I was always talking about my conscience, but one day I realized that what I called conscience was my own bloomin' conceit."[1]

In the United States the doctrine of party government has never taken deep hold in either the opinions or behavior of people in practical politics. Here the older doctrines of political individualism still prevail. The contrast between the two perspectives on proper democratic behavior came out in a recent exchange between a British party leader and an American legislator. In the spring of 1970, R. H. S. Crossman, then a Minister in the

---

[1] Quoted in Alan Beattie, *English Party Politics.* Vol. II (London, 1970), p. 550.

Labour Government, was explaining to an American audience the meaning of the party mandate and how it bound Labour M.P.s to vote together. In the question period after the lecture, a member of the Massachusetts state legislature raised doubts about "the morality of the Member of Parliament voting in a way other than how he believes." "Doesn't he compromise his conscience?" asked the earnest questioner. Crossman's reply suggests the mutual incomprehension of these two firm believers in democracy:

> . . . there is no difficulty here because the M.P. is a member of the party and the M.P. is bound, therefore, by Conference decision . . . If he doesn't like that, he's not in the party and, as for the morality, of course, his duty as a party member is to accept the constitution of the party. I can't understand what you're saying.[2]

Viewed from the perspective of party government, the role of Parliament is modest. If we think of the party program as the means by which a like-minded majority directs the course of government action, there is not much for the legislature to do beyond registering the decision of the electorate in favor of the program and providing a forum from which the competing parties can carry on their continuous appeal to the people in anticipation of the next election. Questions no doubt arise as to who is to interpret this program—the parliamentary party, its leadership, or the party outside Parliament—but the drift of the theory clearly is that all, leaders and followers alike, are instruments of the purposive partisan majority in the country. This linkage subordinates the legislature to a parliamentary majority and the parliamentary majority to a majority of the voters. A similar role for Parliament follows if, taking a more Tory view of the matter, we put less stress on program and more on the choice of a team of leaders. In this view the people have spoken by choosing a prospective Cabinet and especially a prospective Prime Minister. The task of the legislature, therefore, is primarily to support the people's choice, providing the Prime Minister with the majorities he and his lieutenants need to make laws, raise and spend money, and control the administration. M.P.s may have the important function of choosing the Leader and in a crisis of removing him. But so long as he has the post, whether in office or Opposition, he and his lieutenants appear as the center of initiative and decision.

Both versions of party government require high party unity and legitimize strict party discipline. Both tend to make Parliament merely an adjunct of a continuous electoral campaign between the parties, without any distinctive function of its own. Viewed as the product of one election, Parliament becomes an electoral college whose function is to transmit the

---

[2]R. H. S. Crossman, Godkin Lectures (Harvard University, 1970).

people's choice, whether of program or leadership or both, to the seat of authority. Viewed from the perspective of the next election, Parliament is a forum of propaganda, which the parties use as part of their apparatus for winning and holding public support. The idea of party government poses the central question of the study of Parliament today: Is it merely an adjunct of party competition, or does it have a distinctive role of its own? Does it have important functions that are peculiarly parliamentary and that it performs with a substantial degree of autonomy? After a generation or more of reporting with approval or dismay the "decline of Parliament," observers are beginning to see that it does have such a role and does perform such functions.

Sovereignty and Symbolism

References to "Parliament" in discussions such as this mean, for almost all intents and purposes, the House of Commons. In legal theory, however, the Parliament of the United Kingdom of Great Britain and Northern Ireland is not a single body, but consists of three powers: the sovereign, the House of Lords, and the House of Commons. The consent of each is normally required to give legislation its legally binding force, as indicated in the usual enacting clause of a statute: "Be it enacted by the Queen's most excellent Majesty, by and with the advice and consent of the Lords Spiritual and Temporal, and Commons, in this present Parliament assembled, and by authority of the same." The sovereign, it should be emphasized, is legally speaking a part of Parliament and in this connection should be referred to as "The Queen in Parliament" not "The Queen and Parliament." To be sure, her assent is always given to legislation that has been properly passed by the chambers—the last time it was refused was 1707 —and her role in legislation, as in all acts of government, is governed entirely by the advice of Ministers responsible to the House of Commons. Likewise the power of the House of Lords, which until the nineteenth century was the dominant chamber, has been vastly reduced. Under the Parliament Acts of 1911 and 1949 it has only a brief, suspensive veto over legislation (see Chapter 6). And even this limited power is rarely exercised against the will of the Commons. In effect, therefore, the legislative power rests exclusively with the so-called lower House.

This power is very great. Legally speaking, it is unlimited. In few other regimes do we find as complete an embodiment of the modern concept of sovereignty as in the legal theory of the powers of Parliament. In the United States the power of the legislature is limited by various provisions of a written constitution, such as the Bill of Rights, most of which can be used as the basis for court action challenging laws deemed unconstitutional. Britain's unwritten Constitution sets no limits upon the legal power of Parliament. On the contrary, a central principle of the Constitution is Parliament's legal omnipotence. Whatever may be said on other grounds against a law that has been enacted in Parliament, it cannot be challenged in a British court of law as unconstitutional. In the words of Sir Edward Coke, the great seventeenth-century lawyer and judge, the power of Par liament is "so transcendent and absolute as it cannot be confined either for causes or persons within any bounds."[3] Or as DeLolme, the author of a famous exposition of the eighteenth century constitution, facetiously put the matter, "parliament can do everything but make a man a woman and a woman a man." There is perhaps no more striking instance of Parliament's sovereignty than its legal power to determine its own life span, as it did during World War II by putting off a general election until the end of hostilities in Europe. The result was that—apart from changes brought about in by-elections—the same House sat from 1935 to 1945.

The expressive symbolism of the House of Commons is fully in accord with this transcendent authority. Everything about it—its architecture, officials, forms of address, tone and manner of speech, and so on—is deeply impressive, as one would expect of the "Mother of Parliaments." To understand what Parliament is and does, one must sense this expressive symbolism, if only vicariously.

Let us imagine that the reader is sitting in the visitors' gallery of the House for the first time. No doubt his first impression will concern the physical appearance of the House. Even if he does not find it attractive, he will almost certainly find it surprising. In particular, if the visitor has seen other legislative chambers, he will be surprised by the unique size and seating arrangements. From the standpoint of size, it is little more than a glorified town hall. It seats fewer than two-thirds of its 630 members, even though it makes no space-consuming concessions to members' comforts (such as providing desks and individual chairs). All members are seated on long benches, and the M.P.'s lap is the only support for papers. The chamber measures roughly three thousand square feet, while the American House of Representatives, despite a much smaller membership, commands more than four times that much space. The prevailing atmosphere of the House of Commons, therefore, is intimate—except on great occasions (e.g., before an important "division") when, with over 600 members crowding into a space designed for 346, the chief impression is one of excitement and expectancy.

The feeling of excitement at such times is further increased by the seating arrangements. In most of the world's legislative chambers, members sit in semicircular or straight rows, facing a rostrum from which members address the chamber and from which its presiding officer conducts the

---

[3]Quoted in Sir Bernard Cocks (ed.), *Erskine May's Treatise on the Law, Privileges, Proceed ings and Usage of Parliament.* 17th ed. (London, 1964), p. 28.

proceedings. The impression is of an auditorium facing a stage on which individual legislators play the star turn. In the House of Commons, however, members sit on two sets of long benches that are graded upward and *face each other.* The Speaker sits at the head of and between the rows of benches. On his right are the benches of the Government and its supporters—Ministers on the front bench (or Treasury bench, as it is sometimes called), ordinary members ("backbenchers") grouped behind them like obedient and anonymous soldiery. On his left sit the Opposition—the "shadow Cabinet" on the front bench and its own soldiery arrayed on the benches behind. The two groups face each other like football teams in a scrimmage; when members make their verbal cuts and thrusts, they inevitably appear as members of a team—not as figures temporarily elevated in splendid individuality to the national tribune.

Since the present House of Commons is only a few years old (the old House having been destroyed by German incendiary bombs in 1941), neither its layout nor its small size are accidental. Despite certain obvious discomforts, it was decided to make the new House of Commons almost exactly like the old, not alone because of attachment to the past, but because it was widely felt that the physical character of the House somehow affected the character of its proceedings. For example, Churchill, the most insistent spokesman for the small chamber, felt that the whole style of debate in the House would be changed for the worse if the House were enlarged; that the effects of meeting in a large and half-empty hall (and the House is rarely full even now) would be depressing; that the old sense of crowding urgency on great occasions would go; and even that the clean-cut two-party system would be endangered if the seating arrangements were altered.

The next thing the visitor to the House will notice is the general tone of its proceedings. It is here that he will be impressed most by the curious mixture of formality and informality. In some ways the House of Commons is the most formal of all legislative chambers. Its deliberations are governed by procedures most of which are hoary with age and many of which are pure ceremony of the quaintest sort, procedures that either no longer serve a useful function or have long since been adapted to new uses while maintaining their old form. The visitor may, for example, be in the House when it is getting dark. Suddenly the cry goes up: "Mr. Speaker, I call for candles." True, candles have not been used to illuminate the House for decades, but if a member were to say, "Mr. Speaker, how about putting the electric lights on," his request would be without effect. The rules of parliamentary procedure are the product of a long development. In fact until the nineteenth century, almost all the business of the House was covered by usage, with only a small handful of standing orders, as the rules deliberately adopted by the House to regulate its proceedings are called. Since 1832 the number of standing orders has grown immensely, but they do not constitute a complete code of procedure. The greater part of the rules of procedure are still unwritten—to be gleaned from the journal of the House, reports of debates, or the rulings of the Speaker.

If any physical evidence of the continuity of British parliamentary institutions were needed, Mr. Speaker would furnish it. He sits in his chair (on his "throne," perhaps we should say), looking like nothing so much as the frontispiece from a biography of Handel in his flowing wig, black satin knee breeches, buckled shoes and long black gown, a figure straight out of the age of squirearchy. He is an arresting figure, and not only does he look much prettier than his French counterpart, who sits in the bourgeois drabness of modern evening dress, but he is far more authoritative. To cite a simple example: If the French National Assembly gets out of hand, the President of the Assembly rings a bell, an act which often merely augments the prevailing din. But if the House of Commons becomes disorderly— which it rarely does—the Speaker almost always manages to restore order without recourse to mechanical devices. He merely rises from his chair, the rule being that when Mr. Speaker is on his feet all members must be off theirs. And only at times of riotous turmoil does he resort to the ultimate, almost unfailing, method of getting order—putting on his hat. His powers over debate, over the putting of motions and questions, and over members' conduct, are vast and to some extent arbitrary.

But even more important than his formal powers is the readiness with which his rulings are obeyed. No doubt his effectiveness as a presiding officer is in large measure due to the same factor to which the monarchy largely owes its popularity—that his political impartiality is completely established and unquestioned. He is the very embodiment of the rules of procedure and, like the rules, neutral. This neutrality is guaranteed in numerous ways. The Speaker is elected for the life of a Parliament, not for a single session, as in France, and he will be reelected, according to a convention dating back to the early eighteenth century, as many times as he wishes. Thus Speakers, like monarchs, are generally in office for long periods and acquire the usual venerability of age and experience. Although elections to the speakership may be contested by the parties, only men who have not been violent partisans are put up, and the aim is always to secure a unanimous election. Finally, once a man has become Speaker, he is divested of his political personality, so to speak, in a number of ways. Although he continues to be a member of Parliament, his constituency chores are taken care of by another member. He may vote only if there is a draw in a decision, and then only to preserve the status quo. He never takes part in a debate (absolutely never). And his seat is never contested by the other party ("never," in this case, in the Gilbertian sense; there have been four contests for the Speaker's seat since 1714).

But whatever the sources of the Speaker's power, he has it—and does not greatly need it. The normal tone of the House is orderly and polite; it is a chamber with an aristocratic past and with palpably aristocratic habits. True, the prevalent politeness is to some extent backed by rules. For example, in referring to another member, a member speaking in the House must never use his name but must refer to him by a ceremonious title. If he is a member of another party, the usage is "the honorable member for _____" for an ordinary M.P.; "the right honorable member" for a Privy Councillor; "the honorable and learned member" for a lawyer; "the honorable and gallant member" for a former officer in one of the armed services; or "the noble Lord" for the son of a great nobleman who possesses a courtesy title. If the other member belongs to the same party, the title will be varied—for example, "my honorable friend, the member for _____." These ceremonious titles are not conducive to belligerence, however much venom certain members manage to inject into them. Again, the Speaker is empowered to see that members use only decorous language. He may have obstreperous members removed by the Sergeant-at-Arms and, indeed, suspended from the House altogether. A brief but representative list of expressions ruled unparliamentary in the late-nineteenth century includes "cowardly," "a poltroon," "of remarkably fragile honour," "a bigoted, malevolent young puppy," "the reverse of the truth," "bloodthirsty," and "mendacious."

It would be a mistake, however, to suppose that the politesse of the House is merely a matter of rules. The rules and precedents are often overlooked, particularly when they are picayune. Churchill and Bevan, among others, have unburdened themselves of expressions that would have astounded the fastidious Speaker Denison in the nineteenth century. The courtesy and good humor of the House are rather a part of its spirit. They come out most clearly and under least compulsion when a member has made a "maiden speech," his first essay in the House of Commons. No matter how miserable the speech, the next speaker—whether friend or foe—will congratulate him on an eloquent and informative performance and will express the pleasure of the House in hearing it and the hope that the member will be heard from frequently on other occasions.

This courtesy toward the maiden speaker is also a rule, even though it exists merely intangibly, in the spirit of the House. It is part of the ritual by which the House never lets us forget that it is both an ancient and a solemn institution. The House, no less than the monarchy, appeals to the form worshipper, the pomp worshipper, that dwells in most of us. Yet for all its formality, it is, as the visitor will immediately sense, basically an intimate and informal place. Here, of course, is where its size plays an important part. For example, it is not unusual for the great table that supports the golden mace to support also the gangling legs of some elongated frontbencher. Members present in the House of Commons sit in almost every conceivable posture: some, like Balfour, on their shoulder blades; others reclining on their sides. And there is an almost constant coming and going, bowing in and bowing out, and conferring behind the Speaker's chair. But the prevalent informality is most notable in the speeches. British parliamentarians need suffer neither the academic pompousness of German legislators nor the incessant Fourth-of-July oratory of the Americans. The tone of the House of Commons is conversational rather than declamatory, witty rather than learned—it could hardly be otherwise. In so small a chamber, lectures and orations invariably sound ludicrous—except on the greatest of occasions or when delivered by a semilegendary figure like Sir Winston Churchill. Moreover, it cramps the orator's style to be compelled to speak in his place, with others crowded around him, rather than from a special tribune. It equally cramps his style to have neither a desk on which to put things, nor a rail on which to lean. It cramps his style not to be allowed to use a prepared speech or even special notes; the House permits only Ministers making important announcements of policy, where every word counts, to read their speeches. And not least, since all remarks in the House are to be addressed not to other members but to Mr. Speaker, a man can sound ridiculous haranguing a crowd of one. Speeches, therefore, tend to be calm. They also tend to be concise, partly because this is the tradition of the House, partly because the Speaker may immediately suppress all irrelevant remarks and tedious repetitions, and partly, no doubt, because the crush of modern business demands dispatch.

But informality is not all. The House can be a mercilessly discourteous audience, particularly if a member departs from its mores, and it is always a tough audience. A. P. Herbert, never one to tremble before a crowd, called it the "torture chamber," and with good reason. In almost any circumstance members, unless they are completely bored, will keep up a running fire of interjections. If the speeches offend the House, a merciless cacophony may break loose. The would-be orator, for example, will almost certainly be engulfed in a tumultuous rustling of papers, stamping of feet, coughing and sneezing, or, as has happened once or twice, such a continuous chorus of "hear, hear" that he cannot be heard. The House is generally courteous and calm; but it is never easy on speakers in the sense of tolerating nonsense or lack of decorum or blatant unconventionality. The atmosphere of the House, it has been said, is "gentlemanly." If so, it must also be remembered that a gentleman has been defined as a man who is never unintentionally rude.

Class Composition

Like any other democratically elected legislature, the House of Commons by no means represents all occupational and social groups in proportion

Table 5.1 Background of M.P.s Elected in 1970 (in Percent)

	All Parties
Professions	46.4
Business	20.7
Manual Workers	12.4
Miscellaneous	20.0

SOURCE: David Butler and Michael Pinto-Duschinsky, *The British General Election of 1970* (London: Macmillan, 1971), p. 302. Reprinted by permission of Macmillan London and Basingstoke.

to their numbers in the country. It is not, socially speaking, a "mirror of the nation." In Britain, as in legislative bodies elsewhere, the professions are strongly represented. They make up one-half of the membership of the Commons (see Table 5.1). The law profession, however, which accounts for only about one-fifth of all M.P.s, has nothing like the predominance it enjoys in the American Congress, where representatives with legal training often number over half the membership of the two houses. In the House of Commons businessmen and workers just about balance one another, although together they are outnumbered by members of the professions. The category "manual workers," however, deserves comment. At first glance it constitutes a sharp contrast to the heavy businessman contingent in Parliament. It would also seem to contrast with the distribution of occupations in the American Congress, where manual occupations are rarely used to characterize members. In fact, a great many of these M.P.s are trade-union officials who have not worked in a mine or on the shop floor for many years and who occupy managerial posts with responsibilities as great as, and in many ways similar to, those occupied by the businessmen with whom the conventional job description seems to set them in opposition. The miscellaneous category in Table 5.1 includes as its principal constituents farmers and journalists. On the basis of occupation the House, while including a broad representation, tends to be a middle- and upper-class body.

Class analysis, however, is more illuminating if we distinguish the parties.

Table 5.2 Background of Labour and Conservative M.P.s 1970 (in Percent)

	Conservatives	Labour
Professions	45	40
Business	30	10
Manual Workers	1	26
Miscellaneous	24	16

SOURCE: David Butler and Michael Pinto-Duschinsky, *The British General Election of 1970* (London: Macmillan, 1971), p. 303. Reprinted by permission of Macmillan London and Basingstoke.

Table 5.2 compares the two main parties on the basis of occupation. We find the expected and substantial contrast in the representation of businessmen as opposed to workers, each category accounting for a quarter or more of the appropriate party's total. The Labour party does include some businessmen. And among Conservative backbenchers, it must be pointed out, will be found two genuine manual workers. When analyzed, the professions also reveal party contrast. Although the two parties are not very different in the representation of most professions, with regard to teachers there is wide disparity: Only nine count themselves Tories, while fifty-six sit on the Labour side. In the House elected in 1966, the contrast was even sharper: nine Conservative to seventy-two Labour teachers. Lawyers are stronger on the Conservative than on the Labour benches, while, as would be expected, almost all the farmers are Tories.

Table 5.3 Educational Background of M.P.s 1970 (in Percent)

	Conservatives	Labour
Elementary	1	21
Secondary	25	62
Public School	74	17
Eton	18	1
Oxford and Cambridge	52	24
Other Universities	12	29

SOURCE: David Butler and Michael Pinto-Duschinsky, *The British General Election of 1970* (London: Macmillan, 1971), p. 303. Reprinted by permission of Macmillan London and Baskingstoke.

Education tells a similar story (see Table 5.3). Labour is the party of M.P.s who started their education in the government-supported schools and one-fifth of whom never went beyond the elementary level. Those who did go to a university were not likely to go to Oxford or Cambridge. Conservative M.P.s, on the other hand, overwhelmingly went to "public" (i.e., exclusive private) schools and thence to Oxbridge. Still, the strength of university graduates on the Labour benches must not be overlooked, the totals for the two parties being not far apart: 64 percent for the Conservatives and 53 percent for Labour.

These figures on occupation and education measure what an observer in the gallery quickly senses. In terms of social origins, the Labour party in the House is a more heterogeneous and socially representative body, although tending, like parties of the Left generally, to be a party of intellectuals and union officials. The balance between the latter two categories, it may be noted, has shifted in recent years; professional people, and especially university teachers, are noticeably displacing workers. The Conservative party, in accent, manner, and dress as well as in occupation and education, has not so much a middle-class as a distinctly upper-class flavor. Perhaps the best objective clue to this is the high percentage of its members who went to Eton, a school that has produced English notables at least since the battle of Waterloo was supposedly won on its playing fields. On both sides of the House, but especially on the Tory side, sits a powerful remnant of the governing class that won the admiration of Tocqueville and Schumpeter.

Six

The Functions
of Parliament

The extravagance of the legal theory of its powers, the impressiveness of its symbolism, and the remnants of the governing class among its members only make more poignant by contrast the actualities of the position of the House of Commons under Cabinet government. For, in the words of an ex-Minister, it is the Cabinet that wields "the collective sovereign power of the state" (see Chapter 2). To be sure, the Cabinet is responsible to the House, which, if it chose, could deprive any given set of Ministers of this power and vest it in another set. But nowadays the chance of a Cabinet's losing the confidence of the House is very slight.

The Decline of Parliament

Two indexes of this imbalance of power between Cabinet and House—and also, incidentally, of the decline of Parliament—are the historical record of Cabinet defeats and the rise of party cohesion in votes of the House. On the basis of a comparison of the mid-nineteenth century with recent decades, the probability that a Cabinet will be defeated in the House of Commons has declined almost to the vanishing point. In the period 1846–1860 parliamentary independence reached its peak, the House administering eight major defeats to successive Governments. On six occasions defeat led to the resignation of the Cabinet; on the other two the Prime Minister got a dissolution of Parliament and went to the country in a general election. In these fourteen years there were five different Cabinets, each with an average life of less than three years. In 1867 Walter Bagehot stated a cardinal truth of British government at that time when he wrote that the House of Commons "lives in a state of perpetual potential choice."[1]

In the twentieth century the relationship is radically different. The last time a Government resigned because of a defeat in the House was 1923. A year later another Government suffered a defeat serious enough for it to call a general election. In each of these cases, however, the party constituting the Government had only a minority in the House and was dependent upon support from another party to govern. This was the period when the rise of Labour and decline of the Liberals had created a situation of three-party competition, which broke up the normal pattern of two dominant parties. To find an instance when a Government originally enjoying such a party majority in the House lost on a vote that caused it to resign, we must go back to 1885, when Gladstone's Liberals split over Irish Home Rule. In the present age of collectivist politics and party government, we would expect Governments to resign only as a result of defeat in a general election. This has indeed been the case in each of the changes in governing party since 1945: the resignations of Attlee in 1951, Home in 1964, and Wilson in 1970. Labour was in for six years, followed by the Conservatives for thirteen, then Labour again for six—an average for each party of about eight years.

The indexes of rising party cohesion parallel and in part explain this immense increase in governmental stability. Table 6.1 gives this measurement from the mid-nineteenth century to recent times.

Table 6.1 Party Unity 1860–1946 (Measured by Coefficients of Cohesion)[2]

Year	Liberals	Conservatives	Labour
1860	58.9	63.0	—
1871	75.5	74.0	—
1881	83.2	87.9	—
1894	89.8	97.9	—
1899	82.5	97.7	—
1906	96.8	91.0	88.4
1908	94.9	88.3	92.8
1924–1928	88.8	99.2	99.8
1945–1946		99.0	99.9

DATA SOURCE: Samuel H. Beer, *British Politics in the Collectivist Age,* rev. ed. (New York: Knopf, 1965), pp. 123, 257, 262.

---

[1] *The English Constitution,* World's Classics ed. (London, 1928), p. 125.

[2] Starting from the assumption that a fifty-fifty split in a party signifies zero cohesion, we calculate the coefficient of cohesion by dividing by fifty the difference between fifty and the

This measurement of party unity tells us only the extent of cross-voting, that is, when a party member deserts his party and votes with its opponents. It says nothing about threats of cross-voting, abstentions, contrary speeches, conflicts within the party caucus, and other forms of party dissidence. As we shall see, party rebellions and revolts on the back benches have by no means come to an end. Yet the immense rise in party cohesion since the mid-nineteenth century vividly indicates the transformation in parliamentary behavior between the liberal and the collectivist ages. As far as cross-voting is concerned, the independence of M.P.s has declined almost to nil, while the stability of governments has risen to new heights. In the House of Commons today we see two bodies of freedom-loving Britons, chosen in 630 constituencies throughout the United Kingdom, and subject to influences that run back to an electorate that numbers nearly 40 million and that is divided by the complex interests and aspirations of an advanced modern society. Yet day after day, with a Prussian discipline, members troop into the division lobbies at the signals of their whips and in the service of the authoritative decisions of their parliamentary parties. However we may ultimately assess the shift in the balance of power between the executive and the legislature, such behavior constitutes a profound transformation.

A third body of evidence showing the degree and manner of the Cabinet's dominance relates to its control over the business of the House. According to the standing orders and the unwritten rules, the procedures of the House presuppose on the one hand a Government—that is, not merely a number of official members, or Ministers, but a unified ministerial body having a program that it will put before and carry through the House —and on the other hand an Opposition, similarly organized and capable of exercising responsibility for sustained and systematic scrutiny of what the Government proposes and does. In historical perspective these characteristics of the present procedure of the House of Commons simply embody, at this stage in political development, the ancient bipolar conception of authority. In that conception there are two main elements in British government: One is the central, initiating, energizing element—formerly the monarchy and today the Cabinet; the other is the checking, criticizing, controlling element—the Parliament and, nowadays especially, the Opposition. This bipolar model constitutes the basic structure around which the procedure and work of the House are organized.

The standing orders of the House divide its business into two very

---

percentage of party members voting on one side. Thus when 90 percent of the members of a party are on one side, the CoC is 80 percent. In this analysis abstainers are not counted. Only the votes of those who took one side or another are examined. In Table 6.1 the divisions analyzed are in nearly all cases those in which the Government of the day put on its whips, whether or not the other parties did likewise.

unequal branches, private business and public business. *Private business* consists mainly in the passage of private bills, of which some fifty or sixty are enacted each session. A private bill relates to a specific locality or to an individual firm or other corporate body—for example, the authorization of some activity by a local authority. It is handled in a semijudicial manner and takes up very little of the House's time. *Public business* comes under two main headings, private members' business and Government business. *Private members' business* consists of bills or motions introduced by unofficial members, that is, M.P.s who are not members of the Government, but who may be members either of the Government party or of an Opposition party. Private members may freely introduce bills; the problem is to get time for them. M.P.s draw lots to see in what order their bills will come up. But how much time will be allocated to these bills, or whether they will be given any time at all, is subject to the discretion of the Government, which may reduce this time by a simple resolution of the House. In the early postwar years, when the Government was carrying through large legislative programs, the time for private members' bills and motions was cut on average to as little as two days per session.

Apart from the provision made for private members' time, the standing orders of the House allot the rest of the session to the Government, which may distribute its business among these days for the most part as it sees fit. The allocation of this time for *Government business* constitutes an important part of the work of a Cabinet, the two main sources of conflict among Ministers being money for their programs and parliamentary time for their bills. It is not a committee of the House, such as the rules committee in the typical American legislature, but the Government that controls the allocation of parliamentary time, and the House learns about the allocation of time from the Government every Thursday when the Leader of the House announces the order of business for the coming week.

Historically, growing control over the time of the House and increasing allocation of time to Government business parallel the other changes that transformed the nineteenth-century Parliament. That century was marked by a continuing struggle between Cabinet and House for control over the parliamentary time table. One reason for the frequent defeats of Governments in those days was their lack of control of the business of the House. But in the course of time, and especially after the Irish members pushed to extremes their use of obstructionist tactics, the House developed means for severely controlling debate and empowered the Government with substantial control over its business.

The Cabinet's control over the business of the House is qualified by conventions, pressures, and various prudential considerations. A Cabinet may decide to provide time for private members' bills not only in order to be fair, but also in order to avoid having to take sides on a hotly controversial issue. In this way the Labour Government allowed a private member's bill abolishing capital punishment to go through in 1964 on a "free vote," that is, without the Government itself taking a stand. For similar reasons Governments have left to private members the bills easing the laws regarding divorce, abortion, and homosexuality. Moreover, apart from time spent on bills and motions, other occasions are considered to be largely at the disposal of private members: for example, the daily Question Hour—although it must be said that the actual interchanges at that time appear hardly less partisan than the set debates between Government and Opposition.

Of crucial importance are the conventions obliging the Government to set aside from its own time a very substantial part for the use of the Opposition. During the annual debate on the reply to the Queen's speech, the second part of the debate is devoted largely to amendments moved by the Opposition. Later in the session, some twenty-six days, nominally devoted to debating the estimates of proposed expenditure put before the House and called the Supply days, are made available to the Opposition for criticizing administrative policy under virtually any heading it chooses. Most important is the long-established convention that the Government will never fail to accede to the Opposition's request for time to move a vote of censure on the Government. In addition, of course, front-bench spokesmen for the Opposition, like backbenchers speaking for themselves, take part in replying to the Government in debates initiated by it.

The purpose of these examples is to show that the initiative in parliamentary business is far more widely distributed than would be expected from considering only the near monopoly of parliamentary time by Government business. One authoritative estimate, based on an assessment of where the initiative lay during the 1950s, gives the following distribution of time for the average annual session of 159 days: private members, 35 days; the Opposition, 32 days; the Government, 69½ days; indeterminate, 22½ days. Enjoying such rights to control parliamentary time, the Opposition cannot fail to be consulted by the Government when the weekly timetable is being framed. While the Cabinet makes the final determination, it does so only after consultation between Government and Opposition whips and with reasonable regard for the requests of the latter.

Criticism and Control

The forms of procedure used in the House can be classified under three headings, according to the explicit purposes for which they are used: (1) criticism and control of policy, (2) legislation, and (3) control of finance and expenditure. As the previous discussion should have made clear, the ostensible purpose of a procedural form in the House of Commons does not necessarily indicate its actual function; and as we shall see, one of the most fascinating and elusive problems in the study of that body is to determine from its proceedings at any time or over time what political functions are actually being performed. It is appropriate to look first at criticism and control of policy, since this class of proceedings suggests the oldest function of the House, the airing and redress of grievances. When medieval kings first called Parliament into existence, largely in order to enhance their revenues, the members of the lower House soon learned to demand some quid pro quo in return for their grants. The proceedings that descend from this ancient transaction will be discussed under the heading of control of finance. But the task of bringing to the executive's attention conditions that call for action and of criticizing what is proposed to be done about them has become a more general function of the House.

A major opportunity for discharging this task is provided by Question Hour, which occupies the House almost immediately when it convenes at 2:30 P.M. on the first four days of the week. The occasion makes an exciting start of the day's sitting. Members crowd in and leaders are well represented on both front benches, the Prime Minister himself necessarily being present on two days when questions directed to him are taken. Any M.P. may submit a question to any Minister regarding a matter for which the Minister is responsible, and Question Hour is one of the remaining ways in which the individual responsibility of Ministers is still expressed and enforced. The questions are submitted at least forty-eight hours in advance and are printed on the daily order paper. Ostensibly they are requests for information. But when that is the questioner's only object, he is more likely to write directly to the department concerned or to put down his question explicitly as a request for only a written answer. The questions for oral answer are the ones that raise the level of interest and partisan combat. For despite the fact that the putting of questions is left mainly to backbenchers on both sides, the scoring of party points is a main purpose, and former Ministers, although more likely junior than senior ones, will be found among the questioners.

The topics range from some very specific act, or failure to act, to major policy positions of the Government. Two recent examples illustrate the range:

> Mr. George Cunningham (Islington, South-West): To ask the Secretary of State for the Home Department, when he expects to be able to release the site of Pentonville Prison to the Islington Borough for building purposes.

> Mr. Woodhouse (Oxford): To ask the Secretary of State for the Home Department, if he will introduce legislation to amend the Commonwealth Immigrants Act 1968 to remove the clauses discriminating on racial grounds against citizens of the United Kingdom born in former colonies.[3]

---

[3]Order Paper. Questions for Oral Answer (July 23, 1970) Nos. 45 and 46.

While the initial question itself will often have a sharp polemical edge, it is especially the supplementary questions used to follow up the attack that have the desired effect of scoring the point, embarrassing the Minister, winning the headline, impressing the Leader, and so forth. The whole business of putting a question is conducted with rapid-fire precision: The Speaker merely barks out the name of the M.P., who thereupon rises in his place and states the number of his question on the order paper. If the supplementaries are not too drawn out, as many as fifty or more questions can be gotten through in one period. Although briefed by his civil servants, the Minister may find these few minutes a severe test—perhaps more of his verbal than his administrative ability—but still a severe test, with considerable bearing on whether his reputation goes up or down. It has been reported that a British Prime Minister, after referring sourly to the lofty unapproachability of President de Gaulle and of the effect on him of the deference of his "court," added that if the President of France had to come down to the House twice a week and stand up to a running fire of questions, this deferential attitude would surely be attenuated.[4]

Unlike the French system of interpellation, questions put in this manner do not lead to debate and a vote. If the answer given by a Minister is considered unsatisfactory, even after supplementaries, members have several methods available to prevent the matter from being buried. If they feel it urgently needs airing, they can attempt to get a debate under standing order nine. This rule has recently been liberalized to permit such a debate if the Speaker finds the subject "to be so pressing that the public interest will suffer if it is not given immediate attention." Such an emergency debate, which, needless to say, is a fairly serious reordering of the Government's timetable, will take place either that evening or, at the Speaker's discretion, the afternoon of the following day.

The actual form under which the debate takes place is a motion to adjourn the House. Adjournment motions are used in a variety of ways to provide opportunity for criticism by backbenchers and by the leaders of the Opposition. In the daily half-hour adjournment debate, which takes place between 10:00 and 10:30 in the evening, the topic, as at Question Hour, must be within the responsibility of a Minister, who is given notice so that a reply can be prepared by his department. Members win the right to initiate such debates partly through their luck in drawing lots and partly through the Speaker's selection of topics from those proposed by members.

Two other types of opportunity for criticism of policy are of major importance. The debate on the address in reply to the Queen's speech comes each fall at the culmination of the ceremony associated with the

---

[4]Ronald Butt, *The Power of Parliament* (New York, 1967), p. 324.

opening of Parliament. M.P.s and peers crowd into the upper chamber where the Queen reads a short speech—extremely short compared with a President's state of the union message. Written by the Government and announcing both its legislative program for the coming session and its policy on major questions, such as international affairs, this speech initiates a debate in the House of Commons, which starts with a confrontation of Government and Opposition and runs on for perhaps six days. Subjects for each day's debate are arranged through "the usual channels," that is, by the whips of the two parties. The last half of the debate is given over to the initiatives of the Opposition and occasionally backbenchers.

Another type of occasion on which Government and Opposition are explicitly pitted against one another is the debate on a motion of censure, or other motion of confidence. In moving a vote of censure, the Opposition will spell out the nature of its complaint, normally an allegation of some large failure of public policy. A motion of confidence may also be moved by the Government, perhaps at a time when things have not been going too well and the Cabinet feels that it must not only provide an opportunity for criticism, but also give a lead to opinion in the House and in the country. Confidence, which is of the essence of the relationship between executive and legislature under a parliamentary system, may be called in question in the course of other debates. That fateful debate of May 7 and 8, 1940, which took place as the German armies swept across Europe and which led to the fall of Chamberlain and the installation of Churchill as Prime Minister, took place on an adjournment motion. It was turned into a vote of confidence when on the second day Herbert Morrison, a leader of the Labour party, rose and declared that he was neither satisfied with Chamberlain's explanation of the Government's failures nor confident that the Government was aware of its shortcomings. Whereupon the Prime Minister, Neville Chamberlain, replied: "I accept the challenge . . . and call on my friends to support us in the Lobby to-night."[5] In the ensuing division, while Chamberlain won, the Government's majority, usually around 240, fell to 81, when 41 members from the Government benches voted with the Opposition and about 60 others abstained.

Legislation

"The chief function of parliament," said the famous lawyer of the last century F. W. Maitland, "is to make statutes." Unquestionably, legislative proceedings occupy the House of Commons more than any other type of proceedings—perhaps as much as half of its time. In a year the Parliament

---

[5]360 *H. C. Deb.* 1266 (8 May 1940).

will produce some fifty or sixty public acts, of which perhaps half a dozen originated with private members and the rest with the Government. There are normally five stages in the passage of a bill by the House of Commons. As in American procedure, the *first reading* is largely perfunctory. Only the title of the bill is read, and the Minister in charge (assuming it is a Government bill) names the date on which the second reading debate will take place. Here is a crucial difference from American procedure that goes to the heart of the difference between the two political systems. In the American Congress, after a bill is introduced, it is sent to a committee, whose deliberations may greatly affect its content and its fate. These procedures, reflecting the separation of powers, show the independence of the American legislature and the powerful position of its committees. To find a comparable function in Britain we would need to look at the way in which the Cabinet, or a Cabinet committee, deals with proposed legislation before it ever goes to the House.

In the *second reading* debate, to which one parliamentary day is ordinarily devoted, the House is asked to approve of the bill as a whole before it is sent to committee for detailed consideration. For this reason members may not offer amendments that change the content of the bill, but only amendments which in effect involve its total rejection. Thus in contrast with Congressional procedure, it is not in order for a member of the House of Commons to move to strike all sections of the bill after a certain clause and add new provisions. The explicit purpose of this stage is to give the House the opportunity to decide in principle whether it wants such a bill, a decision that will restrict the nature of amendments that may be offered in committee. In fact, a good many of the speeches made at this time will be concerned with only some of the bill's provisions, as members reflect their special interests and competencies and perhaps prepare the way for amendments that they will move at the committee stage. Needless to say, the Government wins its inevitable majority at the end of the day, and the bill goes to committee.

At this point, if the bill involves the expenditure of public money, an additional stage is inserted between stages two and three. The House must approve what is called a *financial resolution,* which like any other matter involving a charge on the public funds, must be moved by a Minister of the Crown. The approval of a financial resolution should not be confused with voting an estimate of departmental expenditure. The latter is normally part of the annual financial business by which money to cover government expenditure is appropriated. A financial resolution, on the other hand, is voted only in relation to a specific bill that involves public expenditure. The financial resolution is comparable to an authorization of expenditure, in congressional parlance, while the voting of the estimate is like congressional appropriation.

The *standing committees* of the House, to which nearly all bills are now referred, are miniature Parliaments. They consist of twenty to fifty members who are presided over by an impartial chairman and led by a Minister who heads a partisan majority proportionate to the majority in the House as a whole. The proceedings, however, are far more relaxed and less partisan, and amendments, normally referring only to details of the bill, are often accepted by the Government in committee. But even when amendments are turned down at this third stage, they sometimes reappear on the Minister's initiative at a later stage.

Usually eight standing committees are appointed. In keeping with their parliamentary character, most are not assigned special fields of policy, but are simply designated by letters of the alphabet. They are constituted specially for each bill: A nucleus of members interested in or expert in the subject matter of the bill are initially chosen, along with as many other members as necessary to get the right party balance. The rise of Celtic nationalism, however, has affected the committee system of the House. The Scottish Standing Committee, consisting of members from Scottish constituencies, takes the committee stage of all Scottish bills. Enlarged to include all Scottish M.P.s, as well as a few others, this committee becomes the Scottish Grand Committee, to which Scottish estimates and the second reading of purely Scottish bills are referred. There are also Welsh standing and grand committees.

In the *report stage* the bill as amended in committee comes back to the floor of the House. On the order paper, which gives the agenda for the sitting, will be various amendments, possibly including amendments rejected in committee as well as new substantive amendments and new clauses. At this point the Speaker has the power to select the amendments to be discussed (the power of "kangaroo"), which he may use to prevent repetition of arguments already aired in committee. The Minister in charge may again accept amendments; he may also use the full party majority available to him from the whole House to reverse a change that his narrower majority in committee has failed to control.

After going through the bill in the report stage, the House then gives the bill its *third reading*. Needless to say, this does not mean that the bill is actually read before the House—some of these bills run to hundreds of pages! What happens is that a debate takes place on the Minister's motion that the bill be "read a third time." At this stage (the fifth, assuming there has been no financial resolution), debate is again presumably on the general principles of the bill. It resembles the debate on second reading, and the opportunity to amend is similarly narrowed to proposing rejection of the bill as a whole.

Legislative procedure in the House of Lords is similar to procedure in the Commons, taking a bill through the same five basic stages. The Lords' suspensive veto is almost negligible, and the principal use of the upper chamber in law making is to provide an opportunity for extended consideration of noncontroversial amendments. If the Commons will not accept a Lords' amendment and the Lords refuse to back down, the provisions of the Parliament Act of 1949 come into play. Under these provisions the bill will become law in the form desired by the Commons, providing the Commons has repassed it in the same form in two successive sessions, one year having elapsed between the second reading on the first occasion and the third reading on the second occasion. With regard to finance, the Lords' power is even slighter, since any bill certified by the Speaker of the House as a "money bill" must be passed by the Lords without amendment within one month after being sent up; otherwise, it will go to the sovereign for the royal assent without needing to be passed by the upper House.

The ultimate phase of law making, the royal assent, is signified to Parliament in a ceremony that retains a medieval charm. Normally the Queen does not indicate her assent in person, but by means of a commission signed by her and listing the bills to which she assents. Upon receiving such a commission, the Lords sends its ceremonial officer, the Gentleman Usher of the Black Rod, to signify to the Commons that its attendance is desired. When this message is delivered—and it may break into the middle of an important debate—the Speaker, at the head of a straggling line of M.P.s, goes across the Palace of Westminster to the upper chamber. The commission is then read, as are the titles of the bills, and the royal assent to each is signified by a clerk in Norman French. Assent to an appropriation bill is signified by the words, "La Reyne remercie ses bons sujets, accepte leur benevolence, et ainsi le veult." For all other public acts, the formula is "La Reyne le veult."

In controlling the legislative process, the Government has at its command several potent instruments of parliamentary procedure. These derive largely from changes made during the latter part of the nineteenth century, under the impact of Irish obstructionism, the increase in government business, and the heightening of party conflict in Parliament. In 1881, in reaction to filibustering by the Irish, Gladstone introduced the rules from which modern closure and the guillotine developed. *Closure* means that the Government can apply its majority to stop debate. It can only do this, however, when the Speaker finds that every section of opinion has had a chance to speak on the matter before the House and when not only a majority, but at least one hundred members are present and voting in favor. This instrument is available not only in the House but also in standing committee, where the Minister can use it to prevent dilatory talk and to hasten a bill on its way.

Closure itself may not suffice where a determined minority exploits its rights by arguing every amendment and every possible line of dissent. To cope with such efforts, the Government may utilize a *guillotine,* or "allocation of time order." Such an order, which is voted by the House, is a timetable specifying precisely how much time is to be allotted to each stage of a bill, or even to discussion of groups of clauses in standing committee. The passage of such an order means that when the time allocated to a certain phase has expired—regardless of the extent or coverage of the debate—the Speaker puts the question, and the House, having given its inevitable answers, passes on to the next phase indicated in the order.

Delegated Legislation

The exercise of powers of delegated legislation is, on the one hand, law making. On the other hand, the procedures of the House that attempt to give it the means to assert its authority in this sphere of law making constitute opportunities for criticism and control. As government intervention grew with the rise of collectivism, the sheer increase in rule making, the need for flexibility in changing and adapting these rules, and the increasingly technical and complex character of the rules made it more and more difficult to keep all law making on the floor of the House. In consequence, the practice of delegating to Ministers the power to make rules with the force of law grew rapidly. By 1920 the rules and orders issued under delegated powers filled five times as many pages as the statutes passed that year by Parliament. Today the welfare state and managed economy continue to produce vast quantities of legislation in this way. The "statutory instruments" embodying such acts of executive law making number between 2,000 and 3,000 a year, and some are of very great length and complexity.

As far as parliamentary control is concerned, statutory instruments fall into four classes. With regard to some rules of minor importance, no special steps are taken to bring them to the attention of Parliament. A second class are merely laid before the House, that is, put on file in its library. A third class not only are laid before the House, but also are subject within a certain period of time to being nullified by the House's passing a "prayer," that is, a request to the Queen to quash the rule. Finally, there are those rules which do not come into legal effect until the House has taken action by an "affirmative resolution" to approve them.

In attempting to cope in some way with the mass of rules laid before it, the House has had since 1944 the assistance of the Select Committee on Statutory Instruments—commonly called the "Scrutinizing Committee." While it may not comment on questions of policy or even efficiency, the committee is charged with calling the attention of the House to statutory instruments such as those which impose charges or make an unusual use of the power originally conferred. Assisted by a small expert staff, the committee examines a large number of instruments each session, sometimes as many as a thousand. It will call the attention of the House to perhaps half a dozen; among these, however, one that is felt worthy of a debate will be found only very rarely.

Finance and Expenditure

The third category of proceedings in the House of Commons in addition to criticism and control of policy, and legislation is the control of finance. It will take up perhaps a third of the typical session. In Britain as elsewhere the financial business of the legislature consists of two sorts of activity: appropriations (supply, as the British have traditionally called it) and taxation (ways and means). The process of appropriation begins every year sometime in February when the estimates are introduced in the House. These are departmental requests for money needed in the impending financial year. They are collated and reviewed by the Treasury and presented to Parliament—in the case of the armed services, presented by the appropriate departmental Minister and in the case of other services, by the Financial Secretary to the Treasury. Ultimately the estimates are embodied in the annual Appropriation Act, which is usually not passed until some time in late July or early August.

For all this business the House has set aside a total of twenty-six days —the Opposition days—which are fitted into its work schedule at various times from February until the middle of the summer. On most of these days the House, sitting as Committee of Supply, concerns itself with the estimates of a particular department. These debates, however, are not normally on financial matters, such as how much money should be provided for a department or for one of its services. Instead, the debates center on departmental policies and programs.

Thus in the past a grant to the Ministry of Housing and Local Government has been the peg on which was hung a debate over whether or not the Government was making an efficient use of manpower in its public housing program. The Foreign Office estimate has been used to set in motion a wide-ranging discussion of the Government's actions in international affairs. Before the Post Office was hived off, its estimate could be used to raise the question of increased charges for the use of telephones (which, like all telecommunications in Britain, come under the Post Office).

It is not unknown for such a debate to center on what the Opposition regards as excessive spending on a government service, such as the vastly expensive National Health Service. That these debates do not normally deal with expenditure, however, is made plain by the usual method of inaugurating them. The Opposition moves for a nominal reduction—say £100—in the amount proposed to be appropriated. A hundred pounds is negligible in a departmental program running to millions of pounds, yet by long tradition a vote on an estimate, no matter how insignificant the amount, is a matter of confidence. This means that the Government will take special care to muster a majority and that the vote itself will make no difference in policy or expenditure. At the same time, because the estimates cover practically the whole spectrum of government action, they provide a highly flexible matrix for structuring criticism. Hence, while it is no doubt convenient for the Government to be sure of its appropriations for the coming year, it is also convenient for the Opposition to have at its disposition the twenty-six days devoted to criticizing such aspects of Government policy as it chooses to select.

In any one year most of the estimates will not, of course, be discussed. Most departments, however, can expect to come under some scrutiny, broad or narrow. Debates sometimes may range widely over a department's policy during a substantial period of time; more likely, they will take up some special aspect. And indeed, a Supply day can be used for what might be called "targets of opportunity," that is, grievances such as strikes, bureaucratic gaffes, and breakdowns of public service, which are typical in the huge modern polity and which can readily be blamed on the Government of the day. Behind the ostensible purpose of these debates, which is to decide how much money should be voted for government purposes, lies the function of providing an opportunity for the Opposition to pursue its scrutiny and criticism of government action in a flexible and systematic manner.

Proposals for taxation, as we have seen in our discussion of administration, begin in the executive branch. On the bureaucratic level the center of origin would be that small division in the public sector group of the Treasury that since 1967 has had the task of coordinating Treasury work on the budget. The budget is under consideration almost continuously throughout the year by a high-level official committee of the Treasury. Final decisions are made by the Chancellor in consultation with the Prime Minister. After their decisions have received the approval of the Cabinet, the Chancellor presents them to the House in his budget speech around the beginning of the fiscal year—in Britain April 1.

The British give a narrower meaning to the term budget than do Americans, who use it to refer to both the revenue and expenditure side of government finance. Strictly speaking, when the Chancellor presents his budget, he puts before the House only his proposals for raising revenue. Since he is, however, the Minister responsible not only for prudent housekeeping, but also for management of the national economy, his presentation will be concerned with both expenditure and taxation as the basic elements of fiscal policy. Today no less than in the days of Gladstone —a Chancellor "who could lead his hearers over the arid desert, and yet keep them cheerful and lively and interested without flagging"—the budget speech is a great parliamentary and national occasion.

After the budget speech, which is likely to last two or three hours, the House immediately passes a series of tax resolutions that authorize the Government to collect all new taxes immediately. The ensuing debate, first on the budget and then on the finance bill, which is brought in to give effect to the new revenue proposals, occupy perhaps fifteen days of parliamentary time. Like the Supply days these days are distributed over the remainder of the session. The final outcome of the two processes of legislative activity is the Consolidated Fund (Appropriation) Act and the Finance Act, both finally enacted toward the end of the session, in late July or early August.

Proposed Reforms

This system of procedure regarding expenditure and taxation clearly bears the stamp of an earlier generation before Governments were greatly concerned with the economic influence of government finance on the national economy. As we have seen, under this older and narrowly financial approach, the Treasury was concerned with economy, efficiency, and a balance among department spending programs in accordance with Cabinet priorities. Like the relevant Treasury procedures, the financial procedures of the House of Commons had also developed during the latter part of the period of liberal modernization, and in spirit and form they are often identified with the great reforming chancellor, Gladstone.

On the parliamentary side the procedures of Gladstonian finance surely gave the House of Commons the opportunity to control both expenditure and taxation. The rise of party discipline, however, severely limited the significance of these procedures. Moreover, in recent years the growing use of government fiscal activity to manage the economy could not be readily expressed through them. To take a crucially important example, under these procedures all expenditure was voted on an annual basis—as if Parliament could, and did, from year to year decide what the total expenditure would be. In fact the massive programs of the modern polity —building roads, houses, schools, hospitals, and so on—mature over a period of years and can be only marginally altered by the annual financial exercise (see Chapter 4).

For more than a decade the Treasury has been adapting its procedures to this need for long-term calculation and control of expenditure as well as to other needs of economic management. Recently the House of Commons has also begun to respond, and at this writing it would seem that reforms of major importance are in the process of being made. Precisely what the new system will be cannot be predicted. Yet it is possible to suggest the general lines that reform will probably take. In the first place, M.P.s will be given the information needed to show the interplay between public finance and national economy for a period of several years. This would mean information regarding prospective government expenditure as well as assessments of the likely course of economic growth. So informed, M.P.s would be able to share with Ministers and civil servants in that confrontation of public expenditure versus national resources which is at the heart of the task of economic policy making. As a step in meeting this need, the Government is already providing the House annually with a report on the probable expenditure for the next five years. Moreover, if informed judgments are to be made, not only must a global estimate of expenditure be provided, but also some indication of how it will be allocated to the main areas of government action. This is now being done not only within the executive for its use, but also for the use of Parliament by means of the annual white papers on public expenditure.

Finally, if the House is to make intelligent use of such new and fairly complex and technical bodies of information, it will need appropriate machinery. From 1912 it had a committee specially charged with reviewing expenditure proposals presented to Parliament, the Select Committee on Estimates. This body was created when the House revealed its inability to control expenditure by means of its debates on the estimates. While the committee likewise found it impossible to learn enough about proposed expenditure in time to feed this information into an effective discussion, it performed a useful service, especially in recent years, by its many inquiries into the economy and efficiency of projects involving heavy spending. This ad hoc approach, concentrating on economy, did not meet the new needs of economic policy making. In consequence, following the proposals of a select committee of the House, the Heath Government set up in place of the Estimates Committee a new Select Committee on Public Expenditure. It considers the long-term projections of expenditure submitted to the House, operates through six subcommittees corresponding to broad fields of government activity, and inaugurates an annual two-day debate.

These subcommittees may take the place that some reformers had expected would be filled by a new set of specialist select committees. Under the Wilson Government six such specialist committees were set up: three "subject" committees to consider science and technology, race relations and immigration, and Scottish affairs; and three "departmental" committees to investigate the ministries responsible for agriculture, education and science, and overseas aid.[6] These committees had the power to send for persons, papers, and records, but did not take part in legislation or appropriation. They took evidence sometimes from Ministers and often from civil servants. They employed specialist technical and professional advisers. Dashing the high hopes once held by their advocates, however, the new committees did not catch the fancy of the House. "It must be conceded," concluded a recent report, "that when—too rarely—their

---

[6] *Select Committees of the House of Commons* (October, 1970), Cmnd. 4507, p. 4.

reports have been debated, the degree of interest shown by other Members has sometimes been disappointingly small." While the subject committees have been kept, the departmental committees have been abolished. In accord with the present high esteem enjoyed by output budgeting and cost-benefit analysis, the new expenditure committee will work through subcommittees that are neither subject nor departmental, but functional. Each of the functional subcommittees is expected, as a principal duty, to examine "the implications in terms of public expenditure of the policy objectives chosen by Ministers and assess the success of the Departments in attaining them."[7]

Conceivably, the future procedure of the House in financial affairs might take the form of a three-stage process. The new select committee on public expenditure would annually receive the two basic sorts of information regarding public expenditure and economic growth. It would examine these and make a report to the House, perhaps even going so far as to present alternative proposals regarding not only the overall size of the public-sector expenditure, but also the priorities between different main blocks. This report would provide the foundation for an annual debate, presumably in the autumn or early winter. In the second stage the House would, as at present, debate the estimates. These would be presented, however, in two forms: the conventional line-item form and an output budgeting form, conforming as far as possible to the categories of the public-expenditure projections. Clearly, if this could be done, it would greatly facilitate the kind of policy discussions that take place on the Opposition days. M.P.s could see much more clearly what the actual priorities of government policy are and could more intelligently criticize the use of national resources for any objective or field of objectives.

The final stage would consist in a postaudit by a parliamentary body. There would be no great departure from the present procedure. In charge of the annual audit of appropriation accounts of the departments is the Comptroller and Auditor General, an official who is independent of the executive, holding office during good behavior and removable only by resolutions of both houses. He and his staff examine departmental accounts to check on not only their legality, but also their economy and efficiency. It is with such matters that his reports to the House are normally concerned. On this basis the Public Accounts Committee of the House conducts its own inquiry, summoning before it and examining the responsible financial officers of various departments and reporting its findings to the House. The new form of the estimates, which would be reflected in the departmental accounts, could only make the work of the committee

---

[7] *Ibid.*, p. 5.

more effective in assessing the government's allocation of its resources. While the Public Accounts Committee would continue to audit the accounts of departments, the Select Committee on Nationalized Industries would also continue to perform a similar task with regard to the accounts of the nationalized industries.

The present trend in procedural reform is bringing Parliament abreast of the executive in the way problems of financial and economic policy are conceived, much as certain procedural reforms of the Gladstonian period brought the Parliament of the Liberal era abreast of the reforms that were then creating a new Treasury. If we think of the role of American legislative committees concerned with finance—as some British advocates of reform quite explicitly do—we can also see the prospect of the new select committee's alternative proposals for spending becoming an alternative to the Government's own program. Beyond that we can see the possibility of the new committee's emerging as a kind of rival executive to the Cabinet. It is not idle to consider the prospect of such rivalry, dim and distant as it may be. Indeed, the fact that Ministers and civil servants are alert to it as a possibility is a reason why it does not eventuate. By anticipation they ward off the threat.

The point is illustrated by the fact that a quarter of a century ago a reform proposal much like the one recently adopted was rejected. In brief, the proposal was to set up instead of the estimates committee a committee on public expenditure that would work through subcommittees and would be assisted by "trained clerks," that is, specialists. Although the Labour Government was in a vigorous reforming mood at the time, it reacted to these proposals just as any other British Government would have reacted—negatively. Herbert Morrison reflected the attitude of Labour in the answers he gave to questions from the select committee on procedure that was considering the proposal:

> Q: You would never suggest that in the final resort the House of Commons was responsible to the Government of the day?
> A: To the Government of the day?
> Q: Yes?
> A: That would be against the whole doctrine. The Government is responsible to the House. On the other hand, the Government has to try to lead the House.
> Q: Then why is it, that when you get into the field of departmental inquiry, you take the attitude that the civil servant is a superior person, and that the power of the representatives of the House, the power of the trained clerks, I think you said, would be too great, and would be resented in the Departments . . .
> A: Because then we get into the argument as to who is responsible for executive current administration, the Government or Parliament. I say it is the Government that is responsible. It is responsible to Parliament, but if Parliament is going to set up another duplicating set of administrative experts to take an interest in

current administration, there is going to be a clash between Parliament and Government, which I think would be bad.

Parliament's business is to check the Government, throw it out if it wants to, go for it, attack it, criticise it, by all means, but Parliament is not a body which is organised for current administration—not in this country. They have had a go at it in France and the United States, and I do not think too much of it.[8]

---

[8]Select Committee on Procedure, *Third Report* (October, 1946), Minutes of Evidence, p. 111.

Seven

The Power
of Parliament

The previous chapter makes clear how very faithfully the model of party government embodies some of the most important dimensions of British political behavior. We see how the ostensible purposes of much parliamentary procedure usually conceal quite different functions. We also see that whatever the proceedings, the Government almost always controls the initiative and the outcome. Under any of the three headings—control of policy, legislation, or control of finance—it could well be argued that the function of Parliament comes down to criticism, nothing more and nothing less. In this perspective Parliament neither makes laws nor controls finance and policy. If a person wants to know what laws will be passed during a coming session, he does not take a poll of M.P.s, he reads the Queen's speech. If it says that "My Government" proposes to introduce legislation for a certain purpose, the chances are overwhelming that by the same time the following year a statute to this effect will be on the books. Similarly in the daily business of the House, if we want to know what is going to be discussed during the coming week, we cannot do better than to listen to the Leader of the House when he announces the parliamentary timetable on a Thursday afternoon.

The Continuous Electoral Campaign

The power to criticize is no mean power. In the context of the British party system, it means that the appeal to the electorate in the next election is constantly foreshadowed in the clash between Government and Opposition. The disjunction between the legislative leaders of the parties and the leaders of the parties in the national election that characterizes the American system is completely bridged in the British party system. The leaders of the disciplined forces of Government and Opposition in the House are also the leaders of the party organizations throughout the country. The party battle, centering on the daily clash at Westminster, is simplified and dramatized: There is no mystery as to who is responsible, no difficulty in identifying the alternative team. Under the British party system the House is the principal forum from which the parties appeal to voters for their support in the next election. "Governing has become a prolonged election campaign," writes Bernard Crick. "Parliament," he continues, "is still the agreed area in which most of the campaign is fought" and the principal device by which "the Parties obtain something like equal access to the ear of the electorate in the long formative period between the official campaigns."[1]

This is all in accord with the doctrine of party government that finds the main functions of the legislature to be, first, to register the decision of the voters at an election, and, second, to provide the forum from which the two antagonists carry on propaganda and, it may be hoped, political education. Not that one should exaggerate the attention given to Parliament. The newspapers that carry reasonably full reports of parliamentary debates are read by only about a tenth of the adult population. About the same percentage has been identified as the "serious public," meaning those who are "very interested" in political affairs and who follow them between elections.[2] As opinion leaders such political strata perform an important function in forming the opinion that is expressed at elections. In pointing to the interaction between these strata and the continuing controversy in the House of Commons, the model of party government brings out an important dimension of the process of social choice in Britain.

Yet this view of the House and its functions is not quite right. To some critics it is correct factually but not normatively. These critics lament the decline of Parliament from its supposed preeminence in its great liberal period. They propose reforms which, although they cannot undermine the vast stability of government in this day of the collectivist party, will some-

---

[1] Bernard Crick, *The Reform of Parliament* (London, 1964), pp. 25–26.

[2] Richard Rose, *Influencing Voters: A Study of Political Campaigning in 1964* (London, 1967), p. 169; and Rose, *Politics in England* (Boston, 1965), p. 89.

how recapture for Parliament a voice not only in criticizing, but also in influencing government policy. But this reformist perspective, like the party-government view itself, is also not factually correct as a true and rounded portrait of what goes on in the House. Any first-time visitor to the gallery of the House must feel that something very important is going on in the House itself, quite apart from the reverberations of its proceedings in the outside world. The excitement, the tension, the strain are the tip-offs. This would not be the atmosphere if the House were a mere electoral college and sounding board. On the contrary, something important is at stake, and the outcome is not cut-and-dried, but uncertain and risky—hence the effort to influence the outcome, creating strain in the protagonists and tension and excitement among combatants and spectators. After all, why do so many busy and important politicians spend so much time in and around the House if nothing politically important is going on? As we have seen, Ministers spend about a quarter of their time there, which is as much as they spend in their departments in the actual business of running the government. A Minister will no doubt use some of this time speaking in such a way as to influence votes in an election several years hence. But educating the public is obviously only one of several considerations that keep him in Westminster.

We can hardly fail to sense the power of the House. To be more specific and say just where its power lies is not so easy. We must begin with a look at the parliamentary parties. The political party was the source of Parliament's new behavior, marking the transition from a liberal to a collectivist phase of modernity (see Chapter 9). It is, therefore, in the analysis of party, the instrument of the new control, that we will find the contours and limits of this control. That means, first, looking at the relations between Governments and their own backbenchers and, second, examining the interaction of the organized Opposition and the Government. Not that the individual M.P. acting on a nonpartisan basis may not at times accomplish notable things; he may remedy a grievance or secure the passage of an important law, as noted in our discussion of the activities of private members. But whether or not the independent M.P. was ever as important as some critics of Parliament believe, he is not the lever by which government is moved today and the enlargement of his powers cannot be the means to enhance the role of the British legislature. Party sets the conditions for present parliamentary activity and for any conceivable reform.

Party Organization

For an American the most interesting and puzzling aspect of the behavior of the parties in Parliament is party discipline. Party discipline refers to a system of sanctions by which the parliamentary party induces recalcitrant members, or perhaps merely slack and apathetic ones, to act in concert with its authoritative decisions. The most dramatic of these sanctions is the "withdrawal of the whip," which means that the member is expelled from the parliamentary party with consequences that may include the termination not only of his hope for ministerial promotion, but also of his parliamentary career. For the party to have at its command such severe negative sanctions may well seem to explain the phenomenal cohesion of the parliamentary parties. At first glance party discipline is to party unity as cause is to effect. The use of these powers needs to be examined against the background of party organization in the House.

While the two parliamentary parties, Labour and Conservative, differ significantly in spirit and method of operation, they have important similarities. At the head of each stands a Leader who is elected by the members of the parliamentary party, but who is also recognized as Leader of the party outside Parliament as well. When his party wins a general election, the Queen automatically makes him Prime Minister. In Opposition he is the head of a leadership group, the shadow Cabinet, which sits on the front benches of the Opposition side of the House—that is, to the left of the Speaker—and which carries on a continuous and organized attack on the Government. Along with other members who assist them— rather as other members of a Government assist the Cabinet Ministers— the shadow Government may be a sizable body. In 1965 under Edward Heath it consisted of some seventy-two persons. While Conservatives leave the selection of its members to the Leader, the shadow Government of a Labour Opposition consists not only of spokesmen chosen by the Leader, but also of certain members—the Parliamentary Committee— elected by the whole body of Labour M.P.s.

In addition to its leadership group, each party has an organization reaching into the back benches—in American parlance, a "caucus"—which normally meets once a week during the session. On the Conservative side this organization is called the Conservative and Unionist Members Committee, or the 1922 Committee. This nickname derives from the fact that the Committee was founded after the election of that year by a group of backbenchers who intended it to be—in the words of one of its founders —"a rein upon the leaders." At first exclusively a backbenchers' organ, communicating with the leadership through the traditional whips, the committee in time drew the leaders into a quite close relationship. In recent years the Leader himself has often appeared before it, even when he was Prime Minister.

The Parliamentary Labour party (P.L.P.) consists of all Labour M.P.s, both leaders and backbenchers. When in Opposition, the P.L.P. annually elects the Leader, deputy leader, chief whip, and twelve others who, with representatives from the Lords, constitute the Parliamentary Committee. When Labour is in power, it has no Parliamentary Committee, but a Liaison

Committee of backbenchers and Ministers presumably keeps leaders and followers in touch. Moreover, Ministers regularly attend meetings to explain, and if necessary defend, what the Government is doing—sometimes virtually appealing for a vote of confidence.

In both parties backbenchers are also organized into a series of functional committees concerned with various fields of public policy that parallel departments or groups of departments. When Labour is in Opposition, the chairmen are usually shadow Ministers for the respective departments, an arrangement that links backbenchers and the leadership group. The committees discuss current policy questions, take votes, and make reports to the parliamentary committee. While the Conservative committees do not formally take votes, a whip is attached to each, and through him, as well as through the committee's secretary, reports will reach the leadership.

The whip is the final element in this structure, and the oldest in point of origin. He descends from the early days of Cabinet government in the eighteenth century, and his name is taken from the hunting field, where the "whipper-in" is the man who manages the hounds. The Conservative Leader always appoints the chief whip; the Labour Leader appoints his party's chief whip only when he is Prime Minister. The chief whip is a busy man, and when his party is in power, he has eleven paid assistants, as well as a number of unpaid assistants. Of old, the job of the Government whips was "to make a house, keep a house and cheer the minister." Their primary task is still to make sure that enough party members are available in the House or nearby in the lounge, library, tearoom, or bar to enable the Minister to win the divisions necessary not only to impose the Government's will, but also to keep the wheels of British government from grinding to a halt. It is exacting work. Every two hours the Government whips report to Ministers the number of members available before each division, giving a precise count of the prospective votes on each side along with an indication of the expected Government majority.

All this takes advance planning of the business of the House and the attendance of members. In carrying out their duties, the Government whips act under instructions from the Leader of the House, normally a Minister and member of the Cabinet. In this role they not only inform members, but also persuade, cajole, and, if necessary, warn those who are indisposed to accept authoritative party decisions. But they are also most emphatically a means of communication between backbenchers and the leadership. From what they learn at party meetings and in everyday, informal contact with backbenchers, they keep the leaders informed of the views, grievances, and general temper of the party. The whips let the leaders know what their followers will not stand, a crucial reality that by anticipation deeply affects what any Government attempts.

This whole mechanism of party organization provides two crucial things: first, a means of making authoritative decisions in the name of the party and, second, a means for seeing that these decisions are known and carried out by the party members in the House. The two parties operate in much the same way when in power. The authoritative decisions on tactics and policy come from the Cabinet and are communicated to M.P.s by the whips and by Ministers at the various party meetings, as well as by ministerial statements to the House itself. In Opposition the procedures differ significantly. On the Conservative side it is understood that the Leader has the final say, although, of course, in regular meetings with his shadow Cabinet—as in his dealings with the 1922 Committee—he cannot fail to take account of political realities. On the Labour side authority reverts to the Parliamentary Labour party. The standing orders under which the party operates most of the time specify that "the privilege of membership [in the P.L.P.] involves the acceptance of the decisions of the Party Meeting." (Indeed, these words would seem to bind not only all members, leaders, and followers when the party is in Opposition, but also by clear implication members of any Labour Government as well.) At the regular weekly meetings of the party, with the Leader and Parliamentary Committee giving a lead, the major questions of the business to come before the House are debated and brought to a vote, whose outcome in turn governs the vote of the party in the House. It is not strange, therefore, if some observers find that the most interesting and important debates are not on the floor of the House but "upstairs," that is, in the party caucuses.

Party Discipline

In the use of disciplinary powers the parties also differ. The Conservative Leaders have the power to withdraw the whip, but have proved far less inclined to use that power than has the P.L.P. Although rebellions are at least as common on the Tory as on the Labour backbenches, in only one instance since World War I has a Conservative member been expelled from the parliamentary party. In the Labour party such a question can be decided only by the P.L.P., whether or not the party is in office. When the standing orders are in force, they make an exception for a member only on the ground of "deeply held personal conscientious conviction," and then only to the extent of permitting abstention, never cross-voting.[3] Matters of conscience have been held to include such questions as Sabbath observance, temperance, gambling, and conscription.

These disciplinary powers would seem to have a formidable potential, vesting the whole power of Parliament in a majority of a partisan majority.

---

[3] For text, see *Annual Report,* 51st Conference of the Labour Party, 1952, p. 201.

Conceivably, this arrangement could lead to that ultimate democratic horror—minority government issuing from majority rule. In fact, precisely because this ponderous mechanism does work in a context of democratic politics, its powers are far more limited than they appear to be. A purge of party rebels presents to the electorate the spectacle of a divided and quarreling party and disheartens the organized partisans of the electioneering apparatus outside Parliament. Within the parliamentary party it is a threat to others who also may at some time want room for protest. Considerations such as these severely limit the use of disciplinary powers.

But rebellion can lead to serious consequences for the individual. The classic cases go back to Attlee's first Government after the war. As tension with Russia mounted, a number of Labour M.P.s on the Left became very disturbed and sharply attacked the Government's foreign policy. In 1948 the "cannibalization" of the Social Democrats of Czechoslovakia by the Communists after the Russian-backed coup of that year did much to quiet their dissent. Still, at the time of the Italian general election in April, when the Labour Government was officially supporting the noncommunist parties in the election, thirty-seven Labour M.P.s were prevailed upon to sign a telegram encouraging the left socialist allies of the Communist party of Italy. Fifteen of the signers, when approached by the National Executive Committee of the Labour party, declared either that they had not signed, had signed under a misunderstanding, or had since retracted. Twenty-one others, having been informed that "unless they individually undertake by first post Thursday, May 6, 1948, to desist in future from such conduct they are excluded from membership in the Labour Party," gave the required pledge. The M.P. who had gathered the signatures, however, was promptly expelled from the party, as were, a year later, three others who had given the pledge but had continued with disapproved activities. Deprived of national party endorsement, all stood as independent socialists at the next general election, in 1950. One had strong support from his constituency party, but all were overwhelmingly defeated by official Labour candidates. To be sure, the initiative in these cases was taken by the National Executive Committee (N.E.C.), the whip being withdrawn after, rather than before, its action. Still, the ultimate fate to which withdrawal of the whip might lead was made vividly clear. It may be doubted, of course, whether the whole action made any difference to a parliamentary party that at this time enjoyed a majority of around 191 over the Conservatives and of around 128 over all Opposition parties.

The narrow limits of disciplinary powers are illustrated abundantly by their inability to calm the prolonged and fierce dissension on the Labour Left during the early 1950s. The rebels, led by Aneurin Bevan, a former Minister and a contender for the succession to Attlee, could count on a solid core of about a quarter of the P.L.P. When the issue was popular, this number could be raised to almost half. The peak of the Bevanite rebellion and influence was reached in 1954 during the struggle over the party's position toward a German contribution to the proposed European Defence Community. At the party conference in the fall of 1953, the Attlee-Gaitskell faction won a majority for a favorable response, but only because of a last-minute switch by a small trade union, and by the narrow margin of 3.3 million to 3 million votes. At a meeting of the P.L.P., a motion to support the same position passed, but only by 113 to 109. Although the party then compromised by deciding only to abstain from voting and not to support the proposal when it came before the House, six left-wingers broke party discipline and voted against it. In consequence, the party did withdraw the whip. But there the matter rested; such was the support for the rebel viewpoint in both the parliamentary and extraparliamentary parties. Within three months the whip was restored.

In the Labour party the harsh procedures of party discipline have been used only on very small groups against whom the great mass of the party in and out of Parliament will rally. When the party was unified to this extent, however, such coercions were hardly necessary. When the party was seriously divided, as in the days of the Bevanite controversy, the mechanism of party discipline did little, if anything, to heighten cohesion. In short, when these powers should have been useful, they were ineffective, and when they were effective, they were not really necessary. Perhaps the tendency to splinter, inherent in an ideological party of the Left, makes such procedures and the threat of them necessary. Yet we may suspect that Labour probably would fare no worse if, like the Conservatives, it let the power of withdrawing the whip atrophy.

Back-bench Influence

On few generalizations do former Ministers agree more than on their report of the constant, anxious, and even deferential attention Cabinets give to the opinions of their backbenchers. Reporting on his experience in the Wilson Government, Richard Crossman recalled that each Cabinet begins with a discussion of next week's business and parliamentary matters. Members of the Cabinet, being themselves members of the House of Commons, "are constantly aware of the troubles we are having over the road in the Palace of Westminster [with the Labour backbenchers] and are discussing how they should be handled, what will be the next cause of trouble. This is a constant preoccupation of a British cabinet—its sensitivity to the House of Commons."[4]

---

[4] R. H. S. Crossman, *The Myths of Cabinet Government* (Cambridge, Mass., 1972), p. 47.

Herbert Morrison, Leader of the House under Attlee, points out a particularly important dimension of this interaction of leadership and backbenchers. After recognizing the fairly numerous occasions when overt activity by backbenchers has succeeded in causing the withdrawal or modification of a proposal put forward by the Government, he distinguishes another category of back-bench influence that is actually of greater importance, although harder to detect and evaluate—the cases where Ministers respond to backbenchers by anticipating their reactions. Ministers have many channels through which they are made aware of the opinions of their own backbenchers, and in considering projected legislation or policy, any sensible Government will take these opinions into account. Their concessions are made not merely in advance of parliamentary proceedings, but in the course of developing the proposal within the executive. "Such concessions," Morrison concludes, "of course, cannot very well be recorded in the columns of Hansard."[5]

The importance of anticipation must be kept in mind when considering the record of overt back-bench pressure on Governments. For the interaction of backbenchers and leaders takes place against a background of possibilities, often unmentioned, yet vividly present to the minds of participants and conditioning their present behavior. Writing of this background of thought among Conservatives at the time of the Suez Crisis in 1956, Richard Neustadt reports:

> The Tories had been traumatized in 1940 when abstentions on their own side yielded Neville Chamberlain so relatively narrow a majority as to impair beyond recall the public image of his Government. He went. By this route Tory Premiers have ever since feared to go.[6]

Conservative Revolts

"Over and over," wrote one Conservative ex-Minister with reference to the 1950s, "I have seen cases where the Government were forced to swallow their pride and to back down on some issue under the pressure of backbench action."[7] A few examples will indicate how much importance should be attached to this pressure. In 1955 the Minister of Agriculture, Fisheries, and Food backed down on a proposed reduction of the whitefish subsidy. The reason, it appears, was that he found not only the Labour party opposing the reduction, because it harmed "the small man,"

---

[5]Herbert Morrison, *Government and Parliament: A Survey from Inside* (London, 1954), p. 167.

[6]Richard E. Neustadt, *Alliance Politics* (New York, 1970), p. 83.

[7]Enoch Powell, "1951–1959: Labour in Opposition," *Political Quarterly* (October–December, 1959), p. 336.

but also a number of his own backbenchers. Highly critical Conservative M.P.s from the fishery constituencies met with the Minister; some M.P.s even threatened to defy the whips and vote against the statutory order making the reduction. As a result, the Minister withdrew the order and issued a new one, which changed the proposal by restoring half the cut originally proposed for the smaller vessels.

In 1957 the Government withdrew the clauses of the Electricity Bill of that year, which would have given the Central Electricity Authority power to manufacture electrical plant. The Monopoly Commission had reported that private manufacturers made a practice of fixing prices of such equipment, and the clauses in the bill were intended to enable the public corporation to act if prices were fixed against it. Pressure centering in the back-bench Conservative Fuel and Power Committee caused the Minister to accept arguments he had previously rejected and to give in to back-bench demands.

A more notable instance of such influence took place in the same year during the course of the passage of the Government's controversial Rents Bill. Under Clause Nine some 800,000 tenants renting properties at "middle class" rents were to have their rents decontrolled six months after the passage of the bill. The Labour party opposed this clause along with the whole bill. In addition a number of Conservatives were uneasy, not over the principle of decontrol, which they favored, but over the short period of notice for the tenants affected. On the other hand, the Minister, his permanent secretary, and other officials favored getting through the period of dislocation as quickly as possible. Tory backbenchers used the standing committee stage for a prolonged demonstration of their dissidence. The Minister finally agreed to extend the period of decontrol from six months to fifteen months. A short time later, when mounting outside pressure was added to parliamentary criticism, he acted to give the courts power to delay evictions for hardship.

The case of the Shops Bill in 1956–1957 also involved a good deal of pressure from outside Parliament and is a good example of how departments work out noncontroversial legislation with the pressure groups concerned. The bill, which provided for earlier closing hours in retail stores, had been prepared by the Home Office under the Labour Government and was introduced under the succeeding Conservative Government. It was supported by both sides in the industry—the retail trade associations and the shopworkers' trade unions, which had been extensively consulted in its preparation—and by the Labour party. The small independent shopkeepers, however, were opposed, and they quickly gained strong support among Conservative backbenchers. While the bill itself was introduced into the Lords, Conservative backbenchers in the Commons were loud and prolonged in their protests. After much hesitation and under a new Home Secretary, R. A. Butler, who had "the most sensitive antennae for back-bench feeling," the bill was totally withdrawn.[8]

In 1964 the biggest back-bench revolt in the Conservative party since the fall of Chamberlain marked the hotly contested passage of the Resale Price Maintenance Bill (R.P.M.). In this case the most significant measure of back-bench influence came before the bill was introduced, when Conservative M.P.s had prevented Government action for a period of ten years and then, thanks to the fears of the Cabinet, were granted substantial concessions in the bill to be introduced. The controversy went to the heart of important issues of economic policy and Conservative party philosophy. R.P.M. is the practice by which manufacturers oblige retailers to sell their branded goods at stipulated prices. This was clearly in contradiction to the defense of competition and the free market, of which Conservatives made much in their clashes with socialistic Labour. In 1961 the president of the Board of Trade brought a proposal for abolition of R.P.M. from the Economic Policy Committee to the Cabinet. There it was defeated on the straight political grounds that it would split the party in Parliament and outside. The next year, when the Prime Minister himself brought the matter up, he was warned off by his Ministers, who were aware of the intensity of back-bench opposition.

The coincidence of two events precipitated Government action. One was the arrival at the Board of Trade of Edward Heath, a forceful and obstinate man; the other was the introduction of a private member's bill to abolish R.P.M. Faced with the need to define his own position regarding the bill, Heath prepared a Government measure for abolition. In the Cabinet his opponents, fearing back-bench reaction, forced a compromise. Opposition in the House was still intense. Some of the leading opponents were connected with interests that would be adversely affected, including a vice-president of the National Chamber of Trade and a high official of the Pharmaceutical Society. But the Opposition extended well beyond such "interested M.P.s." When Heath met with the back-bench Trade and Industry Committee, three-quarters of the hundred or so present were against his bill. He conceded nothing either to them or to the 1922 Committee. On the second reading of the bill, twenty-one Conservatives voted against the bill and fifty abstained, some twenty-five abstaining for the purpose of showing their opposition. In the committee stage Heath defeated a crucial amendment by only one vote. Finally, a few further changes—which, however, did not touch the fundamental principles of the bill—were conceded, and the bill passed into law.

---

[8]Ronald Butt, *The Power of Parliament* (London, 1967), p. 227.

Labour Revolts

After the R.P.M. revolt Heath said that if he had lost the crucial vote in standing committee he would have resigned. Much more than the resignation of a Minister and the defeat of a bill was at stake in the controversy over trade-union reform that wracked the Labour party in the spring of 1969, as the Wilson Government approached its end. When Labour had previously been in power, under Attlee, the left wing of the party was the seat of much dissidence. The rebels, however, were never ready to push a break with the leadership to the point of risking an overturn that might bring in the Tories. Hence, their activity subsided abruptly when Labour was returned with an overall majority of only six in the election of 1950. But the rebels of 1969 were ready to face the prospect of a return of the Tories. One reason was that they represented not so much the left wing of the party as the trade-union section of the party. This rebellion bespeaks the special power of trade unions in the Labour party when the "interests of labor" are at stake, as well as the conditional nature of the power of a Cabinet and of party leaders generally in the British Parliament.

As we have seen in our discussion of economic planning (see Chapter 4), the Wilson Government was engaged for most of its existence in a largely fruitless effort to control inflation. A major branch of its policy in this field consisted in attempts to subdue the wage-push component. As it became clear that incomes policy and fiscal measures would not suffice, reform of industrial relations was seen as having a possible contribution to make. A principal source of the pressure on wages was the rising frequency of unofficial strikes at the plant level. Indeed, the typical strike in the sixties was unofficial, called by local leaders without the support, and very often even without the knowledge, of the national organization. Early in 1969 the Government presented a white paper outlining to Parliament proposals for trade-union reform, of which the principal one would give the Minister of Employment and Productivity power to impose a twenty-eight-day cooling-off period on unofficial strikes, backed by the threat of a financial penalty against unions or individuals who did not comply. In his budget speech the Chancellor made it clear that this measure was an essential of the Government's economic policy. The Prime Minister backed him up, saying it was an issue of confidence and that its defeat would lead to a general election.

From the time it was first announced the measure met with opposition in both the parliamentary and extraparliamentary party. The principal source of opposition was the trade unions. "The Labour party," Ernest Bevin once told the party conference to its face in 1935, "has grown out of the bowels of the T.U.C." As we shall see, this fact of history is reflected in the overwhelming dominance of trade-union votes, representatives, and finance at all levels of party organization outside Parliament. In addition to these general ties of dependence, some 132 Labour M.P.s had been financially sponsored by trade unions in the election of 1966, a relationship meaning that a union has paid the larger part of each candidate's election expenses as well as having contributed heavily to the upkeep of the local party. Although some left wing M.P.s supported the Opposition, the hard core of resistance to the Government was found among the "interested" M.P.s who had union sponsorship.

Before the bill was introduced, a debate on the white paper in March led to a vote in which fifty-five backbenchers, defying a three-line whip, voted against the Government, while another forty deliberately abstained. Although Wilson and nine other Ministers were members of the twenty-eight-man National Executive Committee of the extraparliamentary party, this body voted its opposition to the white paper by a majority of three to one, including among the opponents James Callaghan, Home Secretary and Treasurer of the party. As the Government persisted, the Trades Union Congress called an emergency meeting of the whole body in June—the first since 1920—at which it, on the one hand, demanded that the Government drop the bill, and, on the other hand, as a concession to the Government, strengthened the T.U.C.'s power to suspend a member union because of unofficial and jurisdictional strikes.

Wilson rejected these concessions as inadequate to the problem, and negotiations between the Government and the T.U.C. continued into June, when the Prime Minister asked the Cabinet for authorization to go ahead with the legislation. The chief whip reported, however, that the measure had no hope of passing Parliament, almost all loyalist M.P.s having gone over to the Opposition, thanks in part to the T.U.C. concessions. From this point in the meeting the split in the Cabinet grew, until only Wilson and Barbara Castle, the Minister in charge of the bill, remained in favor. After a brief resistance, and helped by a face-saving declaration by the T.U.C. that it really would use its powers against unofficial strikes, Wilson gave in completely, and the bill was dropped.

In this instance of party rebellion, the influence of the trade unions had changed a major policy to which the Government had publicly and firmly committed itself. Crucial to the effectiveness of this influence, however, was the fact that back-bench M.P.s were ready to defeat their Prime Minister and Cabinet in the House of Commons. R. H. S. Crossman, a Cabinet member at the time, summarized the whole affair in these words:

> The Industrial Relations Bill which we lost was a bill in which we were going to give the trade unions enormous concessions in return for their allowing us to introduce sanctions against unofficial strikes. The sanctions proposed were not very effective, but we lost the Bill because when the crunch came we did not

take the risk of having a vote in the Parliamentary Party. So the Bill was dropped. The Parliamentary Party had defeated the Government . . .[9]

Opposition Influence

In reassessing the role of Parliament, observers have given a good deal of attention to the influence of backbenchers on their party leaders. Less new ground has been broken in the examination of the interaction of Government and Opposition. In most accounts this is still described as a clash between two unyielding partisan bands, which may affect votes at the next election but not policies of an incumbent Government. This familiar stereotype, however, needs to be viewed with some skepticism. We cannot disregard the hypothesis that the Opposition influences the Government.

Let us grant that much of the party battle in the House is directed at the voters outside. If each of the parliamentary parties were committed to a fixed program by ideology or some form of party control, this process of appealing to the voter could have the effect of changing policy only by means of a general election. Indeed, it is fair to say that in many of the sketches of party government this is presumed to be the principal mechanism by which voters control governments. The alternation of parties is considered the essential means of changing policy. Yet if we relax the assumption that the parties are committed to fixed programs and recognize that within limits they will change their programs in order to win votes and rule more effectively, the mechanisms of interaction become far more complex and much truer to life. In this view the Government, anticipating the electoral gains of the other side, adjusts to the strong points brought forward by the Opposition—as the Opposition also adjusts to the popular programs enacted by the Government.

When examining control of the economy, we had occasion to remark that those crucial swings of British Governments back and forth between planning and management have not been mediated by the obvious mechanisms of party government (see Chapter 4). Ronald Butt, an acute student of Parliament, finds in this area an important example of the influence of the Opposition. Writing of the conversion of the Conservatives to planning under Macmillan, Butt observes that while this shift was influenced by the successful example of France,

it also owed something to the existence of a party in Britain which would naturally capitalize on the fashionable switch-back toward planning the economy. In the climate of opinion in the early sixties, the existence of a Labour Party with a plan to control the heights of the economy without wholesale

---

[9]Crossman, *op. cit.,* p. 118.

reliance on nationalisation was an incentive to the Conservatives to produce a counterbalancing policy. . . . In this broad sense, therefore, the voice of the Opposition contributes to the policy-making of Government in any given Parliament and is not simply a factor in deciding what the composition of the *next* Parliament should be.[10]

We need not suppose that British Governments have always behaved in this way. In the aristocratic period public opinion as a force for determining the outcome of elections and fate of Governments was negligible. Cabinets rose and fell on the basis of shifting parliamentary support, and when a general election did occur, the Government that had been in power was invariably returned to office. It was only in 1841 that for the first time a Government dissolving and appealing to the country lost its majority. Subsequently, during the liberal period of Parliament, Governments at times were defeated in the House and then appealed to the country, which might or might not support them. With only primitive party organizations, neither Government nor Opposition could have calculated accurately which way the opinion of voters would swing, even if it had tried. Having adopted a position in Parliament, the Government might well find itself taking its first reliable sounding of opinion the hard way, at the hustings. In time, however, the elaborate organization and communication systems of the collectivist age made it possible for Governments and Oppositions to tune their parliamentary performance far more finely to the anticipated voices of the people. The main source of the Opposition's influence on the Government took the form not of changed votes in the House, but of anticipatory reactions among Ministers. Such behavior is harder to identify and measure than cross-voting in the House or shifting majorities in the country, but it is no less real for that.

Over these same generations of transition from aristocratic to liberal politics the Opposition was becoming a more and more formidable body. Its history goes back to the beginnings of the modern age, when the medieval practice of ventilating grievances was supplemented by a new kind of opposition, which grappled with questions of policy. Toleration of such opposition was fully accepted in the eighteenth century, although the idea of a "formed opposition" in Parliament, that is, a body of men consciously acting together in opposition to the King's Government, was frowned on (see Chapter 8). Actually, the institution of an organized Opposition carrying out a systematic, united, and prolonged attack over the whole range of Government policy arose only at the end of the nineteenth century. Governments were weaker by far in mid-Victorian Parliaments than they are today. But this was not because the Opposition was stronger. On the contrary, it consisted of a coalition of shifting groups even more incoherent than the Government majority.

---

[10]Butt, *op. cit.,* p. 301.

In comparison with the unorganized Opposition of a hundred years ago, the present-day Opposition not only provides more responsible criticism, but also exerts more influence on the incumbent Government. As we have seen, each party when in Opposition has a front-bench structure that marshals continuous and often expert opinion on its side in the House and reaches out to further support from professional sources in the party organization and associated circles in the country. Endowed by parliamentary procedure with constant opportunities for attack and counterproposal, a body so equipped and organized is a massive and formidable reality for any Government. If one is to say that Parliament has declined in the past hundred years, one must reconcile this view of the trend with the fact that the Opposition has risen to new heights of prominence and power.

If today individual M.P.s complain more about their lack of power—and perhaps they do—the reason is not far to seek. The backbencher of the present day, like the ordinary citizen, expects a great deal more for himself. A hundred years ago, in mid-Victorian days, aristocracy was still a great power in the land; between the Earl who might be Prime Minister and the offspring of even well-to-do gentry on the backbenches of the Commons the social distance was known and respected. Neither in the society at large nor in the House of Commons did egalitarianism enjoy a good name. Today equality has become such a cult as to make backbenchers less satisfied with what may actually be a greater share of power.

The model of party government is an instructive guide to the realities of parliamentary behavior, providing we do not succumb entirely to its persuasive simplicities. The House does act as an electoral college, transmitting the outcome of an election into the establishment of a Government. It also serves as a forum for propaganda in the continuous election campaign of British politics. Yet this conventional picture is far from complete. It neglects the dynamic interplay of backbenchers, Government, and Opposition. Above all, it must be revised to allow for the fact that any Government—and indeed any Opposition—will continually adjust its program and general stance in the light of many circumstances, not the least of which is its anticipation of the next election. Shifts in public opinion may thus greatly affect policy without being expressed in changed votes. The mechanism is still that of party responding to popular control, but it does not depend on the unreal assumption of parties committed to fixed and unchanging programs.

Moreover, this interaction between parliamentary and electoral forces is only one major instance of how Parliament is continuously involved in the process of opinion formation in the country as a whole. Ronald Butt observes that "the most profound impact an opposition can make on parliamentary politics may be when it provides a focus for great national debates on matters which deeply divide or disturb the community." In his opinion the outstanding example in post-war years was the Suez affair in

1956. Noting how deeply the policy embittered the conflict between parties in the House, he asserts that "their arguments not only led, but to a great extent created, the debate in the nation." Britain's imperial power had been in decline for years. But the failure of the Suez policy was a rude shock "exposing to the Conservative Party and to the nation Britain's reduced position in the world."

> What was to be the Conservative attitude to prestige politics in the future? What new role could be found for Britain, to solace the nation for its lost world power? For good or ill, all these questions arose from the battle in the House of Commons over Suez. The schism in the nation was largely created by the schism in Parliament.[11]

The Inner Circle

To stress the linkage of parliamentary activity with opinion formation in the polity as a whole should not, however, be allowed to obscure those processes which are performed in a much narrower arena. As in the Suez debate, the force and content of various currents of public opinion may be substantially determined by what goes on in the House. But the House does not only affect the substance of opinion. It also generates, sustains, and imposes upon individuals, factions, and parties special standards of conduct and style. And these standards may be at variance with those engendered by the struggle for power in the wider arenas of electoral politics.

A gifted observer once spoke of the Chamber of Deputies of the Third French Republic as a "closed arena," a way of emphasizing the importance of the political forces generated autonomously within the chamber itself.[12] In a carefully limited sense the term can also be applied to the House of Commons. It has its own political subculture, which governs a life that is no less communal for being intensely competitive. As a human community it has its own standards of excellence and norms of conduct, as well as an elaborate system of sanctions and rewards to enforce them. The power of these sanctions cannot be doubted by anyone who has watched a pack of critics drive a Minister into a corner at Question Hour and has then seen him flinch and flounder amidst triumphant cries of "Answer! Answer!" The House of Commons owes too much to the English public school to be entirely gentle. Commenting on the trials of Anthony Barber, the Conservative Chancellor, during his first months in office, the

---

[11] *Ibid.,* p. 305.

[12] W. L. Middleton, *The French Political System* (New York, 1933), Chapter 5.

London *Economist* spoke of "the remorseless interest of the House of Commons in seeing a man at a disadvantage brought down."[13]

If the House no longer makes and unmakes Governments, it continually makes and unmakes reputations. The House still functions as the principal arena for leadership selection in the British political system. Ability to cope with the party conference and the TV camera, not to mention such matters as sheer managerial competence, have a bearing on a politician's advancement. But perhaps, above all, he must be a "good House of Commons man," showing achievement according to the special and complex standards known to that community and to some, but not many, outsiders. For this community does blend with a small, special public, which is linked by communication centers such as the clubs of Pall Mall, the university common rooms, and the offices of the quality newspapers and weekly political journals. No self-respecting Minister or civil servant can enjoy having acts of injustice or stupidity for which he is responsible exposed to the scrutiny and comment of these circles. Nor can he be insensitive to their praise, with its hint of a footnote in history. "Fame is the spur." But while the electorate can vote power, only a more discriminating public can confer fame. Indeed, the two sets of standards, those which lead to success in the House and those which lead to success in elections, may well be in conflict. The kind of demagogy that wins votes outside may destroy a reputation in the House. The Reverend Ian Paisley could win a dominating position in Northern Ireland with his harsh appeal to religious prejudice, but in the Commons he was received with cold disregard. The House has its own standards, which with a real degree of autonomy it imposes on the behavior of politicians and parties.

The House of Lords

If by the modernity of tradition one means an extreme reluctance to part with any institution with a claim to antiquity, the British retention of the House of Lords is a prime illustration. This body, which originated as the great council of barons of the medieval king and which includes members with such titles as baron, viscount, and earl—not to mention bishop and archbishop and even marquess, duke, and prince—still meets regularly in its ornate chamber at the west end of the palace of Westminster and carries on a large volume of legislative and supervisory business.

Its powers, as we have seen in the discussion of legislation, have been reduced almost to nil. Yet its activities are still sufficiently important to

---

[13] *Economist* (London), Feb. 27, 1971, p. 17.

demand brief mention. Along with other steps reforming and modernizing British government, several important changes in the composition of the Lords have recently made it a more useful body. Prior to the reforms of 1958 the Lords had some 860 members, of whom about 800 were hereditary peers; 26, bishops of the Church of England; and 9, Lords of Appeal. The last named are lawyers appointed to the House for life to permit it to discharge its functions as the highest British court of appeal, and when appeals are heard only these law lords attend the sessions. The principal reform made in 1958 was to make possible the granting of nonhereditary life peerages. The same act provided that women, who were previously barred from membership, could also be admitted as life peers. A later reform made it possible for a peer to surrender his peerage, a right exercised especially by those who wished to clear their way for a seat in the House of Commons. In 1964 an expense allowance was provided, reflecting the modest circumstances of many contemporary peers. This allowance is currently 4½ guineas ($11.28) per day. While he was Prime Minister, Harold Wilson, in accordance with his announced intention, created no hereditary peerages; and as of this writing Edward Heath has followed suit. Both, on the other hand, added substantially to the number of life peers.

Mainly by the creation of life peers, Governments have somewhat redressed the imbalance of parties in the Lords. In 1967 its membership was calculated to consist of 350 Conservatives, 100 Labour members, and 40 Liberals, with 96 Independents. Most peers do not attend, and the hard core of debate is sustained by a daily attendance of some 200, almost all of whom are life peers. While the rules of the Lords are more relaxed and the weight of business less pressing, party organization prevails in the upper, as in the lower, House. When votes are taken, party unity is strongly in evidence.

With regard to legislation, the Lords have several ways of making themselves useful. First, it need only be mentioned, they have a part to play in the enactment of private bills and review of delegated legislation similar to that of the Commons. Second, peers may introduce private members' bills without having to surmount the kinds of obstacles that would confront them in the Commons. On the other hand, the fact that these bills have no future unless the Government is willing to give them time in the lower House keeps their numbers low. Third, the Lords retain their suspensive veto. Actually they almost never reject bills that have come from the House of Commons—however much they may criticize them—yet when they do, even their slight remaining powers may in the right circumstances make an important difference. For example, in the 1955–1956 session a private member's bill abolishing capital punishment passed the Commons, the Conservative Government of the day taking no stand, but finding time for the bill and permitting a free vote among its backbenchers. The House of Lords, however, rejected the bill. Under the law governing the Lords' suspensive veto, the Commons would have had to repass the bill in the subsequent session. The measure failed because the Government was not ready to provide the parliamentary time, although it did enact its own bill limiting somewhat the use of the death penalty.

The House of Lords is also useful as an originating chamber. As such it may save a little time in the Commons by providing the forum for the initial debates on a bill. About a quarter of all bills, and sometimes more, are first introduced in the Lords—although they may never be money bills, and usually are bills of only lesser importance. Finally, perhaps the most important legislative function of the Lords consists in its activity as a revising chamber. As bills from the House of Commons go through the upper chamber, many amendments are put. Often this is only for the purpose of enabling the mover to voice a point of criticism, whereupon he withdraws his amendment. At the same time, the legislative process of the Lords affords the Government a chance to tidy up or improve proposed legislation. Sometimes peers find legal or other flaws in bills that have escaped the scrutiny of both the executive and the Commons; often changes first suggested in the Commons are actually inserted in the Lords, after the Minister has had time to "take them into consideration," that is, to discuss them with his civil servants and the affected interest groups. And, of course, the passage through another chamber gives Ministers and civil servants a further chance to perceive and repair their own errors of omission or commission with regard to a bill.

Aside from its functions as an originating and revising body for legislation, the Lords has also created something of a role for itself as a chamber for debating large questions of the day. Recent additions to its membership have broadened the social spectrum represented. We now find in the Lords professors, journalists, and trade union officials, as well as company directors and lawyers. These talents have their opportunity in fairly frequent general debates on broad questions of public policy.

If we cannot speak of the decline of Parliament, we surely can speak of the decline of the House of Lords. It is fair to say that until 1832 the upper House was the dominant chamber. In the "balanced constitution" of the aristocratic period it enjoyed its position of parity and, moreover, thanks to the patronage of its members, a large influence over many members of the Commons. In the liberal period it still provided Prime Ministers, the last having been the Marquess of Salisbury, who retired as Prime Minister in 1902. As late as 1910 it could precipitate a constitutional crisis of the first magnitude. In that year the Lords not only rejected a finance bill that the Liberal Government regarded as especially important, but they also rejected a subsequent bill that proposed to limit their powers. In the course of their resistance, they forced two dissolutions before they gave in by accepting the limitation of their power by the House of Lords Act of 1911.

It is hard to recapture the atmosphere of an England that could permit, legitimize, and take seriously this prolonged resistance to measures sanctioned by all the norms of popular government on the part of a body whose members were overwhelmingly hereditary, Conservative, and rich. Today that England of the aristocracy and of the governing classes of the Victorian bourgeoisie has declined to the vanishing point, and with it the House of Lords. The House still provides a place for ancient ceremony, as when the Queen opens Parliament each autumn. For a moment the chamber is peopled with gorgeous costumes, animated by medieval ritual, and suffused with nostalgic splendor—for all the world to see, now that the proceedings are put on television. But as the brief ceremony ends and as these university dons, former borough councillors, and ex-civil servants turn in their rented coronets and ermine-trimmed robes, we realize that even in England things sometimes change.

Eight

The Foundations of Modern British Parties

In a highly developed modern polity like Britain, the pattern of interests matches in scale and complexity the pattern of power. As we have seen, the instrumentalities of the state penetrate deeply into British society. Spending half of the national product and employing a quarter of the labor force, the public sector also intermingles with the private sector, creating what the Fulton Committee called "a proliferation of para-state organisations" that mobilize and direct resources in the service of the purposes of the state. The field of activity in which these purposes arise, compete, and are adopted is no less extensive. In this age of collectivist politics its principal actors include political parties and pressure groups, but it should be clear from previous chapters that Parliament, Cabinet, and bureaucracy also play major roles in articulating and determining the ends for which state power will be used.

Basic Conditions of Mass Politics

A comparison covering about a century and focusing on the general elections of 1874 and 1970 suggests the immense growth of public participation. In 1874 the population of the United Kingdom, which then included the whole of Ireland, was some 32.4 million. By 1970 the United Kingdom, although its Irish portion now included only the six northern counties, had a population of 55.3 million. At the time of the general election of 1874, the registered electorate of the United Kingdom numbered under 3 million. By 1970 it had risen to nearly 40 million. A more significant indicator, however, would be the number of persons actually voting. In 1874 this was 1.6 million, or 5 percent of the population. In 1970 it was 28,344,807, or 51.2 percent of the population.

These figures vividly reveal what is meant by the mobilization of interests and the rise of collectivist politics in the modern state. Even though the Reform Act of 1867 had extended the vote to the skilled urban workman, the participating electorate in 1874 still constituted only a small number of the members of the polity. But it is the absolute figures that are the most suggestive. With a total vote of 1.6 million, they mean that the average vote per constituency in the United Kingdom was 2,500, the size of the House at that time being 652. To be sure, just about half the seats were uncontested. Even when we allow for this, the average vote per contested constituency was only 5,000. No words could suggest more vividly the simplicity and organizational informality of the electoral process in contrast with the situation a century later when, on average, 45,000 voters took part in the choice of each M.P.

But the mobilization of interests has meant much more than simply a rise in the number of persons taking part in processes of political choice. For the typical participant there has been a great increase in the facets of his total activity involved in these processes. More of his interests, ideal and material, have become the subject matter of political discussion, electoral campaigns, and government decisions. His life has become far more "politicized." This too has meant an increase in scale and complexity of the polity.

One indicator of increased politicization can be found in the subject matter of electoral campaigns. The 1874 election turned out a Liberal Government under Gladstone and brought in a Conservative Government under Disraeli. Although Disraeli's Government did proceed to enact a series of far-reaching social reforms, during the campaign he had referred to social questions in only the broadest and vaguest way. This was before the day of party manifestoes, but in his election address to the voters of his constituency Disraeli mentioned the subject of reform, going no further, however, than to express his continuing concern with "all measures calculated to improve the condition of the people." This unexceptionable sentiment was not quite so meaningless as it seems out of its historical context. The "condition of the people" question had been given some content by Disraeli in previous utterances. But even in his famous Crystal Palace Speech of 1872, a notable declaration of Conservative purpose at home and abroad, he had stayed on the level of broad generality with regard to his domestic policy. On that topic he said:

It involves the state of the dwellings of the people, the moral consequences of which are not less considerable than the physical. It involves their enjoyment of some of the chief elements of nature—air, light and water. It involves the regulation of their industry, the inspection of their toil. It involves the purity of their provisions, and it touches upon all the means by which you many wean them from habits of excess and brutality.[1]

This reticent approach to campaign promises was entirely in accord with the Tory ideal of not tying the hands of the statesman and meant that, as a contemporary of Disraeli's remarked, "there was no special measure which he had received a mandate to carry through, no detailed policy he had advocated which the country was enabling him to execute."

In 1970 a general election also resulted in a change of Government; Labour under Harold Wilson was defeated by the Conservatives under Edward Heath. Entering this campaign, the Conservatives issued a party manifesto entitled "A Better Tomorrow," which ran to some thirty pages. Its domestic proposals took up 90 percent of the space and are far too lengthy to be more than summarized here. Their wide range and high specificity, however, are obvious from the following summary:

ON THE ECONOMY. Cuts in income tax and surtax; abolition of the Selective Employment Tax and the betterment levy; possible replacement of purchase tax by the Value Added Tax; repeal Industrial Expansion Act; reduce government involvement in nationalized industries; phase out Regional Employment Premium; no statutory wage control; forbid all unjustified price rises in the public sector.

ON INDUSTRIAL RELATIONS. Legally binding agreements between employers and unions; secret ballot and cooling-off period of not less than sixty days for disputes seriously endangering the national interest.

ON FOOD AND FARMING. Introduce import levies; keep support system at a declining cost for at least three years; keep annual review and production grants.

ON HOUSING. Abolish Land Commission; encourage council house sales; renegotiate subsidy system to concentrate assistance on worst areas and change it to provide adequate rent rebates for those who cannot afford fair rents.

ON EDUCATION. Concentrate on primary school building; local authorities to decide on secondary organization for themselves; encourage direct grant schools; raise school leaving age.

---

[1]Quoted in W. F. Monypenny and G. E. Buckle, *The Life of Benjamin Disraeli, Earl of Beaconsfield,* rev. ed. in 2 vols., Vol. II (London, 1929), p. 530.

ON SOCIAL SECURITY. Introduce scheme based on negative income tax; pensions for those over eighty; improve benefits for disabled; ease earnings rule for pensions; make pension rights fully transferable; make public service and armed forces' pensions increases payable at 55.

ON IMMIGRATION AND RACE RELATIONS. Single system of control over all immigration from overseas; limit future work permits to specific job in specific areas for specific period; assist voluntary repatriation; extra help to local authorities with large immigrant populations.

ON LAW AND ORDER. Modernize law on public order, obstruction and forcible entry; oblige those causing injury or damage to compensate victims; inquiry into law of trespass; review Official Secrets Act.

This comparison between the elections of 1874 and 1970 suggests, though it does not quantify, the multiplication and variegation of interests that have occurred during the past hundred years. As we have seen when discussing the dimensions of political development, such an increase in demands asserted in the polity also constitutes an increase in scale, quite apart from any change in the number of participants. The effect is to multiply manyfold the increase in scale and complexity brought about by the massive rise in numbers.

Such developments constitute the basic conditions of mass politics in the collectivist age. We can think of them as posing a problem: How is it possible for such a huge agglomeration to function as the main agent for determining the ends of the polity? How can so many people with so many different demands be joined together in such a way that they exercise effective, ultimate control over their government? These are the questions that come to the mind of the person concerned with testing or vindicating democratic theory. A more relaxed and analytical way of putting the question is to ask what broad model (if any) best describes how demands arise and come to be adopted in the system.

In this book the doctrine of party government has been put forward, hypothetically, as providing a model likely to reveal the main structures in the pattern of interests. It is important to realize that other models could be tried out, some of which are compatible with the party government model and some of which are not. A brief review of them will sharpen the concept of party government and may be helpful in the course of the analysis in revising the concept to fit realities.

One possibility is that mass politics tends to become what the name immediately suggests: a mere aggregate, an atomized mass without substantial structures, formal or informal, to give it shape or direction; responding with volatility and confusion to the erratic stimuli of the mass media and dangerously susceptible to the appeal of the demagogue and the Caesar. This line of analysis, which has been developed in recent decades by students of "mass society"—such as Ortega y Gasset, Emil Lederer, Hannah Arendt, and others—goes back to earlier critics of modern society, who saw in mass politics a severe threat to social and political cohesion.

Another, blander model comes from the students of pressure groups—the Bentley model. The basic units, according to this view, are a plurality of groups, normally based in the economy and usually giving rise to organizations, such as trade unions, trade associations, and professional organizations. Parties can be analyzed into coalitions of such groups, and have no significant role or influence of their own, their so-called ideologies or philosophies being reducible to composites of the particular demands of their component groups. A mechanical balancing of group forces produces decisions that constitute the pattern of policy. As it shifts, this balance produces, at best, compromises reflecting the strength of the demandant groups; at worst, immobilism and inaction when such compromises cannot be struck; and, on average, a meandering but tolerable sequence of government interventions.

Various types of elitism are compatible with these models. In Britain, throughout its various phases of modernization, party government has been associated with, and perhaps has presupposed, a governing class in some form. This association is clear, for instance, in Schumpeter's discussion (see Chapter 1). The Marxist idea of a ruling class of capitalists has been applied to Britain, as in the later writings of Harold Laski. Of interest to current analysis is the technocratic possibility. Technocracy is something more than the rule of bureaucrats—the possessors of the skills used by, and organized in, the pattern of power. Although technocracy was long foreseen, it is most instructive as a concept of analysis when taken as a product of the current, acute phase of the scientific revolution. The vast increase in scientific knowledge in recent decades, along with the institutionalization of research and the use of its findings directly in making and implementing policy, has elevated people with special knowledge to an entirely new plane of influence. The complexity and technical character of public policy—military, foreign, and domestic—makes them indispensable. At the same time, their technical knowledge—of weapons systems, spaceships, medical science, economic problems, and so on—enables them to perceive problems and propose solutions well beyond the conception, or even the comprehension, of most citizens. Herein lies the possibility of a new kind of elite, embracing the top professionals in the public and private sectors and transcending, and possibly manipulating, the party system.

All these approaches have something to contribute to the analysis of British politics. But there are several reasons for taking the party government model as the leading hypothesis. One reason is that conventionally it has provided most American political scientists with their main instrument for interpreting British political institutions, in which, moreover, some have found a model for the reform of American politics. Although the hope, once widely entertained, of creating "a more responsible two-party system" in the United States has greatly diminished, the idea of such a party system is still put forward by some reformers as a goal and used by many teachers as a device for bringing out the distinctive traits of the American system.

A more important reason for taking seriously the party government model is that in one version or another it is the way Britons generally think they are governed. Surveys of opinion show that the electorate overwhelmingly sees elections as contests between the two main parties, enabling the victor to constitute a Government, which in turn produces a distinctive kind of policy output. "The individual elector," write Butler and Stokes, "accepts the parties as leading actors on the political stage and sees in partisan terms the meaning of the choices which the universal franchise puts before him."[2] Moreover, typically, the voter not only holds the party in power responsible for government policy, but also regards a change of party as an effective means of achieving the economic and social conditions he values. The behavior of British voters corresponds with these perceptions. In Britain there is no real equivalent for the term "independent," which many American voters use to characterize their political identity. A Gallup survey in 1966 asked British voters whether they considered themselves Conservative, Labour, Liberal, or Independent. Only 3 percent chose Independent. In the United States a similar question in a Gallup survey in 1967 drew the response "Independent" from 31 percent of the sample.

In recent history the general election of 1945 illustrates the power of party. Clement Attlee, the Labour party Leader, could not compare in personal appeal with Winston Churchill, the wartime Prime Minister, who campaigned amidst an outpouring of gratitude and respect. While the crowds turned out to cheer Churchill, however, at the polls the people voted for the Labour party and its program, sweeping out Churchill's Conservatives in a crushing defeat.

Party and Modernity

For the student of political development there is an even more weighty reason for considering party the major structuring influence on the pattern of interests. This is the obvious link between the party system and political

---

[2]David Butler and Donald Stokes, *Political Change in Britain* (New York, 1969), p. 23.

modernity. In Britain the rise of parties coincides with the beginnings of modernization. Conventionally, the two-party system is dated from the emergence of Whigs and Tories in the conflict over the Exclusion Bills of 1679 and after, which attempted to bar the succession to James II, then duke of York, because he was a Catholic. The Conservatives of today are directly descended from those Tories and are sometimes spoken of as the oldest political party in the Western world.

The historical association of political parties and modern polities is clear. The important question is analytic and theoretical: Is there some intrinsic connection between modernity and party? Are there conditions, cultural or structural, that are inherent in modernity and that produce a party system? Conceivably, party could be a type of structure inherent either in all polities or in all developed polities, modern or not. On the other hand, they could be much more transitory than is usually thought, characterizing a certain period in the development of the modern polity, but tending to wither away or decompose at a later stage. If there is an intrinsic connection between party and political modernity, some understanding of this connection should throw light on the role parties play in the process of social choice, and on the limitations of this role.

Political parties are bodies of men seeking to win positions of authority in the polity. But political formations characterized by this goal can be found in most regimes, nonmodern as well as modern. Thus the baronial factions in the court of a feudal king competed for the great offices of state and other avenues of influence within a political and social system that itself remained unchanged. Modernity, however, brings into existence a new pattern of political culture and a new form of polity and, in consequence, a new structuring of the pattern of interests.

One characteristic of the new pattern of interests—and an important condition in making a party system possible—is suggested by Sigmund Neumann's observation that the rise of political parties correlates with the rise of the modern legislature. He wrote,

> It is not . . . accidental that the beginning of modern political parties is closely tied up with the rise of a parliament. When political representation broadens and a national forum of discussion develops, providing a constant opportunity for political participation—wherever those conditions are fulfilled, political parties arise. This happened in England in the revolutionary seventeenth century; in France on the eve of the great Revolution of 1789; in Germany around 1848. Even where contingent influences may create political groups of an awakened intelligentsia, as in the nineteenth-century tsarist Russia, they assume political dimensions only where some degree of participation is possible.[3]

---

[3]Sigmund Neumann, *Modern Political Parties* (Chicago, 1956), pp. 395–396.

Parliaments predate modernity and, indeed, as institutionalized meetings of the estates, were a normal feature of medieval regimes in Europe. It is the modern, not the medieval, legislature, however, that correlates with the rise of political parties, for it is only in the modern legislature, freed from medieval restraints by the conception of sovereignty, that law making on the requisite scale takes place. In the English case the essential functions of the medieval Parliament were the redress of grievances and the grant of supplies. Not that statutes were not enacted, but their scope was so limited that a whole school of medievalists has been able to maintain that the Parliament of those times should be regarded not as a "legislature" but, in accord with the term used by contemporaries, as a "court." Thus C. H. McIlwain's classic work elaborating this theme is entitled *The High Court of Parliament.*

As modernization progressed, the legislature shed these medieval restraints and law making was extended to matters that had previously been untouched. Legislation establishing religious toleration was perhaps the most radical innovation. Also, the regime itself might be modified, as it was by the great acts regulating the succession to the Crown in Britain, the Bill of Rights of 1689, and the Act of Settlement of 1701. As for the arena in which these questions were raised and decided, factions that resemble parties may form where the royal council of a sovereign monarch is the only forum in which the law-making authority can be influenced. But a representative legislature like the British Parliament, with elections subject to the influence of groups and opinions in the country, is more likely to produce what we call political parties. In this way Tories and Whigs, originating in the struggle over the Exclusion Bill, continued to find the center of their conflicts in the Parliament, where laws were passed and money appropriated. The modern party and the modern legislature are intrinsically related.

The modern political party presupposes both the legitimacy of law making and a structure, such as a legislature, giving some significant number access to participation in the exercise of this power. The feature of modernity that is our concern, however, is political parties—in the plural. A plurality of parties is not likely to arise unless another condition obtains, namely, the acceptance of opposition on basic matters of public policy. As we have seen in discussing the rise of opposition in Britain, modernity does involve this condition, legitimating disagreement that extends beyond mere presentation of grievances to principles of public policy. Under the Tudors this condition did not obtain, the initiative and determining influence in "great questions of state" being reserved for the monarch. By the early eighteenth century it was entirely legitimate for members of Parliament to criticize and oppose even those proposals brought forward by the sovereign's Ministers, and by the late eighteenth century such opposition was common. Such acceptance of differences of opinion over the common good seems inherent in the premises of modernity. Modernity departs fundamentally from any notion of a final and fixed social order buttressed by tradition. The voluntarist spirit, as it makes will the source of law, thereby also opens the way to the toleration of different conceptions of authority and purpose (the common good) within the ruling community. Scientific rationalism would seem even more influential, given its adaptability to the notion of the piecemeal discovery of truth.

Modernity legitimizes differences of opinion over the common good and creates the expectation that such differences are inevitable and even desirable. Toleration of opposing views comes to be founded on the belief that controversy is a necessary part of the rational discourse from which public policy should emerge. Such a premise is essential to the eighteenth-century idea of parliamentarianism, the notion that the legislature is a forum for deliberation where decisions are made by mutual persuasion among men with diverse viewpoints. This notion of the common good as something arrived at by rational discourse and mutual persuasion is central to Edmund Burke's conception of the role of the legislature and its members. In his speech of 1774 to the electors of Bristol—the voters of his constituency—he declared that Parliament was not "a congress of ambassadors from different and hostile interests, which interests each must maintain as an agent and advocate against other agents and advocates." It was rather "a deliberative assembly of one nation with one interest, that of the whole—where not local prejudices ought to guide but the general good resulting from the general reason of the whole." In consequence, he continued, while a member of the legislature ought to give "great weight" to the wishes of his constituents, he ought never to sacrifice to them "his unbiased opinion, his mature judgment, his enlightened conscience."[4]

This passage breathes the orderly reformism of which Burke was the first philosophic champion and for which British politics became noted. It involves a crucial prerequisite of party government: the acceptance of opposition and criticism on matters of public policy on the grounds that controversy is a legitimate phase in the determination of truth. This premise of the party system did not suddenly appear, but unfolded slowly as men grudgingly accepted opposition as inevitable, then as tolerable, and finally as desirable and even indispensable. Yet the essential doctrine—the idea of the piecemeal discovery of truth mediated by argument—goes back as far as Milton's *Aereopagitica* (1644) and runs through modern political thought to its classic formulation in John Stuart Mill's essay *On Liberty* (1859). Its crucial importance as a cultural premise of the party system and of party government can be seen if we consider the practical tendencies

---

[4]Edmund Burke, *Writings and Speeches,* Vol. II (Boston, 1901), pp. 89–98.

of the contrasting view that there is one Truth, fixed, permanent, and neither needing nor permitting criticism. This is not only a premodern idea; it also finds lodging in the utopian strain of modernity, which sees in one great truth the definition and justification of a final and unchangeable political and social order. The natural vehicle of this belief is the one-party state.

In these ways modernity lays the foundations, cultural and structural, for the rise of political parties. Yet the actual existence of parties was bitterly resisted for many decades. Even in the late eighteenth century, the Fathers of the American Republic rejected with abhorrence the prospect of such bodies arising in this country, condemning them as "factions" and seeing in them a great threat to popular government. Modern as these men were in spirit and ready as they were to accept and tolerate differences of opinion, they thought government could and should be carried on without the emergence of organized bodies of partisans.

Likewise in Britain, although individual opposition had long been tolerated, the idea of a "formed opposition" was repugnant to common opinion in the aristocratic polity of the late eighteenth century. Some voices had been raised in defense of parties, but the first powerful case was put forward by Burke in 1770. In his *Thoughts on the Present Discontents* he defended parties, largely on the pragmatic grounds that if men are to act effectively they must act in concert. Moreover, he defined what he was defending in a classic formula: "Party is a body of men united, for promoting by their joint endeavors the national interest, upon some particular principle in which they are all agreed."[5] The legitimacy of the modern political party cannot be logically deduced, so to speak, from the premises of modernity. But assuming conduct oriented by the norms of modernity, and given the structural fact of a legislature with its growing political community outside, political parties were a natural, if not inevitable, consequence.

This discussion of the connection between modernity and party is important because it tells us something about the nature of political parties. They have been defined in many different ways: as nothing more than groups of men who seek to win power, differing only as "ins" and "outs"; as mere coalitions of special interest groups; as combinations seeking only to acquire and distribute patronage; and so on. These definitions point to traits that can be found in most political parties in the modern world. No doubt some political formations called parties are exhaustively characterized by such definitions. But to start from the cultural and structural dynamics of modernity shows that inherent in these dynamics is a distinctive kind of political formation. These dynamics tend to produce political for-

---

[5] *Ibid.,* Vol. I, p. 110.

mations consisting of bodies of men acting in support of different conceptions of the common good and in conflict with one another. In short, modernity tends to produce as a regular feature of the polity organized opposition over important matters of public policy. It is not necessary to say that such political formations must inevitably arise or that they cannot be offset; the example of the modern dictatorship shows that this is not so. The essential point is that political formations as characterized in the Burkean formula have grounds that are deep seated in modernity.

Party and Development

Political parties are intrinsically connected with change. Moreover, they reflect the fact that change in the modern period takes the form of development. In the context of the present analysis, the important characteristic of modern development is that it is marked by a series of stages that show a trend. This is a distinctive mode of change. It does not apply to change that consists in a mere continual repetition of the same forms of behavior. It does not apply to change consisting of a succession of discrete and dissimilar moments without connection. Moreover, it is incompatible with a mode of evenly incremental change in which each moment is, so to speak, equally a "stage" and a "transition." This last distinction is crucial since it involves the question of whether the "stages," "periods," and "eras" that students of development find in historical change correspond to realities or are simply imposed upon a continuous flux for the sake of making it more intelligible. Quite possibly some stretches of historical change must be so treated; they are merely prolonged transitions that cannot be divided into periods. But other stretches of historical change do satisfy this requirement of the concept of development.

The course of political modernization in Britain, for example, falls into three or four stages, which do not merely serve the convenience of the student, but reflect realities in behavior and attitude. This means that certain times are times of relatively full realization of a given political order and other times are times of transition between such periods of realization. The seventeenth century, especially the earlier part, was a time of transition to modernity, and the aristocratic polity flourished in the eighteenth century. In the nineteenth century the liberal order in economy and polity achieved a kind of fulfillment, although, of course, elements from the previous stages strongly survived. Moreover, within this liberal and individualist period, it makes sense to distinguish two phases: an earlier one marked in the polity by narrow suffrage and a policy of laissez faire, and a later phase of Radical democracy, when the active political community was greatly enlarged and when substantial though piecemeal interventions in the economy by the government were sanctioned. The twentieth century, which has become collectivist both in public policy, with the rise of the welfare state and managed economy, and in political formations, with the emergence of distinctive forms of political parties and pressure groups, constitutes the fourth stage of political modernization.

The significance and distinctiveness of this kind of historical change is illustrated by a striking characteristic of modern British political history. This is the recurrence, toward each mid-century, of a marked lull in political conflict. In the 1950s this decline in party conflict was so marked that many people spoke of "the end of ideology." Certainly, there was a great change from the interwar period, when even a moderate such as Clement Attlee could declare that "the issue before the country is Socialism versus Capitalism—and Socialism is not a matter of degree." By the 1950s, although not without bitter resistance from within, Labour had receded from its old premise of wholesale nationalization and comprehensive planning; while the Conservatives, to the surprise of everyone but themselves, had accepted the welfare state with its heavy burdens of taxation and the managed economy with its broad intervention in the private sector. The two leading spokesmen for the Conservatives and Labour, R. A. Butler and Hugh Gaitskell, respectively, had such similar views of both means and ends that the term "Butskellism" was coined to indicate their consensus. Compared with the interwar years, British politics in the 1950s showed a great decline in class antagonism. The questions dividing the parties became marginal, statistical, quantitative—questions of "more" and "less" rather than great social theories in conflict. Correspondingly, general elections consisted not of pitched battles between opposing social philosophies, but of small raids on interest groups. One American journalist wrote of the general election of 1951 as "the lull before the lull."

A quite similar pattern of consensus in attitude and behavior characterized the earlier mid-century lulls. After the "roaring forties" of the nineteenth century, the fifties led to that period of calm and balance that some historians have called the "Victorian compromise." Chartism with its menace of working-class violence and even revolution had withered away. The main pillars of aristocratic economic privilege had been pulled down with the repeal of the Corn Laws. Prosperity abounded under the new regime of laissez faire. As for politics, the parties were at a low point of cohesion, and, indeed, a kind of multipartism reigned in Parliament. In 1859 Lord Derby, the Prime Minister, declared that although he was not ready to say that parliamentary government itself had come to an end, with regard to a two-party system in which leaders commanded the votes of their followers and exercised a species of parliamentary discipline, "those days are gone, and are not likely to return." In sharp contrast with the bitter contention raised before 1832 by the issue of extending the franchise, now the prospect of giving the vote to the skilled urban workman merely excited a sluggish competition between the parties, which was won almost by accident by the Conservatives when they succeeded in passing the Reform Act of 1867.

The 1750s succeeded a time of no less instability and bitter party combat, although perhaps at further remove. The furious strife of "the great parties" of the late seventeenth century—to use Burke's characterization —bequeathed to the early eighteenth century a period of party combat that involved vital questions of foreign policy, the position of the Church of England, and, most ominous of all, the question of a Jacobite succession. As late as 1746 Bonnie Prince Charlie, the son of the Stuart pretender, was able to land in Scotland, invade England, and keep the field for a year. But the Tory party, which had already lost its capacity for coherent political action, was hopelessly compromised by "the Forty-five." It lingered on as a collection of country squires and a disembodied tradition, while the Whigs, broken into aristocratic "connections," fought one another and monopolized successive Governments. It was an issueless politics, in which the active political community accepted with hardly a question the aristocratic polity and the mercantile system for protecting and fostering British agriculture, industry, and, above all, commerce. So quiet were the times that at the opening of Parliament in 1753, the King's Speech, after requesting supply, had nothing further to recommend to the attention of the assembled houses than the increase in the "horrid crimes of robbery and murder." Quite naturally, when we take a detailed look into the politics of these years, we find only a politics of interest and connection, not of party or principle. This is also true of similar moments in other stages of political modernization. As in other periods in which party and party conflict decline, the reason in the mid-1700s was not an "end of ideology," but rather a "consensus on ideology." After long contention a certain political and economic order had been established that was widely accepted in the active political community.

Each of these periods of consensus marks the realization of a certain identifiable political order, possessing in each case a distinctive political culture and distinctive patterns of power, interest, and policy. For the student of political parties the important fact is the connection of party with such an order. On the one hand, party has been a main instrument in the establishment of this order. The party struggle preceding the period of consensus and realization involved changes in attitudes and behavior that helped constitute the new order. In this way party is an important means of political development, and the party struggle an important arena of political modernization. At the same time, a party that has contributed to the establishment of an order becomes identified with that order and, as the party of the status quo, defends what it had so large a part in bringing into existence (not that parties ever fully realize their initial visions). Societies and polities cannot be fabricated *de novo;* and an established order includes many elements and shades of meaning proceeding from sources other than the conscious orientation of a political party. The party of the status quo acquires a commitment to an order with complex origins.

Without trying to assign causal primacy to either, we can see the connection between modern development as a mode of change and the modern party as a type of agent of change. The Burkean party is characterized by a distinctive conception of the common good (authority and purpose), which is supported by a body of men acting in concert during some substantial length of time. The action of such an agent of change is one reason why modern political development is marked by stages, a mode of change in which a distinctive order rises, flourishes and is transformed in a new transition. Likewise, the fact that there are such established orders constitutes a source of the conceptions of the common good that are characteristic of the Burkean type of party. When historical change consists in mere flux, or in a succession of discontinuities, this type of political formation cannot function. It is appropriate that Burke, with his strong sense of modern historical development, should also have perceived the type of political formation it entails.

To summarize the analysis up to this point: The cultural and structural conditions of modernity that give rise to British political parties are threefold. First, the emergence of sovereignty—the power and legitimacy of law making—and the vesting of sovereignty in a body with substantial participation creates the objective possibility that differences may arise over the nature of the common good among the active members of the polity. To legitimize law making does not, however, necessarily legitimize controversy over law making and the toleration of opposition to those chiefly charged with it. Modern attitudes provide this second prerequisite of parties by sanctioning efforts for change based on changing human wishes and new perceptions of truth. Third, there is a structural interdependence between the character of modern development and the organization of opposing viewpoints. As we have just seen, organization means that these viewpoints are advocated over a period of time and that they constitute coherent outlooks on the political and social order. The opposition of early modernity took an organized form because it was confronted by an established order: that is to say, by social and political arrangements that endured over a substantial period of time and themselves constituted a coherent polity and society. At the same time, throughout modern political development an important reason why such established orders have been brought into existence has been that they were sought and maintained by political parties organized around conceptions of the common good.

Party, Pressure Groups, and Class

To understand the conditions that must obtain if parties are to come into existence does not tell us what the parties stand for or what their aims are. Understanding the prerequisites of the party battle does not explain its content and issues. To shed light on this question, it is plausible and conventional to look to influences from the environment of the polity, especially the economy. One of the most striking characteristics of modernization is a rapid and immense increase in the power of the state. Historically, this increase in power has proceeded largely from development of the economy. It can hardly be doubted that so dynamic a sector of modern society has a profound effect on the polity. In European history the classic instance is the impact of industrialization, which brought into existence powerful new classes, the commercial and industrial bourgeoisie, who through several turbulent decades disrupted and transformed—often by revolutionary violence—the old political and social order of the aristocratic and monarchic age.

The relationships of economic groups and the polity in the course of economic modernization can be stated in general form. Economic development proceeds through specialization. Advances in technology produce new divisions of labor with corresponding innovations in capital equipment and land use. As the new skills and techniques are put into practice, new occupational groups come into existence. The specialization that brings about the increase in productive power of the modern economy means at once greater differentiation, making a more complex economy, and new occupational components, constituting the new strata of the changing economic order.

These new strata are a principal basis of the growing power of the modern state. Their skills and resources are increasingly mobilized as the modern state extends its control over the environment. They provide personnel for the bureaucracy, civilian and military, and their growing wealth enlarges the resources on which the state may draw by taxation. At the same time, the emergence of new strata also brings about changes in the pattern of interests. Conflicts between strata arise—for instance, the classic conflict between older agrarian interests and a new and growing group of middlemen in an expanding economy. There is also a possibility of conflict between the activities of new strata and the established policies of the state, such as the restrictions in the early phases of modernity upon the movement of labor and goods. From such situations, which recur continually in the course of modernization, new demands on the polity arise. Emerging strata, their economic power perhaps enhanced by organization, attempt to use state power to protect and promote their interests in relation to other strata and to state policy itself.

This brief sketch, which puts into historical perspective the familiar interest-group model of politics, reveals a great deal about the politics and political issues of modernizing states. In the British case each of the main stages of political development coincided with a distinct economic order. The aristocratic age was a time of agrarian predominance and of rapid commercial progress. The nineteenth century was, of course, the era of industrialization, while the collectivist era in politics and government came when the fully industrialized economy was massing its growing productive power in large corporate organizations. Each of the economic orders had a pattern of economic interest groups, old and new, many of which became pressure groups attempting to use state power to promote their ends. Among the influential actors in modern British politics, we cannot fail to include the capitalist farmers, enclosing landlords, stockjobbers, and merchants of Whig England; the manufacturers, traders, shipowners, railway directors, and banking and insurance companies of the Victorian era; the trade unions, trade associations, and professional organizations of the contemporary welfare state and managed economy. When interest groups take an organized form, they are commonly called pressure groups. In this sense British politics has never been without pressure groups.

To grant the importance of interest groups does not show their connection with political parties and certainly does not imply that parties can be regarded as mere coalitions of interest groups. On the contrary, the two types of political formation, parties and pressure groups, are radically different. There are various important differentiae, but one significant behavioral index is their use of quite different channels of access. In each of the main stages of British political development, the political behavior of the special interests has usually constituted a mode of representation distinct from that of the political parties. In the collectivist polity, for example, the great producers groups of the present economy, organized in specialized associations and affiliated in wider groupings, have developed a system of access to policy making that bypasses parties and Parliament and goes directly to the executive. Close and continuous relations between these groups and the departments and subdepartments of the bureaucracy have created what may be called a system of functional representation, in contrast with the system of parliamentary representation dominated by the political parties. A similar contrast can be found in the political orders of the earlier stages of political modernization.

The connection between party and economy becomes clearer if we look at those broad categories of interest groups constituting classes. Even in England, where the connection between class standing and party affiliation is today, and no doubt has been in the past, exceptionally strong, the correlation is not perfect (see Chapter 11). Nevertheless, during the past generation quantitative studies of the question have shown that two-thirds of the working-class vote has regularly gone to Labour, while an even larger fraction of middle-class voters have supported the Conservatives. A similar connection between party and class can be found in the past. It was the British working class that overwhelmingly provided the leadership that founded the Labour party and guided it through its first decades. In the early nineteenth century the manufacturing and commercial classes lent their support largely to reform, although for a long time they accepted the leadership of aristocratic families that espoused the Liberal cause. During the fierce party fights of the late seventeenth and early eighteenth centuries, the bulk of the aristocracy, which, of course, had its economic base in vast landholdings, were Whigs, while the Tories drew their strength from the lesser landowners and the gentry.

A class consists of a number of similar occupational groups, performing as a whole a major economic function. When such a class has provided the spearhead for political innovation, it has usually been helped by the fact that it embodies new advances in technology. Such was the case with the landholders who benefited from the agricultural revolution of the seventeenth and eighteenth centuries, the manufacturers who emerged during the Industrial Revolution, and the trade union leaders who utilized the new techniques of organization developed in more recent times. In this sense the innovating class commands growing economic power, which it may use in its contest for political change.

As science and technology advance they endow certain groups with new and exceptional power over nature and society. Such were the manufacturing classes of the Industrial Revolution; such too are the managers and professional classes of today's collectivist economy. Their growing skills and resources are means that these groups can use to try to better their position in the polity. But as these examples suggest, the important fact is not whether the rising class is based in the polity or in its environment, in the public or the private sector. Technological development can produce new classes and prepare the way for class conflict in a socialist as well as in a liberal economy.

In the course of modernization, however, technological development has not done more than prepare the way for class conflict and political innovation. What values a new class will champion when it enters politics, or indeed whether it will make an effort to enter politics or passively accept its old status, depend as much on political as on economic variables. The classes that have led the way in British political development have not been simply pleaders for the particular interests of their component groups, but have advocated broad conceptions of the common good. As objectives of political action, a plea for a particular interest and a conception of the common good are quite different. Intrinsically, the difference resides in the fact that a conception of the common good, however biased, makes provision for many interests, while the objective of the particular interest is essentially "more" for the relevant group. In consequence, a conception of the common good provides a normative basis for restraining and directing the interests of even the more favored classes. To be sure, special interest groups and their advocates may also be members of larger political groupings, such as political parties, not to mention the national political community itself. As such their attitudes and behavior will also be affected by norms of the common good. But in the modern polity the function of advocating particular interests becomes differentiated from the function of advocating conceptions of the common good. This is a major reason for distinguishing between pressure groups and political parties.

In periods of innovation, one reason the innovating classes have been able to bring along substantial allies from other groups is that they have appeared as champions of broad perspectives. Burke's conception of a hierarchic society, for instance, expressed not merely a norm of inequality, but also a belief that hierarchy should and could in the long run guarantee the rights and interests of all. In this view the aristocracy without question occupied the peaks of authority and privilege, but there was also allowance for other classes, including those Whig allies, the mercantile and commercial classes. When Burke spoke of "the strength of the nation," he listed the elements seriatim: "the great peers, the leading landed gentlemen, the opulent merchants and manufacturers, the substantial yeomanry."[6] In terms of economic policy, the Whig polity made commerce "the dominant factor" in the existence and well-being of Britain, and the mercantile system, which was designed especially to promote British commerce, had as firm a grip on the minds of the great landowners as on the minds of its more immediate beneficiaries in the commercial classes. These Whig aristocrats were among the first and most vigorous of the modern nation-builders, and they entertained aspirations for national and imperial development ranging far beyond their own direct concerns as landed magnates.

Party and the Intellectuals

As in the case of the Whig aristocrats, the conceptions of the common good that have informed party activity throughout British political development have by no means been mere reflections of the economic positions of the classes adopting them. The mobilization of interests through which new groups have been drawn into the active political community has been a response to many factors besides technological advance. Above all, it has been profoundly affected by that complex process by which, on the plane of thought and opinion, the implications of the premises of moder-

---

[6]*Ibid.,* p. 492.

nity have been explored and put before the public by the intellectual classes of the time.

Along with the process of economic modernization has gone the process of cultural modernization. Both proceed from the same premises, but they do not always lead in the same direction. Industrialization, for instance, is one of the most obvious and direct consequences of modern attitudes. Yet it does not necessarily require democracy and liberty in the political system. On the contrary, the nature of the individual enterprise, as well as the economy as a whole, might well seem to make a hierarchic and authoritarian system of control far more appropriate. Such indeed was the opinion of some early observers, such as St. Simon, an opinion which the experience of both Czarist and Soviet Russia as well as that of many newly developing countries has not disconfirmed. Therefore, if the period of industrialization in Britain and generally in Western Europe was a time of rising democratic forces, the reason is to be found not in the economic process, but in the profound changes taking place in the climate of opinion.

In giving a character to this change, the role of the intellectual classes was preeminent. As we have seen in looking at the rise of free-trade sentiment in Britain, the economists were in the field decades before the groups whose interests were involved began to respond (see Chapter 1). With reference to the great age of reform generally, a major portion of the legislation was inspired by Benthamism, and not a little was actually drafted by Benthamites. In earlier as well as later times, men who explore, articulate, and publicize ideas about the political and social order have played an important role in the development of British political culture. From its earliest days, when John Locke was secretary to Shaftesbury, the founder of the Whig party, to its days of ascendancy, when Edmund Burke was secretary to the Marquess of Rockingham, the Whig aristocracy had close connections with an intellectual world, ranging from philosophers and poets to the pamphleteers and scribblers of Grub Street.

Similarly, as Schumpeter has emphasized (see Chapter 1), in the critical moments during the rise of the working-class political movement in Britain in the late nineteenth and early twentieth centuries, a small band of socialist intellectuals played a highly influential role. Years before there was a Labour party, the Fabian Society, founded in 1884, set out to "permeate" influential public opinion with their version of socialism. The active membership in those early days was drawn from such quarters as belles-lettres, journalism, education, and the Civil Service. While the Society never committed itself to a single program, perhaps because it recognized the difficulty of getting precise agreement among such lively minds, it was responsible for shaping in fundamental ways the great political movement that arose after the founding of the Labour party at the turn of the century. It rejected revolutionary methods in favor of parliamentary ones, although that choice was probably already implicit in the constitutional and law-abiding commitments of British trade unionism. Its brass-tacks, problem-solving approach, much akin to the practical spirit of the Benthamites, also found a home in important circles of the Labour party.

Perhaps the Fabian Society's most distinctive contribution, however, was to propagate and give operational meaning to the conventional social-ist idea of "common ownership" of the means of production. The idea of common ownership was not a necessary outgrowth of the economic conditions of the working class in industrialized Britain. In the United States similar conditions have consistently failed to produce any such political upshot. American working-class politics has taken a social-democratic turn, as in the New Deal, but it has never been in any significant way what is called "socialist" in the conventional European sense. Moreover, not only did the Fabian intellectuals adopt and propagate this idea, they also brought it down to earth in their proposals for a program of bureaucratic nationalization of the principal industries.

In any society the intellectual class is of crucial importance. Its essential concern is with the more general principles that underlie the norms and beliefs followed in the everyday conduct of the society. Through schools, churches, newspapers, and similar organs, intellectuals function as impor-tant agents in the cultural socialization of each generation, "infusing into the laity attachments to more general symbols and providing for that section of the population a means of participation in the general value system."[7] Some also devote themselves to the elaboration and develop-ment of alternative potentialities of the cultural heritage; criticizing re-ceived beliefs and drawing out new models of the social and political order. This process of shaping the tastes, preferences, and ideals of each generation and all classes is crucial to the process of demand creation, which conditions fundamentally the development of both the economy and the polity. It enlists some of the most powerful minds and irrepressible individualities of each age, and from it have issued major perspectives on which political parties have been founded and by which the development of the polity has been driven forward.

---

[7]Edward Shils, "The Intellectuals and The Powers," *Comparative Studies in Society and History,* 1 (October 1958) (The Hague), p. 7.

Nine

The Modernization of British Parties

The premises of modernity have provided the basis for a wide-ranging and complex elaboration of political and social values. The modern spirit itself, with its emphasis on invention and innovation, legitimizes and stimulates this work of intellectual development. The resulting history of political attitudes, whether in formal theories or in the operative ideals of public opinion, is rich and complex beyond the scope of any typology. Ancient prejudices hang on, and the eccentric products of wayward circumstance and imaginative genius continually disrupt our simplifying models. Fully recognizing the extent to which abstractions distort reality, however, we may use a simple four-cell diagram to show some of the main political values entertained by British political parties in the course of modernization.

Values and Party Development

Voluntarism and rationalism respectively provide themes of will and control for elaboration. Thus modern conceptions of authority vary along an axis of greater or less equality, while modern conceptions of purpose can be classified according to whether they make the locus of control the individual or the state. These two dimensions, inequality-equality and collectivism-individualism, create four cells into which the central values of the principal parties of innovation can readily be fitted. The arrows show

155

Figure 9.1 Modern Political Values

	AUTHORITY		PURPOSE	
		Collectivism	Individualism	
	Inequality	Whig ⟶	Liberal ↓	
	Equality	Socialist ⟵	Radical	

the line of chronological succession. (See Figure 9.1.)

Looking at conceptions of authority alone (see Figure 9.2), we can ask of any political order how the common interest and particular interests, respectively, are given representation. The collectivist category provides variations on the theme of functional representation, while the individualist category includes various kinds of voluntary association as the means of access for particular interests. Along the equality-inequality axis, modes of representation of the common good are classified according to whether they are more or less direct. Into the four resulting cells the four main conceptions of authority can again be fitted.

Figure 9.2 Conceptions of Authority

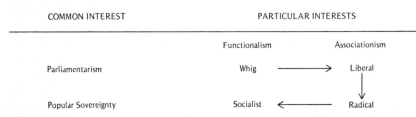

Missing from these diagrams is a major and, indeed, the senior actor in British party history—the Tory party. The Tories are absent because our classifications have dealt with variations of modern political values. The Conservative party, however, is an older and more complex entity.

Its origins go back before the modern period, at least to Tudor England, when the ideal of the hierarchic, corporate, and Christian society, although challenged by the first stirrings of modernity, still inspired the established order. This order, reduced to the status of a party during the transition to modernity in the seventeenth century, has nourished the heart of British Conservatism to this day. While retaining its Tory heart, however, British Conservatism has endured many massive infusions from other political bodies. Typically, these are former innovators who, having become attached to an order that they had a hand in creating, find themselves challenged by champions of further change and so move over to the Conservatives, the traditional party of any established order. Thus, under the impact of the French Revolution, the Tory party, hardly more than a scattering of back-bench squires, emerged as the dominant party of the Younger Pitt because of an accession of Whigs. In the nineteenth century steps toward popular government and less inequality continued to push aristocratic names into the Conservative ranks. Toward the end of the century, as the Radical tide rose in the Liberal party, financial, commercial, and industrial wealth moved strongly toward the Conservatives; for instance, the number of businessmen greatly increased among Conservative M.P.s. With the rise of Labour, in turn, the Conservatives picked up further support from Liberal voters, perhaps the larger part of them. During the post-World War II period it was shown that when Liberal voters moved to other parties, support was two-to-one in favor of the Conservatives.

As a result of this long accumulation and complex inheritance, the Conservative party is much harder to understand than its younger and simpler competitors. It is right to stress its ancient heritage—for example, its disdain for equality and its readiness to accept collectivist measures for the sake of security. At the same time there is both a strong Liberal tradition and a strong businessman's stratum in the party, which can be used to rationalize and support a sharp turn away from government intervention and toward use of the market. Moreover, when we recall that the Radical current in the Liberal party included a high regard for the "little man," the powerful support that many Conservative backbenchers gave to Resale Price Maintenance, against the free market and in favor of the small shopowners, makes ideological as well as electoral sense.

But the term ideological can be applied to the Conservatives in only the most tenuous sense. An array of diverse and contradictory perspectives inhibits simple theoretical formulations of purpose. Conventionally, the Conservatives have been regarded as the party that has no ideas but which can govern. Its diverse heritage helps account for both characteristics. The absence of ideology makes it more flexible, with the result that Conservatives have sometimes been able to perceive and to adapt to circumstances that baffled their more single-minded rivals. But this ability to govern is also something more positive than mere flexibility. Putting it a bit formally, we might call it a multiple capacity for perception deriving from a complex tradition. In any case it is not accurate to think of the Conservatives as nothing more than the party of the status quo. On the contrary, they have often been agents of modernization. While not propagators of grand theory, they have often been the authors of the concrete measures by which modernity was forwarded. The roll of innovative British statesmen would be sadly incomplete if it did not include the Tory names of Pitt, Canning, Peel, Disraeli, Neville Chamberlain, R. A. Butler, and Harold Macmillan.

One effect of these ambiguities of Toryism has been to complicate the pattern of party development. The basic mechanics of the process are clear: A party of innovation having close ties with an economic class mobilizes a coalition that is instrumental in establishing a new order in politics and policy; in due course the innovators defend this order against the challenge of a new party of change. But the peculiarities of the British party of order, the Conservatives, mean that frequently it too has been responsible for significant innovation. Thus in 1846 Peel completed the major work of liberalizing British economic policy by repealing the Corn Laws, although he split his party in the process. A generation later the Conservatives, under Disraeli, often took the lead during a new phase of social reform that was reflected in the rise of Radical influence on the Liberal side. During the interwar period Conservatives laid the foundations of government control on which the managed economy of the present day was built. In the early 1950s under the influence of Butler, the Conservatives not only accepted, but in significant ways expanded, the welfare state they had inherited from Attlee's Labour Government. In the early 1960s Harold Macmillan initiated a new effort of economic planning, which the Wilson Government accepted and built on. In 1971 Edward Heath's Conservatives led Britain into the Common Market against resistance strongly represented in the ranks of Labour.

It would be entirely out of keeping with the Tory spirit to see in this behavior anything exceptionally high-minded. The motive is often simple prudence. As Disraeli said, "The palace is not safe, when the cottage is unhappy." Or as Quintin Hogg warned a Conservative gathering in 1944, "If you do not give the people social reform, they are going to give you social revolution." But among people with power such good sense and prudence are not so common that they can be taken for granted and require no explanation. A major reason in British political culture is the tradition of a governing class, and although the essence of this class is that it has provided leadership for all parties, it has usually had its main strength among the Tories.

The basic values of British parties derive from two sources: the premodern order of Tudor England enshrined in the traditions of Toryism and the developing themes of modernity. These values appear in history in rough order of succession, both as party viewpoints and as the rationales of successive stages of political development. These stages can be characterized as Old Tory, Old Whig, Liberal, Radical, and Collectivist, each of which can be identified with a political party. But although these values and their corresponding political formations and political structures did emerge in succession, they also appeared in rudimentary but recognizable form at the very start of modernization. Each of the five main types of political formation has an analogue among the principal factions that appeared during the political struggles of the English Civil War in the seventeenth century. In the constitutional royalists we may find the first Tory party. Rejecting the frantic personal government of Charles I, their inspiration was the Tudor regime, and like Tories in other generations they had support in all classes of the population. As is common in civil wars, the opposition split and splintered. The aristocratic leaders of Parliament and its armies prefigured the later Whigs. A distinct current of opinion was also recognizably liberal. In *Aereopagitica* (1644) Cromwell's secretary, John Milton, first stated the doctrines of free speech and individual self-development to which, two hundred years later, John Stuart Mill gave classic expression in secular form.

In the struggle that broke out within the parliamentary forces in 1647 after their victories in the first civil war, the clash of democratic with liberal viewpoints is reminiscent of many later conflicts. The Levellers stood for a kind of radicalism, which, although suppressed, broke out again in the American colonies and among the democratic forces of nineteenth-century liberalism. Socialism also had its precursors in Winstanley's "Diggers," who aimed at the abolition of private property in land and the establishment of communal cultivation on a democratic basis.

In cultural history ideas and attitudes often emerge in new and original forms from successive contexts. No doubt this has been true of many of the proposals and points of view that have been put forward in the course of British party development. But the fact that the main perspectives appeared almost simultaneously at the beginnings of modernity suggests a different process. During the modern period the actions and reactions of leaders and groups have not been completely indeterminate and open, but have been contained within the possibilities of a certain cultural complex. This political culture includes both a premodern heritage and the basic premises of modernity, voluntarism and rationalism. As we have seen in Figure 9.1, these premises have various implications; they can be embodied in a number of conceptions of authority and purpose, which are made specific by their place on an equality-inequality axis and on a collectivist-individualist axis. The four resulting potentialities of political modernity correspond to the four main currents of oppositionist opinion in the Civil War. With Toryism they constitute the principal values that were expressed in later party and political development. The modernization of British political culture has been driven forward by the elaboration, systematization, and criticism of these potential patterns of value by the intellectual classes.

Whigs and Tories

A trend toward equalizing power and the conditions of life has marked the evolving aspirations of modernity. But when English parties first burst forth from the political struggles of the Restoration monarchy, it must not be thought that the Whigs, although the party of innovation, were more egalitarian than the Tories. In the late seventeenth century they were overwhelmingly the party of the great aristocrats, and for all their connections with merchants and Dissenters, their vision of the polity and society was as hierarchic as that of any medieval baron or Tudor lord. Nor, in spite of their connection with Locke, were the Whigs rugged individualists. Their conception of the society was not only hierarchic but corporate. Individuals were seen as members not only of the various ranks and orders of men, but also of the local communities of village and household, borough and shire, and it was such bodies rather than isolated individuals that were regarded as the legitimate bases of representation in Parliament. Thus Burke, writing at the height of the Whig ascendancy, attacked the philosophy of natural rights because it proposed "personal representation" and failed to recognize "corporate personality." For many years one of the charges against parliamentary reformers was that they championed "individual representation," which, in addition to its suggestion of universal suffrage, also implied equal electoral districts in place of the ancient, unified communities of the old system.

In their conceptions of authority the conflict between Whigs and Tories centered on the role of the monarch. In the Tudor regime the right and duty of representing and protecting the common good had been vested in the monarch. In practice this meant that the initiative and decisive influence in the great questions of public policy were the Crown's preserve, entrenched in its prerogative. Elizabeth denied to the Commons the initiative in questions concerning foreign policy and war and peace; the royal succession; the religious settlement and the church in general; and all exchequer matters and the royal administration, including even grants of monopoly by royal patent. While the monarch often did need the consent of Parliament with regard to such matters, the main concern of the Commons was special and local interests. In the sixteenth century the medieval notion that M.P.s were delegates or attorneys for their constituencies was still very much alive. Their principal function was to bind their constituencies to make good the grants of supply to the monarch. In return they secured the redress of grievances.

In the Whig Parliament of the eighteenth century M.P.s continued to represent the many corporate interests of the nation and the empire, which made great use of private bill procedure as a mode of access to power. The great contrast was that Parliament now was not only the focus of such functional representation, but also the body charged with deliberating on and determining the common good. As Burke said in a famous phrase, it was "a deliberative assembly of one nation with one interest, that of the whole—where not local prejudices ought to guide but the general good resulting from the general reason of the whole."[1] This did not mean that

---

[1] Edmund Burke, *Writings and Speeches*, Vol. II (Boston, 1901), pp. 89–98.

the monarch was excluded from government. Parliament meant—more precisely—the King-in-Parliament. Yet the difference from Tudor theory and practice was revolutionary: From being the principal representative of the community as a whole, standing above and apart from its three estates —Lords Spiritual, Lords Temporal, and Commons—the monarch now became only one of the three estates, King, Lords, and Commons.

Moreover, and here we get to an even more important difference, this Parliament was sovereign. In Blackstone's words, which stated the Whig orthodoxy, it was "a supreme, irresistible, absolute, uncontrolled authority" whose actions "no power on earth can undo."[2] It was from the era of the Civil War that this notion of a unified and unlimited authority in the state had emerged. Sovereignty had not been a medieval nor even a Tudor idea. Nor for all their talk of divine right was it a Tory doctrine. On the contrary, the old system of religious belief that gave royal authority a sacred foundation at the same time limited the power of kings, as it did all human authority. During the struggles of the later Stuarts the Tories were perfectly consistent, believing in divine right and, at the same time, fearing arbitrary power in the state as represented by a Parliament untrammeled by fundamental law. In the Tory conception of social purpose as well, the religious theme was strong. The old idea of a Christian society unified in its transcendental aim by identical membership in church and commonwealth lingered on. The rallying cry of Toryism was "The Church in danger!"—whether from papists or dissenters. In the first decades of modern party struggle, Tory strength was great in the church and among the lesser gentry, though weak in the peerage and among the mercantile classes.

In comparison, Whiggery was markedly secular. This meant that in religious matters the Whigs were tolerant, not to say indifferent, although they could distinguish Protestant dissenters from Catholics, who might well have French connections. But their secularism was also something positive: a conception of national and imperial development that employed the instruments of state intervention at home and diplomacy and war abroad to forward colonial and commercial aggrandizement. Judged by later standards, the mercantile system and its bureaucratic instruments were unbelievably disorderly and inefficient. Yet they represented a conscious and vigorous collective effort to use the state to enhance the wealth and power of Britain, and under this policy the first British Empire was created. Led by their great aristocrats, the Whigs were strong among nonconformists, merchants, moneylenders, stock companies, friends of the Bank of England, and the mob of London.

---

[2]Sir William Blackstone, *Commentaries on the Laws of England* (1765), Bk.I, Ch.II, Sect. 3.

Liberals and Radicals

Individualism informed both the Liberal vision of social purpose and the Liberal conception of how power should be organized and exercised in the state. In both politics and policy the new age of the nineteenth century broke with the immemorial corporatism of English society and govern ment. Like the Whigs, the Liberals were committed to parliamentarism. The member of the legislature was not a delegate sent merely to reflect the will of the people; he was a representative charged with deliberation on the common good. To this extent the Burkean conception of representation maintained its sway. When we ask *what* was represented, however, a gulf opens between the Whig and Liberal views. For the Liberals gave a new stress in their political thought to the representation of individuals, rather than corporate bodies, ranks, orders, or "interests." In their politics, as their economics, the source of action was the rational, independent man.

In this individualism strong egalitarian implications can be found. From it clearly followed the notion of electoral districts containing equal numbers of voters in contrast with the inequalities of representation based on communities, such as the old boroughs and shires. Moreover, in its ultimate vision of society, Liberalism was radically classless. It was an attack upon aristocracy and hierarchy as well as corporatism. The new order of freedom for which Liberals fought would break down privilege and relieve oppression, the twin sources of hierarchy, and enable each man to make his own way in the world. Although no doubt limited in its values and biased by its class connections, the Liberal idea was nonetheless a conception of the common good. It not only drew a large following from among the rising classes of manufacturers and traders; it was also given leadership by members of the aristocracy and gentry and wide support by the growing proletariat of the cities. It was such a coalition, as we have seen, that put through the great reform of 1832.

Inequality of power, however, was strongly justified on Liberal grounds. Parliamentarism itself puts the power of decision in the small body of the elected, not the large body of electors. Moreover, in seeking to identify rationality and independence among the people, Liberals found a rough-and-ready index in the possession of property. Quite consistent with individualist premises, Macaulay argued against the democrats that it was not by numbers, but by "property and intelligence" that the country should be ruled. As we have seen, although the property qualification was modest, the act of 1832, in practice, enfranchised only 3.3 percent of the population of Great Britain.

As Radical democracy gained strength in the last half of the nineteenth century, a fundamentally different conception was put forward defining how the common good was to be determined. Breaking with Liberal parliamentarism, the Radicals put the ultimate power of decision in "the people." This did not mean simply a miscellany of rational, independent men, but rather a body of individuals bound together by a unified and authoritative will that was sovereign in the polity. In America the doctrine was termed "popular sovereignty" and came into wide acceptance in the days of Jacksonian Democracy. In both countries it meant in practice that all men were qualified to be voters, that so far as possible all decisions should be referred to the voters, and that when there was disagreement, the majority should prevail.

Liberal hostility toward corporate representation was carried on, and indeed intensified, by the Radicals. Opposed to "the people," in the Radical view of the political universe, were the "special interests," or the "sinister interests," to use the Benthamite phrase. "The interests are always awake," said Gladstone in his last and democratic phase, "while the country often slumbers and sleeps." In fact, no developing modern economy can do away with particular interests, certainly not one where, as in Britain in the nineteenth century, a rapid differentiation of the economy was driving it forward to unprecedented productivity. The interest groups so brought into existence often did associate. The Industrial Revolution had only fairly gotten under way when in 1798 manufacturing groups organized as the Chamber of Manufacturers of Great Britain. True to Liberal norms, such bodies were associations, not communities; they were sets of individuals voluntarily joining together for specific and limited purposes, not solidary groups satisfying comprehensive social needs.

Even more characteristic of the Liberal mode of representation of particular interests was the direct presence in Parliament of representatives of these interests. In a sense this was a by-product of the Liberal idealization of rational independence. For the candidate this norm implied a lack of strong ties with party or patron and so necessarily some substantial wealth of his own. "It is because I have made a fortune and am independent that I come here to ask for your suffrages to send me to Parliament," said George Hudson, the Railway King, to the voters when he first stood for election to the House in 1845. As his later actions at Westminster showed, he meant anything but independence of his vast railway interests.

But the Liberal period saw a mobilization of interests that was less directly dependent upon the developing economy and more important for the future development of party organization. The early nineteenth century was increasingly a time of reformist agitation, which, moreover, characteristically took the form of voluntary associations aimed at influencing Parliament in favor of some specific policy or piece of legislation. These were pressure groups, but more often working for a cause than for a special interest (see Chapter 1).

The Radicalization of Liberalism

In the course of the nineteenth century there took place a certain Radicalization of party organization as the techniques of voluntary association used by these pressure groups were adopted by political parties. During the period of Whig consensus the "aristocratic connections" that competed for office and patronage had worked out many of the structures and practices of party government. For example, the whips descend from the aristocratic period, as does the custom of Ministers sitting to the right of the Speaker in confrontation with their opponents to his left. In the nineteenth century British parties not only received a new infusion of principle from the rise of Liberalism, but also gradually acquired new forms of organization, as the franchise was extended, communications improved, and policies touched larger sections of the population.

The culmination of the Radicalization of party organization was the creation of the extraparliamentary party organization embracing what was, for the time, a mass membership, emphasizing a party program, and attempting to influence or even control its M.P.s. The leading example is the National Liberal Federation (N.L.F.), which was launched in 1877 and which was a quite self-conscious fusion by Liberals of the Radical stamp of the pressure groups that were forwarding their various causes. Radical sentiments strongly marked the rhetoric of its founders and legitimized its efforts to give its mass membership a voice in candidate selection, program making, and parliamentary action itself. While the agitation for the first and second reform acts had come very largely from nonparty associations, the Reform Act of 1884 followed the launching of a movement for further reform by the N.L.F., which carried out on a large scale the work of spreading propaganda, organizing meetings, and winning support for the measure. Although the federation, with its annual conference and its concern with program making, at times exercised influence, it never acquired in theory or practice the right to dictate to Liberal M.P.s.

In the earlier part of the century the Liberals had little organization in the country apart from small local associations, and the initiative in the reforms of that period very often came from pressure groups and other voluntary political associations. While not strictly part of the Liberal party, these were part of the Liberal movement that remade the British polity in a new image. With the foundation of the N.L.F. this complex of disconnected elements became part of an integrated whole.

In matters of party organization, the Conservatives demonstrated their usual adaptability. Defeated in the crucial battle of 1832 and permanently split by the events of 1846, they were generally in eclipse during the period of mid-Victorian Liberal consensus. As the franchise was extended and mass democracy was achieved, however, the Conservatives moved toward a position of dominance that has been without parallel in modern times and which on the whole was increasingly confirmed in the course of the twentieth century. As we have observed, this was in part owing to their leadership in some spheres of social reform. The Tories also were quick to pick up the new methods of organization. Indeed, their extraparliamentary organization, including local associations and a large membership, was founded in 1867, ten years before the Liberals acted. Like the N.L.F., this organization also had a representative organization affiliating local associations and staging an annual conference, which after 1885 also began to debate and pass resolutions concerning public policy. Unlike the N.L.F., however, it did not claim nor exercise any power over party policy, the party bureaucracy, or the behavior of M.P.s. Explicitly, it acknowledged that, as ever, the parliamentary party and especially its Leader were the source of party policy.

In the mid-1880s the Liberal consensus was rudely shattered and a new era of party conflict inaugurated. In the House of Commons the new era showed itself in sharp contrasts in behavior. After a long period of slackness and decline, party cohesion rose sharply, reaching present-day levels in the 1890s (see Chapter 6). The Opposition, which had been typically desultory and ineffective, pulled itself together to mount a persistent, organized attack upon the Government (see Chapter 7). There was an abrupt end to the easy agreement between the two front benches that had prevailed in the period of consensus and that had enabled Governments to rely on support from the other side when confronted with revolt on their own. Now the leaders of both parties were obliged to rely almost exclusively upon their own backbenchers, as in the party politics of contemporary Britain.

A new set of issues and attitudes arose along with the new patterns of behavior. The transition to the new stage of party development had been sharply marked in 1886 by Gladstone's introduction of his proposal of Home Rule for Ireland, which split the Liberals and led to a party realignment and a new bitterness between the two sides in the House and in the country. But in the previous decade or so, the rise of radicalism had already heightened tension within the Liberal party and had prepared the way for the renewed outburst of strife. Although wealth was moving to the Conservatives, the Radicals were not much concerned with economic or social reform. The strong political cast of their program is clear in some of their principal proposals, such as the abolition of plural voting, payment of M.P.s, shorter Parliaments, and reform of the House of Lords. Home Rule, which headed their list of proposals, expressed the quintessentially democratic doctrine of self-determination. Their demand that the Church of England be disestablished in Wales, which was now largely nonconformist, reflected not only the religious sentiments of large sections of the Liberal party, but also the democratic principle of self-determination in cultural matters.

Far from supporting the leadership, the Radicals used the extraparliamentary organization of the N.L.F. to develop their program and to support left wing dissidence in the House. In time, as Hugh Berrington has observed, the party educated its leaders, and many of the policies of the Liberal Government that won the sweeping victory of 1906 sprang from proposals brought forward in the party conference in previous decades.[3] Although briefer than the period of Liberal dominance, the period of reform dominated by the Radicals before World War I was as significant as that dominated by the Liberals after 1832. Its culmination was the fierce struggle of the "Lords against the People" in 1910–1911 that led to the reform of the upper House.

The Collectivist Period

It is crucially important to see the Radical phase as a distinct stage of British political development. The reason is to make clear the beginnings and nature of the collectivist period and its political formations. Some writers have assumed that tight party cohesion, sharp parliamentary conflict, mass parties, and programmatic politics arose only when the working class emerged as the base of a socialist political party. All these traits, on the contrary, first characterized the Radical period. Deductively we might think that because of its conditions of life, the working class will produce a more solidary political organization than the individualist middle class. In the course of time this proved to be true. But in the early 1900s the cohesion of the Labour party in Parliament was less than that of the Liberals. One clue is suggested by the fact that the Labour party in these days was not explicitly socialist; on the contrary, its M.P.s, apart from their commitment to the "interests of labour," were enthusiastic Radicals, strong in their support of reforming Liberal Government. The characteristic solidarity of the Labour party in Parliament appeared only after it took on a commitment to socialism. On the Labour side of the House, the index of party voting—that is, votes in which 90 percent or more of the members of a party voted on the same side—rose from 80.4 percent in 1906 to 97.3 percent in the period 1924–1928.

As for harshness of conflict, when we consider the modern period as a whole, it is evident that the intensity of British political conflict has steadily declined. In what was said and done, as well as what was at stake, 1688 and, indeed, 1714—with its Jacobite invasion in the next year—put the inauguration of the Whig ascendancy at one extreme. The struggle over the Reform Bill of 1832 is perhaps matched in bitterness by the conflict

---

[3] "Partisanship and Dissidence in the Nineteenth-Century House of Commons," *Parliamentary Affairs,* 21 (Autumn, 1968), 372.

over reform of the Lords in 1910–1911. In both instances two general elections were called and the monarch had to resolve the crisis by threatening to swamp the upper chamber with new peers. Yet the general election of 1906 that brought the Radicals to power was placid compared with the election of 1830, that led to Grey's reforming Government. And in comparison with the turbulence that accompanied these earlier shifts in political power, we hardly recognize 1945, when a Labour Government, assuming office with a socialist program and, for the first time, with a parliamentary majority, proceeded to put through a series of sweeping reforms to which the Conservatives adapted without missing a step.

Overall the correlation is clear: After Labour introduced a politics that was far more ideological than any that had gone before and that was, for the first time, explicitly based on class, British party conflict came to be conducted with more balance and decorum than ever before. Perhaps the reason for this was the long-run decline of religious issues in politics and the rise of economic questions to the place of main importance. Economic matters can be argued rationally—they are quantifiable and instrumental —but religion touches ultimate values.

The political culture of the collectivist period shows the continuing power of the modern thrust toward equality. This is especially apparent in the ideology of the welfare state, which affirms the need to reduce, or even abolish, economic inequality. The old Radical political ideals also won ever wider acceptance, and democracy was continually broadened in a series of acts between 1918 and 1969 that abolished the last restrictions on manhood suffrage, extended the vote to women on the same basis as it was held by men, abolished the plural votes that some property owners had retained, reduced still further the power of the Lords, and finally, in 1969, gave the vote to eighteen-year-olds.

What was especially new about this time, however, was less its egalitarianism than its collectivism. This new outlook characterized attitudes toward both policy and politics. With regard to control of the economy, the state rather than the individual was seen more and more as the center of power. With regard to participation, a new and enhanced status was attributed to producers groups, and, by socialists, to the main economic classes, workers and owners. These further steps in cultural modernization took specific form in conceptions of authority that made party government and functional representation, respectively, the means by which the common interest and particular interests were to be represented.

Even more sharply than in the past, the development of this period was marked off and shaped by the rise of a new political party. Labour was the party of innovation, and its ideas and actions are the least ambiguous expression of the new attitudes. "The Labour Party," Ernest Bevin once said, "has grown out of the bowels of the T.U.C." Founded in 1868 during the period of the Liberal consensus, the Trades Union Congress affiliated the rising national unions of craftsmen and acted as their lobby before Parliament. Extending its membership to include the newly organized unskilled workers in the 1880s, the T.U.C. decided to strike out on a more independent line when in 1899 it voted to initiate a separate political party. At first calling itself the Labour Representation Committee, the new organization took the name Labour party only in 1906. In these Parliaments before World War I, however, Labour was little more than a coalition of trade unions acting as a pressure group within the vaster Liberal movement. Socialists were affiliated with the party through two small organizations, the Fabian Society and the Independent Labour party. But Labour did not explicitly declare itself socialist until 1918.

Two momentous changes were made that year. First, the party gave itself a national constituency organization. Previously, it had been merely a federation of unions and socialist societies; now it established local organizations in parliamentary constituencies. Also, for the first time the party gave itself a program that explicitly committed it to a "Socialist Commonwealth," based on "the common ownership of the means of production." These two steps served to separate it once and for all from the Liberals. Thereafter Liberals might cooperate with Labour, as when they supported the minority Labour Governments of 1924 and 1929–1931. But Labour was never again the junior partner, nor did parliamentary support become coalition or coalescence, although Liberal leaders of the Radical stamp have often dreamed of some such party realignment.

To a greater degree than any other major party in British history, Labour developed an ideology. This was natural in a party in which intellectuals enjoyed a position of such exceptional importance. For in Britain, as on the continent, intellectuals were highly influential in giving a socialist orientation to the working-class political movement, which in turn was very hospitable to them. In their conceptions of authority, the socialists of the Labour party, like the Radicals, rejected parliamentarism and accepted popular sovereignty, expressed through the verdict of a majority in favor of a party at a general election. But because of their collectivist views they gave to party government a far firmer foundation than the individualist Radicals had. Their approach to policy legitimized a greater degree of cohesion and discipline. Even when the Radical sought so to reform the economic and social system as to eliminate privilege and promote equality, the system he supported was still an individualist system and the reforms he proposed were acts of piecemeal intervention and redress. The socialist, on the other hand, whether believing in wholesale nationalization or only in a managed economy, held that the main decisions of economic policy must be made by a government that would consciously harmonize the decisions with one another in space and time. From this necessity flowed a new and compelling sanction for party unity and party discipline.

This need is evident, but how can it be reconciled with the wide democratic participation that inevitably, it would seem, intrudes a lively, not to say chaotic, pluralism into decision making? The socialist's answer springs from his conception of the class nature of society. In his view political divisions derive from economic class divisions of which, in an industrialized economy, there are essentially two—workers and owners. Such fundamental duality subsumes the complex pluralisms of occupational and other economic groups. Moreover, it roots the solidarity of the party not merely in a meeting of free minds but in objective membership in a class with an overriding class interest. Here are firm grounds for joining and sticking with the party of your class and for reprobating any breach of solidarity. Behavior corresponded with these beliefs. In the great interwar crisis of the party in 1931, when the three top leaders of the Labour Government confronted with economic crisis tried to take the party into coalition with Conservatives and Liberals, the party inside and outside Parliament, almost without exception, rejected their leadership. Although deserted by its three top leaders, the party—in contrast with the Conservatives in 1846 or the Liberals in 1886—did not split. In behavior as in attitudes, the Labour party was a new and distinctive type of political formation.

From Labour's collectivist premises a theory of democracy by party government follows. The working class is seen as having a system of interests and aspirations that are reflected in the party's social philosophy and articulated, as the times require, in its program. Democracy is interpreted to mean, primarily, periodic contests between two such programmatic parties. At such times the voter has a choice that is meaningful in two senses: He has a choice between two coherent and distinctive programs. Moreover, he knows that the victorious party will have the cohesion to carry out the program to which it is pledged. Its "mandate" will be honored. With regard to the inner procedures of the party, there too democracy must prevail. Only the mass membership, representing the authentic voice of the working class, can be entrusted with the task of framing the party program. Discretion as to details, timing, and so forth can be left to the parliamentary leadership. But the decisive will and main thrust of ideas must come from the rank and file.

This whole set of ideas involves difficulties. It cannot be easy to reconcile intraparty democracy with the need for a viable and coherent government program and the doctrine of the mandate with the unpredictability of history. Yet this in general has been the party's official theory of itself, as expressed in the plain words of its constitution, in what speakers at conference say about its powers, and in the public utterances of party leaders. Two-party competition, tight cohesion among partisans, a program deriving from a comprehensive social philosophy, party allegience founded primarily upon economic class and giving the party a mass membership, a party structure providing for intraparty democracy, especially in framing the party program: such are the main elements in the socialist conception of party government.

Functional Representation

Political equality and popular sovereignty constitute strong links in the Radical past with the socialist conception of authority. The new views of how particular interests should be represented, however, broke sharply with the older individualism, as the associationism of both Liberal and Radical outlooks gave way to a new version of functional representation. This term refers to any conception of authority that finds the community divided into various strata, regards each of these strata as having a certain corporate unity, sees each as performing a function in the society, and holds that they ought to be represented in the polity. The idea is medieval in origin and in British political development has taken various forms as the constituent strata have been differently constituted—estates, ranks and orders, interests, classes, and occupational groups.

At the turn of this century there were signs, on both Left and Right, that opinion was shifting toward a new functional pluralism. The same part of the party constitution, the famous Clause IV, which committed the party to "common ownership," went on to voice the syndicalist demand for "the best possible obtainable system of popular administration and control of each industry and service." For a time the guild socialists agitated in favor of a form of syndicalism; even after their propaganda subsided, the idea of workers' control, which they had done much to foster, influenced the trade unions, not being finally put to rest until after Labour took office in 1945. By that time other channels of access had been firmly established for trade unions and other producers groups.

During the interwar years there was growing recognition from other sources as well as Labour ideology of the need for and legitimacy of associating representatives of interest groups with government administration. The National Health Insurance Act of 1924, for instance, provided for the representation of specific interests—such as the medical profession and suppliers of drugs, medicines, and appliances—on the various committees charged with administering the system of social insurance. World War II involved a vast increase in the direct presence of producers groups in government as trade unions, trade associations, and similar groups were used to guide and implement the vast war effort. During postwar years the representation of interests had become so normal and expected that it was a rare and serious charge that the Government or a department had made policy without consultation with the relevant bodies. A major expression of the new role of organized interests was the position given them on bodies concerned with economic planning. At the highest level these included the Economic Planning Board, the National Production Advisory Council on Industry, and from 1962 on the ambitious effort represented by the National Economic Development Council and its score or so of similar bodies for particular industries (see Chapters 4 and 10).

Labour and Socialism

The influence of class thinking on the structure and behavior of the Labour party is easy to illustrate. If we turn to the party's conception of purpose, the question of the meaning and seriousness of its commitment to socialism raises harder questions. We do not have the kind of survey data that would enable us to say, for example, with regard to the roughly 200,000 individual and 2 million trade-union members in 1928, how many would have said they believed in the abolition of capitalism and the establishment of a socialist economy based on common ownership. We do know, however, that the imagery of socialist doctrine—common ownership versus private ownership, cooperation versus competition, planning versus the market, economic security and equality versus individual effort and reward —informed the huge mass of party utterance in the decades after the commitment of 1918. In conference debates, party programs, parliamentary speeches, and countless public meetings there was expressed a reasonably coherent and wide-ranging socialist ideology.

Moreover, we also know that during this time a massive program was developed, comprising a long list of major structural reforms, which, when the party won power, were put into effect speedily and almost without exception or change. In the campaign of 1945 Labour presented a manifesto entitled "Let Us Face the Future." It had been debated and approved at its party conference and was packed with pledges that had been accumulating over the years and that were derived from many different groups within the movement. While in power the Attlee Government of 1945–1951 based its legislative program squarely on the manifesto, and for virtually every paragraph of pledges in the statute book, a corresponding act can be found. Fulfilling its pledges of nationalization, the Government passed the following:

The Bank of England Act of 1946

The Electricity Act of 1946

The Coal Industry Nationalisation Act of 1946

The Civil Aviation Act of 1946

The Transport Act of 1947

The Gas Act of 1948

The Iron and Steel Act of 1949

As pledged with regard to the social services, Labour passed the National Health Service Act of 1946, which nationalized almost all hospitals and set up a free and comprehensive health service. Also, the social insurance system was consolidated and extended by the National Insurance Act of 1946, which provided sickness, unemployment, and retirement benefits as well as maternity grants, widows' pensions, and death grants, and by the Industrial Injuries Act of the same year, which dealt with workmen's compensation. With regard to farming, the Agriculture Act of 1947 established a new system of "assured markets and guaranteed prices." In harmony with its promises in the field of taxation, Labour maintained from wartime, and in some respects sharpened, a steeply progressive scheme of income taxation. Other major reforms included the Housing Acts of 1946 and 1949, the Rent Control Act of 1949, the Children Act of 1948, and the Town and Country Planning Act of 1947.

Even this brief summary conveys a sense of the very great effort and achievement of the Labour Government, especially in its first years. This achievement is emphasized, first, as an illustration of party government. More particularly, it was party government very much in accord with the socialist model, the new pattern of policy being derived from a party program that had been legitimated by intraparty democracy and that had originated not from an elite, but from a plurality of initiatives. Second, Labour's achievement constituted the establishment of the British welfare state. To be sure, the origins of many social services can be traced back to the Radical period, precedents for nationalization can be found in the interwar years, and in originating or developing both sorts of reform, Conservatives played an important role. But Labour's achievement, like its promises, were distinctively different from what the Conservatives offered or would have done. If there was one central point of difference, it was the magnitude of government expenditure. When the Conservatives did face the task of adaptation to Labour's reforms, this prospect of huge continuing expenditure was the bitterest pill. Moreover, as we have seen (see Chapter 4), the expenditure of the welfare state does much to determine the nature of the managed economy. It means that the economy will be profoundly affected by what government does, and, moreover, it tends to ensure that the instruments that government will use to control the economy will be primarily fiscal.

In this sense the new order of the postwar welfare state and managed economy in Britain was very much the creation of the Labour party. Even more than in previous transitions party was the principal agent of political development. Labour did not at that time or in later years, fulfill its original vision of the Socialist Commonwealth. But it is hardly unusual for parties of innovation to be diverted from their early ideals and to find history harder to control than they had imagined.

Conservatives and Collectivism

The Conservative party has found it easier to adapt to the new issues raised by the Labour party, to the establishment of the welfare state, and to the conditions of the collectivist period generally than to some other periods of innovation in the past. Its flexibility has not been flaccid, however, and many values of Toryism have been maintained in the attitudes that shape and justify the Conservative version of functional representation and party government. Some of its older traditions facilitated the break from individualism.

As L. S. Amery, a leading Tory intellectual, observed in 1947, when urging a reform of Parliament that would include functional representation, that conception has a history in Britain going back to the medieval House of Commons when the knights of the shire represented agriculture and the burgesses a variety of localized industrial and commercial interests.[4] Generally, in the rise of the new pluralism in political thought, while the main thrust came from the Left, the Right also produced its advocates. Among them were Ruskin and his follower A. J. Penty, with their ideas for the revival of the guild system. The Conservative version of functionalism also included the proposals of the Whitley Commission in 1917 that joint industrial councils comprising both employers and workmen be established to review and improve industrial relations. Also, as we have seen, the interwar period saw an increasing association of organized producers groups with government administration.

Far more interesting have been the ways in which Conservative attitudes and party organization have adapted Tory conceptions of hierarchy to the conditions of democracy and mass politics. The essential logic is the same as that set forth by Amery, in his interpretation of the British Constitution (see Chapter 1). In that view he attributes a wide scope of independent authority to a "central governing, directing, and initiating element" in government. The role of the voter, on the other hand, is "essentially passive," consisting not in initiating proposals, but in choosing between the two alternatives presented to him at a general election—two alternative sets of proposals, but above all two alternative sets of leaders. Analogously, in a political party there is a real function for a mass membership and an elaborate extraparliamentary organization, but it is essentially to win votes for the leaders, rather than to tell them what to do. Toryism likewise supplies powerful sanctions for party unity in support of the Leader, since this merely translates into a contemporary context the old imperative that order necessitates authority. Thus contemporary conservatism rationalizes a theory of party government appropriate to the politics and policies of the collectivist age.

---

[4]L. S. Amery, *Thoughts on the Constitution* (London, 1947), p. 64.

In the background of Tory thought on authority, class looms large, as it also does for the Socialist, although with quite different meaning. While the Socialist sees classes as economic units that divide the polity horizontally, the Tory sees classes as integrating the polity vertically. Effective leadership requires special talents that will always be confined to a few. A function of the Conservative party is to cultivate, offer, and support such leadership. When it does, it can count on Britons—or at any rate Englishmen—to recognize its claim to their suffrage.

Such expectations have not been disappointed. When Disraeli extended the franchise in 1867, he acted on the belief that "the wider the popular suffrage, the more powerful would be the natural aristocracy." During the following years of Radical and Socialist influence—from 1886 to 1971— Conservatives have held office for three-fifths of the time, or some fifty-two years out of eighty-five. This would have been impossible without a massive following among the lower classes. During the postwar period, survey data show that fully half the Conservative vote has come from the working class. Moreover, among these working-class Tories it has been possible to identify and measure a large fraction—perhaps as much as 25 percent of the total Conservative vote—to whom, precisely as in Tory theory, class is seen as an integrating, not a dividing, force and the Conservative party as the special seat of superior ability.

Needless to say, Conservatives today are more reticent in advancing this claim than they were at the founding of their national association in 1867, when the chairman could say without fear of offense to the many working-men present that "we all of us believe that the Conservatives are the natural leaders of the people." Yet the party cries of the Conservatives still reflect their old self-confidence. In the general election of 1970, while Labour quite expectedly sought to raise fears of Tory landlords, bankers, and other capitalists, the Conservatives pictured themselves as "the party who can," which had not only compassion (conceded to Labour), but also competence. It came down to "Trust us," and at the polls millions of Britons renewed their ancient fealty.

Tory tradition also could be utilized to justify Conservative adaptation to Labour's welfare state. In arguing for the party statement that accepted Labour's main reforms, Anthony Eden, then heir-apparent to Churchill as Leader, could say to the party conference in 1947:

> We are not the party of unbridled, brutal capitalism and never have been. . . . we are not the political children of the laissez-faire school. We opposed them decade after decade.

Justified by such old traditions of state power and collective responsibility and moved by electoral necessity, Tory leaders moved rapidly during the late 1940s to accept Labour's main reforms. At the same time, as we have seen (see Chapter 4), the Labour Government, frustrated in its efforts at physical planning, shifted toward major reliance on the tools of fiscal policy. The result of this typical movement of parties in a competitive two-party democracy was a broad agreement on social and economic policy between the two antagonists, which ushered in one of those phases of consensus and political calm that have been recurrent in British political development. This was the period of Butskellism, when the community of views between the two leading economic spokesmen for the Conservative Government and Labour Opposition vividly illustrated the convergence of the two party positions.

The Collectivist Consensus

During the late 1940s and early 1950s a pattern of politics and policy became established that had new and distinctive traits. Its origins could be found in earlier years, especially the interwar period, but in the first years after World War II, this pattern achieved a kind of fulfillment that is reminiscent of other periods of consensus and stability in British political development. While changes continued both in politics and policy, the basic elements showed strong continuity through some two decades.

While the main stress here will be on domestic policy, it may be noted in passing that a strong movement toward interparty agreement also marked the views of the two parties on defense, foreign, and imperial policy. Labour had come to power with rosy hopes of easy and fruitful cooperation with the Soviet Union. These hopes that "Left can talk to Left" were dashed by the rigidities of Stalinist Russia. But not only did a "socialist foreign policy" prove unfeasible; the expectations of collective security under an effective United Nations were also disappointed. A Labour Government, therefore, found itself compelled to resort to the detested tactics of balance of power, backed up by military force and directed to the service of vital national interests. A socialist Foreign Secretary, Ernest Bevin, was a leading agent in the establishment in 1949 of N.A.T.O., which became, and has remained, the cornerstone of British defense policy.

In imperial policy we would expect sharp differences between the parties. It was not long ago—in 1953—that a young lady addressing the annual conference of the Conservative party could speak of the Empire as "the greatest and most romantic force for good that the world has ever known and is ever likely to know." But not only did the Conservatives accept the Attlee Government's abrupt grant of independence to India; they also pursued a highly conciliatory policy toward the resurgent Egypt of Nasser in the early 1950s. When Nasser seized the Suez Canal, the British military response precipitated a sharp and very bitter division between the parties in Parliament. The rank and file of Labour voters, however, were more ambivalent, which did much to prevent the issue from being pressed persistently by the leadership. Not long after this last imperial fling, it was the Conservative Macmillan who, in his "Winds of Change" speech of 1960, inaugurated a policy that led to rapid and complete independence for Britain's remaining colonies in Africa. Thereafter, partisan arguments sometimes arose regarding the size of Britain's small military commitment "east of Suez" or Rhodesian independence or the sale of arms to South Africa. But although they reflected real differences of sentiment and approach, they did not disrupt an overwhelming agreement toward colonial and postcolonial problems.

The weightiest differences in foreign affairs have arisen over British membership in the Common Market. Neither party has been perfectly consistent in its position. In Opposition the Conservatives under Churchill welcomed the first initiatives toward European union, but once in office stayed aloof until, rather late in the day, they saw that the Common Market was a reality moving from strength to strength. As Macmillan attempted to gain entry, Labour under Gaitskell committed itself to sharp opposition. In spite of this commitment and although de Gaulle had vetoed Macmillan's effort in 1963, the Wilson Government reversed itself in 1967, only to meet with another rebuff. Once again in Opposition, Labour drifted rapidly back into its old position of resistance, leaving to the Tories under Heath the history-making task of taking Britain into Europe.

The consensus on policy and its intrinsic relation to the new pattern of politics can best be illustrated by reference to certain central features of Britain's postwar welfare state. That term has a varied usage. In this work it does not include the system of coordination and control of economic policy that was discussed under the heading of the managed economy, but rather the system of social services. This consists of not only the complex of programs centering on unemployment, sickness, and old age, but also public housing, education, and the momentous commitment to economic security embodied in the pledge of full employment. It was Labour's ambitious efforts in these areas that created the immense financial burden, the acceptance of which by the Conservatives constituted so important a step in British political development. Moreover, once in office the Conservatives not only maintained, they increased welfare expenditure. Looking specifically at expenditure on welfare grants to persons and welfare expenditure by all public authorities, we find a doubling of expenditure under the Conservatives in the fifties. From £1,537 million in 1950, the sum rose to £3,171 million in 1959. The increase was not only absolute, but also relative to personal income. As a percentage of personal income, these expenditures rose from 13.9 percent in 1950 to 16.1 percent in 1959.

The connection with the new politics comes closer to light when we look at the specific items comprised in these totals. They included national insurance benefits, consisting of retirement pensions, widows' and guardians' allowances, death grants, and unemployment, sickness, maternity, injury, and disablement benefits. They also included postwar credits, war pensions, service grants, noncontributory pensions, public assistance grants, family allowances, industrial services for the disabled, and expenditure on education, child care, and the national health services. Another important welfare expenditure not included in the above totals consisted in the housing subsidies, which also rose steeply under the Conservatives from £72 million in 1950 to £116 million in 1959.

It will be no surprise to the American reader that there is a strong tendency for each item in this multiplicity of programs to acquire a body of political supporters consisting of those who benefit from it. As consumers of these programs they have an interest in seeing them expanded and certainly in preventing them from being reduced. It is in the nature of the welfare state to produce a host of such consumer groups whose material self-interest is affected by some measure of government action, actual or prospective. The programs of services producing the "social dividend" are the more obvious examples. But groups are also brought into existence by the "social burden" of the welfare state, especially the various tax programs with their varying incidence on different categories of persons.

Consumer groups are important actors in the system of group politics that the welfare state calls into existence. Such a group politics is by no means incompatible with strong and active parties. Indeed, the two sorts of actors tend to complement one another, the party, under the severe political pressure of competition from its rival, vigorously seeking out groups with actual or potential demands that it may offer to satisfy. Where two parties are fairly evenly matched in electoral support, as in Britain in the postwar period, the resulting process of "bidding" for the votes of consumers groups becomes a principal pattern in the new scheme of politics. Thus the policy statement that was issued in 1958 by the Labour party, in its desperate bid to avoid defeat for the third time in a row, was entitled *Your Personal Guide to The Future Labour Offers YOU* and was conveniently thumb-indexed with references to "Your Home," "Education," "Health," "Age Without Fear" and so on, as if to enable tenants, workers, patients, youth, and other groups to turn directly to the promises beamed to them.

If such consumer groups occupied the center of the political stage in party conflict and won their representation through their voting potential in elections to Parliament, there was also another aspect of group politics that was no less important to the system of the collectivist consensus. The groups in this field were the producer groups of Britain's highly industrialized economy, usually appearing in their organized form as trade unions, trade associations, and professional bodies. It is these groups that won a certain legitimacy from the new acceptance of functional representation. As we have seen in our discussion of the bureaucracy and the managed economy, they also acquired a high degree of institutionalized access. Not only did the new functional pluralism of twentieth-century political culture legitimize a wide role for them as groups to be consulted. The realities of the managed economy meant that the producers who carried on the work of the various economic sectors had to be brought into close cooperation with government. Such groups possessed the expertise and skilled knowledge that government agencies had to command in order to know how to formulate and carry out their policies of intervention. Moreover, the dependence of government upon these sectors for successful implementation of a policy—for example, an export drive or an increase in productivity—meant that their hearty cooperation had to be won if the policy was to be carried out. These facts, as we have seen, often tended to give the producers groups far more than a merely advisory role.

In sum, just as there was a dual aspect to domestic policy—the welfare state and the managed economy—there was a dual aspect to the new system of politics—on the one hand, the politics of parties and consumer groups; on the other, the politics of Governments and producer groups. The two branches of politics, like the two aspects of policy, were not physically separate. The programs of welfare expenditure, for instance, were also instruments of economic management. Depending, however, on how the political situation was viewed—from the perspective of the managed economy or that of the welfare state—the flow of influence was seen to come, respectively, from producers or consumer groups. The two perspectives on the flow of power direct attention to the following relationships: (1) controlled economy: producer groups: functional representation: bargaining for cooperation and (2) welfare state: consumer groups: party government: bidding for votes.

The Relevance of Party Government

At the start of this discussion of British parties (see Chapter 8) it was stated, as a hypothesis, that the model of party government best identified the main structures of the pattern of interests in the age of collectivist politics. No final assessment is possible until we have looked more closely at the past few years—the task of the next chapter. But at this point an intermediate summary is in order.

During modern times parties have been major agents of political development in Britain. While they have often been coalitions of interest groups, they have also usually been more than that, representing conceptions of the common good and showing distinctive views of authority and purpose in the way they think, approach power, and try to change society. In this sense the interest-group model, while instructive in all periods of modernization, is incomplete without recognition of the role of party. This is not to say that party government, as presented in contemporary models, applies throughout the modern period. On the contrary, it is clear from the previous review of party development that a principal feature has been increasing differentiation. As in other modernizing processes, there has been specialization with respect to parties and the party system. Parties have become more clearly distinguished from, and independent of, other social systems, such as family, church, and economy. At the same time they have developed their own systems of communication and control in such a way that their differentiation from other elements of British society has been accompanied by an increasing formalization and rationalization of internal processes. From this process have emerged the highly organized, strongly cohesive, programmatic parties on which the contemporary models of party government are based.

When assessing the role of party, we must note the phase of the political cycle from which data are chosen. According to the concept of party government, parties are important instruments of social choice. Between their promises there is supposedly a significant difference, which in turn is reflected in the character of the policy followed by the party preferred by the electorate. In the 1950s and 1960s, however, there was so marked a convergence in what the parties promised and, even more, in what they did when in office, as to raise serious doubts about these suppositions. A virtue of the historical approach is that it puts such questions in context. In the light of recurrent cycles in British party development, it is not surprising that a period of transition, marked by sharp party strife, should be followed by a time of consensus, when party tensions relaxed and a new group politics supervened. It is in such a cycle that social choice has often been expressed and parties have done their work. This historical approach prevents the lesser role of the Labour party during the phase of consensus from obscuring its functions, first, as a challenge to which Liberals and Conservatives were obliged to respond during the interwar years, and, second, as the principal founder of the welfare state in a burst of innovation after World War II. Seen in this light, the model of party government makes good sense.

Ten

The Continuities of Collectivist Politics

During the postwar period in Britain new patterns of politics were established with a character sufficiently distinctive to justify speaking of them as the system of the collectivist consensus. The first question suggested by this observation is, Do the trends of the late sixties and early seventies show any significant departures from that system? At issue are continuities or discontinuities in functional representation and party government. But inseparable from the developmental approach of this book is a second question concerning how these trends might shape the future of British politics. The history we have looked at suggests that consensus does not last, that it is usually broken up by party realignment, and that new class divisions and new issues then arise during a time of renewed party contention and political transition. These are only possibilities, not laws of political development. They do serve, however, to focus attempts at interpreting the severe challenge to which the collectivist system is being subjected.

Functional Representation

Functional representation is inherent in the highly developed modern polity. Such a political system will mobilize a large share of the resources of the society in an effort to control the social and the natural environment. This mobilization of power at once subjects the resources of the society to greater government control and gives those in immediate command of those resources a new opportunity to influence government. "The greater the degree of detailed and technical control the government seeks to exert over industrial and commercial interests," E. P. Herring wrote many years ago, "the greater must be their degree of consent and active participation in the very process of regulation, if regulation is to be effective or success-ful."[1] The essential political point of this analysis should be kept distinct from a more familiar observation regarding economic modernization. It is well recognized that when technological development brings into exist-ence new producers groups that perform specialized functions in the division of labor, their control over these functions makes it possible for them to organize in order to use concerted action to win advantages from other groups in the economy. Thus, in the past groups of skilled workmen have organized into craft unions in order to bargain with employers. But the managed economy introduces a further source of power for producers groups: The mobilization of their talents by the polity subjects them to the state and, at the same time, gives them influence over it.

Such dependence of controller upon controlled arises not only between the public and private sectors of the modern mixed economy, but also within the public sector. For example, central planners may find them-selves obliged to make concessions in order to win the cooperation of the managers of nationalized industries. Indeed, some observers of nationali-zation in Britain have concluded that public ownership may make an industry even harder to control than when immediate power over its resources was dispersed among many owners. Similarly, within a fully socialized economy top controllers are confronted with the possibility that the bureaucrats in charge of specialized sectors may muster their skill and expertise to show that proposed tasks are impossible and, if coerced, may carry out orders only grudgingly and inefficiently. A major function of the totalitarian party is as an agency of indoctrination and surveillance to reduce the size of this problem. But in a free country the need to bargain with those being controlled is constantly heightened as the managed economy grows.

The root of the power of these functional groups is twofold. First, they constitute bodies of people performing specialized functions who acquire the capacity for unified action by being organized. As we have seen, their power arises whether their organization is part of the public or private sector. Second, the function being performed has come into existence with developing technology and consists in the exercise of specialized skill and expertise. When a government mobilizes these resources in the course of extending its management of the economy, it becomes heavily dependent upon the advice of those in command of the relevant skills and expertise.

---

[1] E. P. Herring, *Public Administration and the Public Interest* (New York, 1936), p. 192.

Advice includes sheer information, for instance, statistical data, without which neither the regulation of a particular trade nor the control of the economy as a whole would be practicable. But the advice government seeks from producers consists also of their technical knowledge and judgment. No Ministry of Economics could have a staff large enough and specialized enough to enable it to make and administer policy without the advice of the producers in the sector concerned. "The form and functioning of British Government," S. E. Finer has written, "are predicated upon the assumption that it will be advised, helped and criticized by the specialist knowledge of interested parties."[2]

Trade Unions

Organization presumably enhances the capacity of a group of people for unified action. Moreover, it is plausible to argue that the more concentrated the organization the better the chances for unified action. Some dimensions of concentration can be measured. One is density, that is, the percentage of eligibles, such as individuals or firms, that have been organized. But if there are many organizations, a high degree of density is compatible with a low degree of unity. Another dimension of concentration, therefore, is amalgamation, that is, how far those organized have been brought together into one body—whether by outright merger, by federation, or by other arrangement. Over time the trend among producers groups in Britain has been toward an increase of concentration in both dimensions.

In the case of trade unions the increase in concentration provides a good indicator of the transition to the collectivist phase of political development. From 1892 to 1953 membership in all trade unions in the United Kingdom rose from 1,576,000 to 9,524,000, an increase from 11 percent to 42 percent of the total employed population. In 1967 the total was 9,967,000, or 38 percent of an employed population of 25,986,000. In the United States that same year union membership was only 23 percent. Amalgamation, which set in strongly after World War I, has reduced the number of separate unions and produced the huge organizations of recent decades. Between 1938 and 1967 the number of unions in the United Kingdom was cut by half, and by 1967, 70 percent of union membership was concentrated in eighteen unions with over 100,000 members each.

These trends are not steady but show significant changes in rate, as can be readily seen in the figures for unions affiliated with the Trades Union Congress. A sharp increase in T.U.C. membership reflected the organiza-

---

[2]"The Political Power of Private Capital," Part II, *Sociological Review*, new series, 4 (July 1956), 14.

Table 10.1 T.U.C. Membership, United Kingdom, for Selected Years Between 1868 and 1970

Year	Number of Unions	Membership (in Millions)
1868	—	.118
1889	171	.885
1890	211	1.470
1911	202	1.662
1920	215	6.505
1938	216	4.460
1946	192	6.671
1952	183	8.020
1969	155	8.875
1970	150	9.402

DATA SOURCE: T.U.C. *Report* (London, 1970), pp. 544–546.

Table 10.2 Strike Data (annual averages) United Kingdom, for Selected Years Between 1892 and 1970

Years	Total Striker-days (in Millions)	Number of Strikes
1892–1896	13.3	760
1907–1911	7.2	570
1912–1916	13.2	890
1917–1921	31.8	1120
1922–1926	41.8	570
1927–1931	4.4	380
1937–1941	1.6	1020
1947–1951	1.9	1590
1952–1956	2.5	2100
1957–1961	4.6	2630
1962–1966	2.5	2260
1967	2.8	2120
1968	4.7	2380
1969	6.8	3020
1970	9.5	4000

DATA SOURCE: Professor H. A. Turner, Cambridge University, England.

tion of unskilled workers in the late 1880s, but from the late nineteenth century until the years before World War I there was hardly any growth in union membership. Then came the years of rapid change, when the unions reached a new plateau of strength and the Labour party struck out for sovereign power. As Table 10.1 shows, between 1911 and 1920 T.U.C. membership more than tripled, and although it fell during the years of slump, it remained more than twice what it had been before the war. In the same years, around World War I, a sharp trend toward amalgamation set in, the average size of affiliated unions rising from 8,000 to 30,000 between 1911 and 1920. A third indicator of profound change consists in the data on strikes in Table 10.2. As Table 10.2 shows, a wave of industrial action began just before World War I and rose to a peak in the years after it. The high point was, of course, 1926, the year of the General Strike. In absolute as well as in relative terms, the figures for days lost in strikes have not been approached even in recent years of industrial unrest. As the data suggest, it was the second and third decades of the twentieth century that saw the emergence of the typical problems and principal actors of the collectivist age.

Labour's peak organization, the T.U.C., has not had a serious rival since its founding in 1868 and has successfully weathered the various surges in union growth without disruptive splits such as the one between the A.F. of L. and the C.I.O. in the United States. From 1894, when T.U.C.-affiliated membership included 65 percent of all unionists, the T.U.C. has increased that proportion—with some ups and downs. In 1953 it reached 85 percent, and in 1967, T.U.C. membership included 88 percent of all unionists in the United Kingdom. Moreover, in spite of the decline of old industries, such as shipping, textiles, and mining, the T.U.C. has maintained—but only maintained—its membership relative to the economy as a whole. In both 1952 and 1969 T.U.C. membership was 34 percent of the total working population of the United Kingdom. Within the T.U.C. itself amalgamation has created a few giants. In 1970, the six largest unions embraced just about half the total affiliated membership (see Table 10.3).

Table 10.3 The Big Six in the T.U.C. (1969)

Transport and General Workers Union	1,531,607
Amalgamated Union of Engineering and Foundry Workers	1,131,252
National Union of General and Municipal Workers	803,653
National and Local Government Officers' Association	397,069
Electrical Electronic Telecommunication Union	392,401
Shop, Distributive, and Allied Workers	316,387
	4,572,369

DATA SOURCE: T.U.C. *Report* (London, 1970), pp. 792–829.

Even more important in the context of Britain's present economic problems, the two largest unions, the Transport Workers and the Engineers ("machinists" in American terminology), were headed by Jack Jones and Hugh Scanlon, respectively, both leaders in the left wing of the Labour party and in the trade union movement and both strongly disinclined to accept or implement an incomes policy, whether administered by a Labour or by a Conservative Government.

In view of the high degree of concentration in the peak organization and in its member units, the T.U.C. might seem to be well fitted structurally to coordinate and unify action on the part of the industrial working class. One of the needs of the managed economy, as we have seen, is efficient, reasonable, and authoritative producers groups that are capable of making and keeping bargains with government on behalf of large sectors of the economy (see Chapter 4). In this respect the T.U.C. has performed poorly. Perhaps the most crucial test came in the period 1964–1966, when a Labour Government attempted to cope with the wage-cost aspect of inflation through voluntary arrangements carried out in cooperation with the T.U.C. In spite of promises and good intentions, the T.U.C. was unable to act effectively and the voluntary policy had to be superseded by drastic legal action (see Chapter 4).

This weakness of the T.U.C. as a coordinating and directing body is of long standing, and many critics have urged the strengthening of its powers, especially those of the General Council, a representative body of thirty-nine that manages affairs between the annual congresses. But the inadequacies that plague the British labor movement today also have a more recent origin. As we have seen in discussing the politics of inflation, individual unions themselves have suffered a loss of authority (see Chapter 4). The leadership of national organizations and national officers has been severely challenged by the rise in power and activity of shop stewards at the workplace and by an upsurge of local bargaining between workers and employers. Local leaders have shown they can sometimes override national officers, as, for example, during the dock strike of the summer of 1970, when the militant leader of the Transport Workers found he was not militant enough for the local leadership, which obliged him to go back on terms he had found acceptable and to champion the stiffer demands pressed on him from below.

The great rise in unofficial, or wildcat, strikes is an indicator of this disruptive localism. As Table 10.2 shows, while the number of striker-days lost is still well below what it was during the great upsurge of unions fifty years ago, the number of strikes now vastly exceeds the number then. It is as if that earlier wave of industrial action reflected the rise of a united working class, while the myriad and uncoordinated actions of the present result from its decline and decomposition. In any case, it is surely an error to think of the deepening economic problems into which Britain was forced by wage-cost inflation in 1970 and 1971 as resulting simply from the irresponsibility or radicalism of national labor leadership. There is good reason to believe that many national leaders, and especially those prominent in the T.U.C., wished to moderate the self-defeating pressure for wage increases, only to find themselves confronted with a crisis of authority within their organizations that undermined their power. At the time of its 1970 meeting, a by-no-means unsympathetic journalist remarked on "the fact that with the rank-and-file running wild, the T.U.C. is facing the gravest crisis of authority in its 102-year history; that Britain is now the victim of the worst strike figures on record; and that it is high time the unions answered the hoary question: What are we here for?"[3]

Trade Associations

During the latter part of the nineteenth century, a new element was introduced into British politics through the formation of nationwide organizations based on a productive function. If trade unions were the leading example, trade associations, linking business firms, followed close behind. Their purposes were to represent employers in relations with trade unions and to provide various economic services for their members; but as government intervention in the economy grew, they also came to advocate business interests at Westminster and Whitehall. Like labor, business organization leaped forward in the years of collectivist transition, around World War I. The Federation of British Industries, which was founded in 1916 and which by the end of its first year included 62 associations and 350 individual firms, had grown by 1925 to include 195 associations and 2,100 firms.

The trend to concentration has been continuous. By the 1950s trade associations in the industrial sector were virtually all-embracing, with 90 percent of the larger firms and 76 percent of the smaller belonging to one or more of the 1,300 industrial trade associations. But as business has lagged behind labor in organizing for economic and political purposes, so also has it, on the whole, displayed a relatively lower capacity for unified action. The T.U.C. was founded in 1868, but it was not until almost one hundred years later, in 1965, that British industries finally established a single peak organization, the Confederation of British Industry (C.B.I.). British commerce was and is separately organized from industry. The Association of British Chambers of Commerce, founded in 1860, had grown by the 1950s to include some one hundred constituent chambers, with 60,000 members, which still left a large number of retail merchants federated in another organization, the National Chamber of Trade

In the industrial sector, the first solid success in interindustry organization came during World War I. This move toward amalgamation still left three organizations in the field: the Federation of British Industries (F.B.I.), which tended to group the larger firms; the National Union of Manufacturers; and the British Employers' Confederation, an overlapping body whose affiliates dealt with labor relations. It was in effect these three bodies that were finally merged in 1965. Of the 108 organizations belonging to the C.B.I., 33 operated solely as employers associations and 75 combined the functions of employers' associations with those of trade associations. After 1965 amalgamations joining the two functions continued. Compared with some other central business organizations, however, the authority of the

---

[3]David Haworth, *The Observer* (London), Sept. 13, 1970.

C.B.I. is weak. In contrast with the Swedish Employers' Confederation, for instance, it does not itself take any part in collective bargaining nor lay down the lines that associations or firms are to follow in negotiating industry agreements.

Like British labor, British business organizations, while having relatively comprehensive membership coverage, have been criticized for not having stronger and more coherent central authority. The Engineering Employers' Federation, which deals with the machine-tool industry, a crucial sector in the British economy with regard to exports and productivity, has been taken to task by a Royal Commission for an old-fashioned structure that "still has no formal place in its constitution for the large companies owning many factories which have come to play so important a part in the industry."[4] Similarly in the Federation of British Industries, the largest manufacturers were underrepresented in its governing body, the Grand Council. When a significant divergence of opinion arose between the larger and smaller firms this differential noticeably affected F.B.I. policy. Such was the case in the early sixties, when big business in Britain on the whole was strongly urging on the Government the merits of membership in the Common Market, while the smaller firms hung back. As a result the F.B.I. posture was a good deal more cautious than the consensus among the larger firms would have justified. As for the recently established Confederation, although its creation represents a major step toward more coherent organization for British business, the new body still has even less authority over its affiliates than the T.U.C. has over its member organizations.

As public policy expanded in this century, business groups, like other producers groups, were drawn into closer contact with government. Government initiative during World War I led to the creation of some trade associations and the establishment of regular contacts with many that continued into peacetime. Total mobilization during World War II vastly extended these contacts and burdened them with vital functions in the wartime economy. Many trade associations were embodied in the government machine and charged with administering specialized sectors of the economy under a system of detailed physical planning and control. At the same time, trade unions were brought into full partnership with government and business. At every level and in most spheres of policy, labor as well as business representatives were included on committees directly associated with the administrative machine. This tight system of planning did not long survive the war, but the arrangements bringing producers groups and government departments together in regular, institutionalized contact did survive. The present arrangement by which every section of industry and every firm has a "sponsoring" department in Whitehall with

---

[4]*Royal Commission on Trade Unions and Employers' Associations, Report* (London: H.M.S.O., 1968) Cmnd. 3623, p. 21.

which it exchanges information and advice, and which it may influence or be influenced by descends from that time.

The system of consultation reached a culminating point with the establishment of the N.E.D.C. in the 1960s (see Chapter 4). The main council, as well as the councils for specific industries, which ultimately numbered twenty-one, included independent experts and representatives from business, organized labor, and government. The main object was to raise the rate of economic growth, and these producers' representatives were brought directly into the government machine, since it had been learned that without their cooperation this primary goal of public policy could not be achieved. During the more ambitious phase of N.E.D.C. planning, an overall rate of growth would be set, as well as growth rates for particular industries, after which the industries would be brought into consultation to determine whether and how these goals could be achieved. After the inflationary crisis of 1966 forced the Government to lower its sights, the industries were asked to work toward more realistic assessments. In February 1969, for instance, the Government produced a "green paper"—the color signifying that its proposals had not yet been adopted, but were only up for discussion—which stated its tentative view of the prospects for the economy up to 1972. The main council then selected particular industries for detailed consultation. Among these were seven covered by industry councils, mechanical engineering, motor manufacture, machine tools, electrical engineering, electronics, chemicals, and paper and board. The specific reports, which came back to the main council in December 1969, provided the foundation for an economic assessment that was made available to government, industry, and the general public. It is said that the Treasury subsequently readjusted its forward view in the light of these commentaries.

The system was useful to the government as a way of winning the consent of industry to its programs. Moreover, it made use of the talents of each industry in criticizing its own performance—in the words of one insider, it was a case of "industry talking to itself." The better trade associations were helpful in this respect. Thus a voluminous report on the wool industry showing that many small firms would not be able to survive had a bearing on government policy toward mergers. The associations were also used to nominate members of the industry councils and to exert moral influence on firms to get cooperation. On the industry side, associations and individual firms found the councils effective in relations with government. Sheer information of what government is going to do over a period of time is crucially important to firms and industries when the public sector is as large as it is in Britain today. An industry might also have specific requests for government action with regard to export guarantees, manpower-training programs, or other forms of government aid. Its contact was usually with its sponsoring department, which was normally a member of the industry council and would take up the matter with the department from which action was desired. If the relationship did not involve bargaining in the sense of negotiation leading to an explicit, binding agreement, it did lend itself to lobbying, in that one party might indicate what it was prepared to do providing the other would reciprocate in some way.

Although the British effort had been in some degree modeled on the French method of planning, the N.E.D.C. system was a good deal less etatist than the French Commissariat du plan. The reason is not because the organized interests were too tough and hard-nosed. On the contrary, British planners even in their more ambitious moods (except in wartime) seem to follow the same consensus-seeking, rather easy-going methods as do the central authorities of organized business and labor. As an eminent civil servant frequently used to remark: "The British like a great deal of rather weak government."

Party Government

Judging by the first year of the Heath Government, the policies of its two main parties are marked by a new divergence. The novelty of this development appears when we look back at the two previous changes of the party in power during the postwar period, the first in 1951 and the next in 1964. In each of these transitions a high degree of continuity in government policy was displayed. By showing that it accepted the welfare state and the managed economy developed by the Labour Government, the Conservative party under Churchill and his successors confirmed the consensus that had been emerging in the late 1940s. A decade later, deepening economic problems led the Conservatives to take fundamentally new initiatives with regard to control of the economy. But again when the Opposition took power in 1964 these initiatives were maintained and developed, with Labour building on Conservative foundations in making its ambitious attempt at national planning and wage-price control.

Party Policy

There was, however, far less continuity between the policies of the Heath Government and its predecessor. With regard to both main branches of domestic policy, the Conservatives broke sharply with Labour. In the field of economic control, the Prices and Income Board was abolished and the Ministry of Technology was replaced by a smaller and less active Ministry of Trade and Industry. In their effort to control wage-push inflation, the Conservatives put their main reliance upon control of the public sector. In this role, according to their view, government, as the employer of a quarter of the work force, has the power to resist inflationary wage settlements on a wide front, at once relieving pressure on the economy and setting an example for employers in the private sector. This policy led to sharp confrontations with the unions, in particular to serious strikes by electricity workers and postal workers in pursuit of wage claims. Among other agencies of economic control the N.E.D.C. was retained, as we have seen, but in the modest role of a channel of communication rather than as a means of planning. In the field of economic control generally, the Heath Government diverged not only from the practices of the Wilson Government, but also from the initiatives of the Conservatives in the early 1960s.

The main thrust of Conservative policy, however, was to restrain public expenditure. This question had been crucial from the moment when the Conservatives, while in Opposition during the Attlee Government, took the essential step of adapting to Labour's revolution by accepting the huge new financial burden it entailed. Thereafter, on social (and political) grounds, welfare state expenditure was protected even in times of economic stringency during the fifties and sixties. The new approach of the Heath Government affected social policy, but its grounds were economic. What might be called the "official" Conservative view of Britain's economic problem under the Wilson Government was that Labour allowed expenditure to rise excessively, financing the new burdens by additional taxation, which reduced incentives for more efficient enterprise and added to inflation by raising the tax component of costs and reducing take-home pay. As a percentage of G.N.P., all taxes (meaning central and local taxes and national insurance contributions) fell slightly in the thirteen years of Conservative rule, 1951–1964, from 37.4 percent to 33.2 percent, only to rise steeply to 44.2 percent during the next five years under Labour. In this same period public expenditure rose from 44 percent to 51 percent of national income. From this perspective, the new divergence between the parties goes back to the middle sixties, when Labour, carrying out its generous campaign pledges, introduced a new rate of increase in public expenditure and taxation.

When Conservatives are asked what expenditures they would cut in their campaign to stimulate the economy, questions of social policy again come to the fore. Some of the things their leaders have said, supported by emerging trends of recent policy, suggest a rationale that sets off the Conservative view from the Labour view and indeed touches fundamental positions in the conflict between socialist and nonsocialist thought. Very simply put, this difference in social policy centers on the question of selectivity versus universality in welfare services. Broadly speaking, Labour's approach in setting up the services was that they should be available to everyone on the same basis. National insurance contributions and benefits would be identical for all. National health services would be free to all. Even public housing would be open to all—without a means test to determine need. The conception of universality expressed in these policies can be seen as derived from the socialist notion of equality. The rationale of selectivity derives from the quite different premise that welfare services should provide not for everyone but only for those in need. Such programs would be "poverty programs" in American terms, directing expenditure to the poor, leaving the provision of such services for people who can afford to pay for them largely to the market and to free choice.

The sharp distinctions implied by this definition of the issue cannot be fully expressed in actual government programs. Yet not only in Britain but in Europe generally, there has been a trend toward selectivity in social services. Sometimes the goal is referred to as a "two tier system," in which certain basic and heavily subsidized services will be supplied to the poor, while those better off are charged more for them, or are left free to make their own arrangements in the private market. In Britain, old-age pensions have been shifted from the universalist basis of the National Insurance Act of 1946, which provided everyone with the same benefits, to an earnings-related basis that provides that people will pay according to income and will be pensioned according to earnings. Initially put forward by Labour, this idea was carried out on a small scale by the Conservatives in the early sixties and then, under the Wilson Government, developed into a far-reaching pension bill that failed of enactment in 1970 only because of the dissolution of Parliament. The Conservatives have also proposed taking further steps toward a two-tier system by enlarging the provision for old age that would be made through private schemes. One barrier to this has been the fact that private pension plans often cannot be transferred when the employee changes employers. An item in the Conservative election program of 1970 proposed that the government take steps to make such plans transferable.

In regard to housing, the Heath Government moved to end subsidies to tenants who could provide for themselves and to relate public expenditure more closely to need. A start was made by charging those who could afford it a more economic rent for public housing. The sale of council houses to tenants was encouraged. On the other hand, the scheme for rebating rents to poorer families was extended to all tenants in public housing and for the first time to tenants in private housing as well. In the national health service, similar changes were made. Characteristic was the decision to increase the charge for prescriptions, but at the same time to extend further the exemption from payment for poorer families. A new family-income supplement scheme was announced, which similarly reflected the Government's concern with the poverty problem. This scheme provided cash payments to families who had members employed in full-time work, but who, nonetheless, were below the poverty line.

Savings on social services constituted a substantial part of the reductions the Conservative Government made in the plans for future expenditure that they had inherited from Labour. Other reductions were made in industrial and agricultural subsidies. As pledged, these prospective savings were promptly converted into tax reductions. Moreover, the first major reduction bore not on the sales tax but on the income tax. In the fall of 1970 the standard rate—a rate paid on taxed income before the scheme is graduated by the imposition of a surtax—was reduced for the first time in eleven years and brought back to where it stood before Labour raised the rate in 1964. The provision of greater incentive to taxpayers to increase their earnings was given as a principal reason for the change. Corporation tax was also reduced, and while depreciation allowances were improved, Labour's scheme for investment grants to business was abolished. Conservatives, reviewing their first steps, claimed that by the end of four years their new policies would mean a reduction in annual public expenditure of a billion pounds, obviating the need for tax increases of some 300 million and making possible tax reductions and, hopefully, more economic growth.

In their complex tradition, the Conservatives can no doubt find justification and precedent for these new departures. Yet objective circumstances as well as party outlook account for the discontinuities, just as they had much to do with the strong threads of continuity in the transitions of 1951 and 1964. British parties are confronted with the realities of getting elected and the realities of governing. Typically at the time of a previous transition, the pattern of policy worked out by the incumbent party gave promise of being adequate to these realities, so it was natural for the successor party to shape its innovations within the outlines of existing policy patterns. The frustrations and failures of the Wilson Government provoked a very different reaction from the Opposition. Circumstances that for over two decades had forced the two parties toward one another now reversed the direction of pressure, initiating a new phase of significant party strife. The parties showed that they were still functioning as instruments of social choice. This is not to say that the pressure of Britain's problems may not force further and unexpected shifts in party positions. These problems, in the private words of one high Conservative, are "almost intractable."

Party Structure

The structures of the two parties consist of very similar elements. The parliamentary side of a party includes the Leader, his circle of lieutenants, and the backbenchers, who are organized into a parliamentary body that acts as a unit and also divides into functional committees. The extraparliamentary side consists of the mass membership distributed among constituency parties—and in the Labour party, certain functional bodies such as trade unions; the annual conference and other intermediate representative bodies; and the party bureaucracy, which takes care of such matters as public relations, research, finance, and organization and which is linked with a body of professional agents serving the local parties. The interesting questions are, What are the relationships among these elements? and in particular, Are there such differences between them as to distinguish Labour and Conservative types of party government?

In theory, there are important distinguishing differences. As we have seen in Chapter 9, differing party conceptions of how authority should be structured and exercised in the larger polity also inform their respective public images. Both socialist democracy and Tory democracy have yielded versions of party government, but one has stressed the role of party adherents in giving direction to the party and its representatives in power, while the other has stressed the necessity for a leadership that will generate the initiative for a governmental record to be submitted to the voters for approval or disapproval. In actual practice there has been a convergence in structure as marked as the convergence in policy. In the first decade of this century the political ways of the two parties were as different as their leaders were distant in social origins. The Conservative Leader Arthur Balfour was a Cecil and the nephew of the Marquess of Salisbury, who had himself only recently relinquished the party leadership. J. Ramsay Mac-Donald, the illegitimate son of a Scots miner, held the post of secretary of the Labour party, which did not yet have a Leader in the traditional sense. Balfour was known to have remarked that on questions of public policy he would as soon take advice from his valet as from the annual conference of his party. The parliamentary work of the handful of Labour M.P.s, on the other hand, was dominated by the initiatives of the extraparliamentary party and the trade unions. Since that time the parties have come to look much more alike, and it is not irrelevant to note that the social origins of their two leaders are also hardly distinguishable. Wilson's father was a works chemist—a salaried technician—and Heath's a carpenter who built up a contracting business, thus enabling the press to refer to the present Prime Minister as the first Tory Leader from the working class.

With regard to the parliamentary parties, a growing similarity (see Chapter 7) has resulted from adaptation by both parties. Most notably, the Labour Leader has come to occupy a position of authority in relation to his lieutenants and backbenchers greatly resembling the present-day Tory model. That change, however, must be considered in connection with the fact that in back-bench organization and activity the Conservatives have in many respects imitated Labour. There remain traces of their differing origins. The Labour Leader must annually subject himself to reelection, a procedure that, although it is a formality when he is in office, may occasion a serious challenge when the party is in Opposition. The Conservative Leader, in contrast, while probably having no more secure tenure, retains his post without need for renewal, although he is subject to challenge. As we have seen in Chapter 7, these structural differences in the parliamentary parties become most significant if we compare the behavior of the parties in Opposition. The formal recapture by Labour backbenchers of the power to determine the party's parliamentary stand gives them more effective and continuous influence on the leadership. In contrast, the Conservative Leader, in Opposition and in office, remains the authoritative voice of party policy; and, while he must carry his backbenchers with him, he is not obliged to subject his proposals to the formal vote of a party caucus, which may accept, amend, or reject them or put forward its own.

It is, however, with regard to relations with the extraparliamentary party that the main differences in Labour and Conservative methods and spirit appear. In this respect, Conservative M.P.s and their leaders enjoy significantly more of that independent authority that in the classic Tory view of the British Constitution attaches to the governing powers (see Chapter 1). In a crucial sense this is simply a result of the contrasts in formal organization. Under the neat, written constitution of the Labour party drawn up by the Fabian Sidney Webb in 1918 and hardly changed since then, there are two sorts of members of the party, affiliated and individual. The affiliated members are organizations, mainly trade unions but also a few socialist, professional, and cooperative societies. The individual members belong to the party through local parties set up in the parliamentary constituencies. Both sorts of members are represented at the annual conference. In 1968, out of a total membership of 6.1 million, the sixty-eight trade unions accounted for 5.4 million and the 656 local parties for 701,000. Accordingly, at the conference of 1969 the union delegates cast about 90 percent of the votes. The unions affiliated with the Labour party do not, of course, include the whole of the British working class or the whole of British organized labor. From a total of 25.6 million wage and salary earners in the United Kingdom in 1970, over 10 million were trade union members, of whom some 9.4 million, in turn, were affiliated with the T.U.C. Yet the party does have the big batallions of organized labor. At the party conference each union casts its vote as a unit—in Britain this is called a "block vote," in the United States it would be called "voting by the unit rule"— so when Jack Jones rises to speak on economic policy or on the Common Market, the leadership listens attentively to the head of a union that pays affiliation fees on 1.5 million members, makes proportionately large contributions to the special funds collected for fighting general elections, casts almost 25 percent of the total vote of conference, and disposes of resources of manpower in the economy at large that are indispensable to the success of any Government.

The formal organization of the Conservative party confronts its leadership with no such concentrations of political and economic power. In contrast with Labour's arrangements, Conservative membership is wholly individual. Organized in local associations based on the parliamentary constituencies, the members of the National Union of Conservative and Unionist Associations—to give the extraparliamentary organization its proper name—annually send "representatives" (they stress this Burkean term in contrast with the Labour term "delegate") to the conference. The less-weighty character of this gathering is suggested by its greater numbers —usually some 3,000 or 4,000 compared with Labour's 1,000 or so— which make serious debate and decision making very difficult, and by the fact that regardless of size, each local association sends the same number of representatives. Industrial Britain is present, as the sprinkling of working-class accents certifies. But overwhelmingly the representatives are solid middle class. Noticeably absent among employers and managers are the opposite numbers of the big trade union leaders. Although the leaders of finance, industry, and commerce are no less partisan in their political preferences and although wealthy men have continued to be a major source of the huge (by British standards) party funds collected by Conservatives, the "top people" from these economic worlds play virtually no part in the public gatherings of the Conservative party.

This disparity in formal representation of the economic powers aligned with the two parties also applies to other elements in their coalitions. The intellectual wing is far more articulate and influential at the Labour conference. It is probably also fair to say that members of Parliament are present in larger numbers and are more active at the Labour conference than at the Conservative one. Given these differences in the "real forces" represented, it is inevitable that conference and the extraparliamentary party in general will have much more influence in the Labour party than in the Conservative party.

The formal allocations of authority in the two parties accord with these realities. Although the Labour constitution, written fifty years ago, still retains its original provision that "the work of the Party shall be under the direction and control of the Party Conference," the extraparliamentary party has retreated deeply from its old practice of "instructing" the parliamentary party. Controversy raged bitterly in the late fifties over the constitutional standing of conference decisions, when conference and leadership adopted conflicting views of British nuclear policy. At the conference of 1960, conference defeated the leadership by adopting a proposal committing the party to unilateral disarmament and virtually a rejection of N.A.T.O. Rather than accept this decision as party policy, the Leader, Hugh Gaitskell, mounted a massive campaign to reverse the decision, which he successfully accomplished at the 1961 conference. One could argue that Gaitskell's resistance showed that conference was not sovereign or, conversely, that his insistence on getting it to reverse itself showed that he did recognize its authority. More interesting, however, was the fact that in accomplishing his end, he deeply compromised his own initial position on major points. Whatever we may say about the authority of conference, this episode showed its great influence on the declared policy of the parliamentary leadership.

To compare the other representative bodies of the two parties is to see the same contrast. On the Conservative side these bodies in theory are only advisory to the Leader and in fact do not significantly influence the positions of the parliamentary party on public policy. The Central Council, which is technically the governing body of the National Union, is only slightly smaller than the conference and meets twice yearly. There is also an Executive Committee, which meets each month and which has a small General Purposes Subcommittee whose membership, like that of the Executive Committee, is largely ex officio. Quite independent of the National Union is the Conservative Central Office, which is responsible to the Leader, who appoints its principal officers. While the chairman of the Central Office is usually a prominent politician, since its reorganization after the defeat of 1964 it has had a permanent head in its deputy chairman, Sir Michael Fraser, who is not only an administrator, providing a center for the large and competent staffs of the party bureaucracy, but also an idea man, sometimes known as "the fount of all knowledge and the supplier of all briefs."

In contrast, the National Executive Committee (N.E.C.) of the Labour party has a position of large, formal authority and substantial influence. Its election by the conference ensures that the real forces present there will also be represented in the committee. The twenty-eight members are chosen as follows: twelve elected by the trade union delegates; one elected by the affiliated socialist societies; seven elected by the constituency delegates; five women elected by conference as a whole; party treasurer, elected by conference, ex officio; party Leader, chosen by parliamentary party, ex officio; and deputy party leader, chosen by parliamentary party, ex officio. Half or more of the members are usually M.P.s, and normally the N.E.C. and the parliamentary leadership, who meet together each month whether the party is in office or in Opposition, work in harmony. Yet the N.E.C. can be a source of difficulties. Not the Leader but the N.E.C. has control of the party bureaucracy, a power which it asserted vigorously in the later days of the Wilson Government by rejecting the Prime Minister's choice for party secretary. It has the power to withhold endorsements from parliamentary candidates, to disaffiliate local parties, and to expel individuals (see Chapter 7). It can take a stand on public questions that differs from the position of the parliamentary leadership, as it did in the spring of 1969, when it declared against the trade union legislation to which the Labour Government itself was committed. Its power in relation to the campaign manifesto gives it an opportunity to influence public policy that is deserving of more extended discussion.

Manifesto and Mandate

When we try to assess the influence of the extraparliamentary party organization, we can focus our question by asking what role that organization had in framing the formal pledges of the campaign and how far these pledges controlled government policy when the party held office. In short, who prepared the manifesto, and did it mandate the victorious party?

The Labour constitution provides that conference shall draw up the party "programme" and that party members, conference delegates, candidates for Parliament, and members of Parliament must "accept and conform" to it. More to the point, the constitution also provides that the parliamentary committee and the National Executive Committee shall jointly decide what items from the programme shall be included in the manifesto issued on the occasion of a general election. Judging by what went on during the last significant phase of policy making by the party, this constitutional formula is still a good guide to what actually happens. In 1961 conference debated and approved a lengthy statement of home policy, *Signposts for the Sixties,* which had been drawn up by the National Executive Committee and which, keying its appeal to "the scientific revolution," stressed economic planning and expansion, land use, social security, educational equality and tax reform. Three years later the election manifesto, *The New Britain,* did draw heavily in tone and in content upon the earlier and longer document.

To identify the sources and influences that were actually responsible for the ideas embodied in these documents is a more complex matter. The pledges did not originate with conference, if by "originate" is meant that they derived from the resolutions put forward by local parties and trade unions. Those energies of the party were brought into play by the struggles between Left and Right over such great symbolic issues as nuclear policy. With regard to these issues, conference did leave its mark on the manifesto. The compromise to which the leadership had been forced in nuclear policy was reflected in the manifesto's virtual pledge to give up "the independent British deterrent." The proposal to renationalize the steel industry went back to repeated confirmations in party pronouncements dating from the interwar years and carried out by the Attlee Government. Although many of the revisionist leaders of the party regarded public ownership as irrelevant to Britain's problems and to socialism, it would have been impossible to omit this pledge, such was the strength of favorable sentiment in the party generally and in conference in particular. (Incidentally, it is worth noting that although the Conservatives had reversed the earlier act of nationalization, they omitted any mention of renewed denationalization in their 1970 manifesto and seemed to be ready to let public ownership stand, subject only to marginal measures of hiving off.)

The initiatives in framing the new policies came from the higher echelons of the Labour party, but they were diverse. The broad thrust to modernize the party and to get away from the old "cloth cap" socialism, with its rigid pledges of universal nationalization, was widely supported among the parliamentary leaders. The actual proposals owed a great deal to the Research Department, which at that time was headed by Peter Shore, an exceptionally imaginative reformer and later a Cabinet Minister. Some of the more complex and technical proposals came from outside experts. For example, the reform of old-age pensions in such a way as to break from the old flat-rate scheme and relate payments to the previous earnings of pensioners was largely developed by Richard Timuss of the University of London and a group of his co-workers. The task of drawing up what proved to be the decisive document, *Signposts of the Sixties,* was given by the National Executive Committee to a subcommittee consisting of four M.P.s and three trade unionists. It was not a radical body, but under the chairmanship of Harold Wilson, then still nominally a leader of the Left, it modified the original draft from the Research Department so as to produce a thoroughly revisionist statement, which it was hoped would appeal to the growing proportion of white-collar workers in the economy. In the years leading up to the election of 1964, the parliamentary leadership was fundamentally united in its outlook and, within broad limits set by party opinion, had its way in determining policy positions.

As for the extent to which a Labour manifesto can mandate a Labour Government, the experience of the Wilson regime is instructive. In spite of the compromise of 1961 that Britain should "cease the attempt to remain an independent nuclear power"[5] and the virtual pledge of 1964 against an "independent British deterrent," after six years under the Wilson Government, Britain still had her own nuclear armament. Broadly, foreign policy and related questions of defense have not shown themselves to be likely subjects for programmatic commitment. The principal reason is that pledges of action and achievement in foreign affairs are not wholly subject to the control of the sovereign nation, but also depend for their success upon the vagaries of other powers as well. That was the bitter experience of the Attlee Government, which took office committed to warm relations with Russia. Under less tragic circumstances, Harold Wilson learned the lesson again when his bid to enter the Common Market was abruptly vetoed by de Gaulle.

When we compare the pledges of the manifesto with the record of government action in various fields of domestic policy, however, their conformity is impressive. R. H. S. Crossman has said:

---

[5] *Labour Party Conference Report* (The Labour Party, 1961), p. 8.

One of the things which most interested me in 1964 was to see the way in which the Mandate was honoured, sometimes embarrassingly. There were one or two parts of the Mandate which I always thought were doubtful. We set about carrying them all out—good, bad, indifferent.[6]

As pledged, a vast system of national economic planning was established; steel was renationalized; a Ministry of Technology was set up; regional planning was developed; a capital-gains tax was enacted; retirement, sickness, and unemployment benefits were increased; health-service charges were abolished; rent decontrol was halted; expenditure on housing, education, and hospitals was increased; a commission was set up to acquire land for public housing; and comprehensive public education was encouraged instead of the segregating of students according to ability. The promises were not as specific, numerous, or radical as those made in the famous manifesto of 1945. Yet the record of performance compares favorably. Since such action usually costs money, the mandate was in large part responsible for the steep rise in taxes from 33.2 percent of the G.N.P. in 1964 to 44.2 percent in 1970. As the party boasted in a review of its record, "public expenditure levels in the social programme have been raised by up to 70 percent in five years."[7]

When we turn to the party's promises on what their policies would accomplish, however, the failures begin to mount up. Inflation was not controlled, nor the pound defended, nor economic growth stimulated, nor unemployment avoided. As in Attlee's time, the party found that it was far easier to expand government services than to control the economy. Indeed, the two aims often came into conflict. As one junior Minister later remarked, "We carried out our mandate on social policy so faithfully that we were unable to carry out our promises with regard to the economy."

The function of manifesto and mandate in the Conservative party can be described more briefly, because the process is not complicated by doctrines such as Labour's powerful belief in intraparty democracy. The parliamentary leadership does have a freer hand. Yet since World War II the party has made increasing use of policy statements and shown increasing concern with election manifestoes. In 1945 the closest thing to a program or manifesto produced by the Conservatives was a brief message entitled "Mr. Churchill's Declaration of Policy to the Electors." But in the wide-ranging party reorganization that followed its crushing defeat in the 1945 election, the policy statement authorized by the Leader, published in pamphlet form and distributed by the millions, became a major feature of Conservative propaganda. Since that time great energy and attention have been given to the development of policy ideas, both as a means of

---

[6]R. H. S. Crossman, *The Myths of Cabinet Government* (Cambridge, Mass., 1972), p. 96.

[7]*Labour Party Conference Report* (London: H.M.S.O.,1969), p. 385.

winning elections and as a basis for governing the country. After the defeat of 1964, the party launched an elaborate review of policy. As many as thirty-six groups were put to work, drawing their members from Parliament, business, and the universities, and utilizing the services of the Research Department. In a new departure, Heath submitted a statement of policy to the conference in 1965, but only for discussion not for approval or disapproval, and no votes were taken. This document showed the new directions of Tory policy that were to be associated with Heath's leadership. It did not mention economic planning or an incomes policy, both of which had been stressed previously by Conservatives, but instead emphasized tax reduction, trade union reform, selectivity in social services, and the Common Market. From it were drawn the main themes of the manifestoes of 1966 and 1970. In the prolonged policy-making exercise leading up to the election of 1970, the voice of the Leader predominated. "He got his own way in policy and he got his own men where he wanted them," was the way one insider summed up the results.

During the first year of the Heath Government, as we have seen, the Tories sought to carry out their campaign pledges with almost doctrinaire rigor. "I take election promises seriously," remarked Heath after a year in office, "and we have been at great pains to fulfill them. I find that many of my colleagues bring a copy of the election manifesto to Cabinet meetings. At the last count we found that we have already redeemed 79 election pledges."[8] One reason for this emphasis was a recognition of the political advantage of promise keeping, and in the spring of 1971 Conservative publications continually directed attention to the correspondence of government action with pledges of the manifesto. While Tory values endow Conservative leaders with a wide sphere of independent authority within the party and within the polity, the leaders' judgment of electoral consequences may cause them to behave like adherents of mandate theory. In the case of Prime Minister Heath, moreover, the system of elaborate program making and his campaign pledges strengthened his hand when he won power. The whole business had been conducted under his close supervision and control and very much reflected the new direction he wished to give Conservative and British policy. Supported by party and by public approval of his proposals, Heath's leadership in policy making was strengthened against fractious Ministers, civil servants, and backbenchers. In this curious manner the democratic mandate enhanced Tory authority.

---

[8] *The Sunday Times* (London), June 20, 1971, p. 10.

Eleven

The Challenge to Collectivist Politics

The previous account reveals changes from the collectivist system, although hardly a profound breach with it. Functional representation has declined from what it was in the fifties and early sixties. Certainly, party conflict has revived as the deepening problems of the economy have been met by a pronounced and even ideological differentiation of party positions. If we look toward the grass roots rather than the commanding heights of the polity, however, mounting evidence suggests more important developments. It does not indicate a clear and indubitable outcome. Yet the signs of qualitative change are too strong to permit us to overlook the question, Is British politics undergoing a system change comparable to the major transformations that marked earlier phases of party modernization? [1]

The flaring up of party strife may simply be a renewal of conflict between two old antagonists who will remain essentially unchanged in an unchanging party system. On the other hand, it may constitute the kind of breach of consensus that in the past has led to the emergence of quite new structures and issues and the transition to a new phase of party development. It is useful and necessary to ask this broad question, for when a state of affairs has lasted a generation or so and we have gotten used to it, it is very easy to assume in the very questions we put to the facts that no major change in that state of affairs is taking place. Yet past history warns against this assumption as applied even to slow-moving, phlegmatic England and forces one to keep in mind that these present changes may not be merely a variation within the collectivist system, but rather a departure from it.

Indicators of such possibilities are of three sorts: strong evidence of organizational decomposition with regard to both parties, a new volatility in voting behavior suggesting the breakup of old class solidarities, and the emergence in substantial numbers of nonparty political groups stressing decentralized and participatory reforms.

Party Decomposition

Signs of party decomposition abound in Western democracies. In the United States in recent years, party identification has dropped sharply and ticket splitting has risen to new heights. Similar evidence of loss of support for parties can be found in France and Germany and, ironically, may be a necessary condition for the recent trend toward a two-party system in each country. In Britain one major indicator has been a decline in the mass organization at the local level.

The term "mass organization" itself deserves some analysis, since, taken literally, it has seriously misled many students of British politics. Each of the parties includes a network of local organizations based on parliamentary constituencies and containing individual dues-paying members. Each party has branches in the wards or polling districts where electioneering for local as well as parliamentary candidacies is conducted. On the Conservative side, an annual general meeting open to all members elects the officers of the association, who, with representatives from the branches and certain others, constitute the governing body, the Executive Council. One of the most important tasks of the association is to hire an election agent who is trained and certified by the Central Office and who will supply professional knowledge of Britain's complex election laws and of techniques for conducting campaigns and winning elections. A party bureaucrat, the agent is little concerned with policy and looks forward to a career as an organizer rather than as a candidate or boss.

In selecting its parliamentary candidate the local association also acts under some guidance from the Central Office. The National Union will suggest names of likely possibilities. (It should be remembered that in Britain the candidate does not need to live in his constituency, and about half the M.P.s come from outside.) Before final adoption of its choice at a general meeting of the association, the approval of a central committee of the Union and the parliamentary party must also be obtained. Actually, approval is virtually automatic, and in their selections the local associations show that the "complete autonomy" attributed to them under the party rules is no misnomer. An American, thinking of his own political system, will not find this autonomy strange, but he will be thoroughly baffled by the absence of open public competition. The solicitation of support by aspirants must be done modestly, quietly, and certainly not through public meetings or campaigning among party members to win their support. The main work is done by the Executive Council and its small selection committee.

Quite similar is the Labour-party variation on the basic structure, which goes back to the nineteenth century and, indeed, was adapted from American innovations in party organization. One difference is that the governing body, usually called the General Management Committee, includes delegates not only from the wards, but also from branches of other organizations, especially trade unions. This body elects an executive committee and other officials, including a secretary who is often the election agent.

This structure, as its Jacksonian antecedents suggest, could make possible wide participation and lively competition within the local parties. British parties have indeed mobilized the electorate to the extent that remarkably large numbers regularly pay dues. In 1969 the Conservatives estimated their individual members numbered 2,225,000, while Labour reported 701,000. This does not necessarily reflect great commitment. In the Labour party the minumum annual subscription is still only $3.00 (£1.20) of which 35 cents goes to the national party. In the Conservative Party it is even less. In effect a delegate committee of perhaps a hundred persons in each local party runs its affairs. This applies even to the selection of a parliamentary candidate, a practice made more remarkable by the fact that three-quarters of the seats are safe, making selection by the local party committee in those cases tantamount to election. The same restraint is carried over to the readoption of an incumbent M.P. Unlike the American congressman, who often has to face a sharp primary contest for renomination, the M.P., once elected, is virtually certain of readoption by his local party at the next election; and challenges, while technically possible, are virtually unknown. Objectively, the structure of British parties makes possible the kind of wide participation and open competition that characterized American parties in the days of the delegate-convention system. Subjectively, however, the norms of British political culture rigidly rule it out.

While the reports of membership given by the parties cannot be taken as enumerations of committed activists, the movements of these figures are indicators of the changing strength of the local party organizations. Taken in this light, the recent trends in party membership reflect severe decline. Membership in the Conservative party, which had numbered 1 million in 1946, and rose to 2.8 million in 1953, sank to 1.5 million by 1969. On the Labour side, the data point to an even deeper slump. From 1928, when it was first reported, individual membership mounted steadily (except during the war years), reaching a peak of about 1 million in 1953. Then the figures began a steady decline that in fifteen years reduced them by 30 percent and has shown no sign of being reversed.

Equally serious is the failure of the trade union section of party membership to grow. Although the figure for trade union membership is in a sense nominal, representing the decision of unions to allocate certain sums from their political funds to the Labour party, a lessening of the will or the ability to increase these contributions signifies a serious loss of momentum. The work force in Britain grows, but the Labour party, like the unions, embraces a diminishing share of its members and of their resources and support. The consequences are sharply focused by the decline in the number of agents. While Labour has never been able to maintain a corps of agents as well paid or as numerous as those in the Conservative party, in 1951 it managed to field 296 full-time agents in Great Britain. By the election of 1970 this number had fallen to 141, in contrast with 396 on the Conservative side.

Class and Voting

The body of party activists has declined in number and performance, especially on the Labour side. Serious as this is for the so-called mass party, its meaning becomes apparent only if it is seen as one expression of a deep-running shift in political sentiment. Another indication is the way British voting behavior in recent years has departed sharply from the established patterns of the collectivist system. The essentials of that pattern were a very high correlation of class and party and, in consequence of this, a steady attachment of two great class-based blocs of voters o their respective parties.

A few years ago a writer authoritatively summed up the consensus among political scientists: "Class is the basis of British politics; all else is embellishment and detail."[1] What this means can be most readily seen in data taken from the Gallup surveys. These surveys divide the electorate into four social classes: upper middle class (6 percent), middle class (22 percent), working class (61 percent), and very poor (11 percent). Table 11.1 shows the strong and persistent correlation between class and party preference. More than half of the two lower classes have regularly voted Labour, with the figure for the very poor occasionally touching two-thirds. The two upper classes are much the more partisan, giving two-thirds to three-quarters and more of their support to the Conservatives. In all advanced countries class is one of the weightiest factors affecting electoral behavior, but comparative study has shown that it is exceptionally important in Britain. Compared with three other English-speaking countries—the United States, Canada, and Australia—Britain has the highest level of class voting. Table 11.2 shows the contrast with the United States.

---

[1]Peter Pulzer, *Political Representation and Elections: Parties and Voting in Great Britain* (New York, 1967), p. 98.

Table 11.1 Class and Voting, Great Britain (in Percent)

	Upper Middle Class		Middle Class		Working Class		Very Poor	
	1950	1966	1950	1966	1950	1966	1950	1966
Conservative	79	79	69	66	36	34	24	19
Labour	9	5	17	14	53	46	64	51
Liberal	10	6	14	7	11	5	12	5

DATA SOURCES: Henry Durant, "Voting Behaviour in Britain, 1945–1964," in Richard Rose (ed.), *Studies in British Politics* (New York: St. Martin's, 1966), p. 123; and *Gallup Political Index, 1966* (London: The Gallup Poll).

Table 11.2 Class and Voting Preference, U.S. and Great Britain (in Percent)

	United States (1960)		Great Britain (1959)		
	Republican	Democratic	Conservative	Labour	Liberal
Nonmanual	55	45	72	19	9
Manual	40	60	27	63	10

DATA SOURCE: Robert R. Alford, *Party and Society* (Chicago: Rand McNally, 1963), pp. 348, 352.

A more sophisticated analysis of the relationship has been presented in a recent study.[2] It shows that British voters tend strongly to think in terms of two classes, the working class and the middle class, and to use occupation rather than wealth, education, or other marks of status as their basis for assigning individuals to one or the other class. When occupations are ranked according to prestige, they tend to fall into two broad groupings, the working class and the middle class. The line between the two groupings, however, does not fall precisely between manual and nonmanual occupations, which is the boundary commonly used in correlation studies. The British voter himself tends rather to draw the line within the area of nonmanual occupations. Those in nonmanual occupations with supervisory tasks, such as draftsmen, local government officials, and secretaries with subordinates, are assigned to the middle class, along with the lower and higher managerial occupations. But on the working-class side of the cleft are those in routine nonmanual occupations, such as policemen, shop assistants, and transport inspectors, along with skilled and unskilled manual workers. The importance of this classification becomes apparent when party identification is related to occupation. The lower nonmanual workers, although generally regarded as working class by British voters themselves, prove to be much more strongly Conservative than the voters in the manual occupations (see Table 11.3).

---

[2]David Butler and Donald Stokes, *Political Change in Britain: Forces Shaping Electoral Choice* (New York, 1969), Chapter V.

Table 11.3 Party Self-Image by Occupational Status, 1963 (in Percent)

	Higher Managerial	Lower Managerial	Supervisory Nonmanual	Lower Nonmanual	Skilled Manual	Unskilled Manual
Conservative	86	81	77	61	29	25
Labour	14	19	23	39	71	75

SOURCE: David Butler and Donald Stokes, *Political Change in Britain: Forces Shaping Electoral Choice* (New York: St. Martin's, 1969), p. 77. Reprinted by permission of St. Martin's Press, The Macmillan Company of Canada, and Macmillan London and Basingstoke.

Like the Gallup data, Table 11.3 shows the strong correlation between class and party preference, Conservative strength increasing and Labour strength decreasing as we move up the occupational scale. But it is also evident that even in class-bound Britain there are marked deviations from a strict class-party correlation. At the upper end of the occupational scale, among the managerial groups, Labour has a significant following. We find here those "middle-class radicals" who have been important and influential in the Labour party since the great days of the Fabian Society. From the interwar period, when the reorganization of the party opened up individual membership to them, they have provided a disproportionate share of Labour M.P.s and Labour Cabinets. In the postwar period, their role increased. While Ministers from working-class backgrounds provided half the membership of Attlee's Cabinet, by October 1969, in the Wilson Cabinet, there were none. Similarly in the House of Commons, one of the most striking changes has been the increase in the number of Labour M.P.s from middle-class backgrounds, especially teachers and university lecturers (see Chapter 5).

In a more general sense, this political splitting of a higher class has been of crucial importance to the operation of the British polity. A necessary condition for the functioning of the governing class has been the fact that substantial numbers of people from a higher class have supported and given leadership to the parties of innovation that drew the bulk of their support from lower social strata. Whigs, Liberals, Radicals, and Socialists have numbered them among their leaders.

We might think it more peculiar, and therefore especially deserving of study, for a member of the middle or upper class to side with a socialist party than for a member of the working class to accept the leadership of a party strongly based in the professional and managerial elites. Nevertheless, it is not the middle-class socialists but the working-class Tories who have attracted more attention from political scientists. As the Gallup data show, Conservatives have continued to win the support of a third of the manual workers. This comes to about one-half the total Conservative vote. Today, as in earlier decades of British democracy, the working-class Tories have been essential to Conservative success. Among these millions, the figure of principal interest has been the deference voter. The term "deference voter," like the motivation it tries to capture, is complex. It derives from the comments of nineteenth-century observers, and the tone of the relationship is caught in such nineteenth-century portraits of interclass harmony as those of Gurth and Ivanhoe or Samuel Weller and Mr. Pickwick. In the motivation of the deference voter there is sometimes an element of pure ascription: the notion that the right to rule belongs to certain persons simply because of who they are—"They're my guv'nors," as working-class Tories sometimes still say. But the deference voter normally does not disregard consequences. He identifies the people to whom he defers by certain well-known signs of class status: accent, upbringing, occupation, and education, not to mention handwriting, table manners, and time of dining—a whole style of life. At the same time, he thinks instrumentally, taking upper-class status as a probable indication of superior political competence, as these responses illustrate:

> They [i.e., the Conservatives] have some of the best brains in the country. They are altogether more successful and brainy than the Labour, and they have a great deal of experience behind them. They've a tradition of governing and leadership behind them for generations.
>
> They have been brought up to rule, to take over leadership. They have been educated to a certain extent to take over. They have no axe to grind for themselves. They look out for other people.
>
> The Tory people are the brains of the country. They know how to get things done. Everyone of them is a man you can look up to and respect.[3]

The peculiarity of the deference voter is that he finds the guarantee of Tory competence in upbringing or, as he often says, in "breeding." In popular form, this is precisely the theory of Tory democracy, with its premise of a governing class brought up in a tradition of public service (see Chapter 9). The distinctiveness of the deferential outlook appears in contrast with the attitude of other working-class Conservatives, who are sometimes called "secular" or "pragmatic." The latter also hold the Tory party to be of superior competence, but their judgment is based not on the superior upbringing of the Tory politician, but on his demonstration of ability by achievement in business, government, or other spheres.

The attitudes of the deference voter descend from Britain's distant past and reflect the adaptation to the institutions of democracy of the premodern belief that inequality and hierarchy are necessary conditions of social order. In accord with the historical origins of their attitudes, deferential voters accept the existence of class stratification; but instead of seeing class

---

[3] Robert McKenzie and Allan Silver, *Angels in Marble: Working Class Conservatives in Urban England* (Chicago, 1968), p. 109.

as a divisive force, they regard it as an integrating one. Whereas the socialist working-class voter is likely to see class as dividing society horizontally and separating parties, the deferential working-class Tory sees it as vertically uniting one level of society with others. Deferential voting is thus one kind of class-based voting. Numerically it has constituted perhaps a quarter to a half of the Conservative vote among the working class. As class declines as an important political force in British society, not only will working-class support for Labour be affected, but so also will this large bloc of support for the Conservatives.

The New Volatility

The correlation between class and party preference (or voting) remains high, as shown by the data for the general election of 1970 in Table 11.1. Yet there are many powerful indications of a severe weakening of class as a force determining political attitudes. In a study of groups of voters who had entered the electorate at different times in the past, Butler and Stokes found that among both working-class Labour voters and middle-class Conservatives the belief in politics as a conflict of class interests increased for each successive age-cohort (groups of persons born during a certain period) of the interwar and wartime years and declined markedly among those who first entered the electorate after 1951. Perceptions of difference between the parties followed the same trends, the proportion of respondents seeing a "good deal" of difference declining in the postwar period.

In this connection the number who replied "Don't Know" when asked what party they would vote for in a general election is also significant. As Table 11.4 shows, the "Don't Knows," after rising gradually in the postwar period, took a sharp surge upward during the late 1960s. This suggests a weakening of attachment to party and, given the strong class orientation of British voters in the past, supports the notion that class is losing power as a determinant of party preference. Likewise, the steady decline in turnout at general elections, which fell from 84 percent in 1950 to 72 percent in 1970, is compatible with a decline in partisan attachment. The bearing of turnout on the role of class appears especially when it is noted that turnout fell markedly in solid working-class areas, particularly mining areas, while it rose slightly in almost all other types of constituency. The contrast with political behavior a decade or two ago is suggested by the 1960 Gallup poll, which concluded that no more than 20 percent of the electorate had ever changed parties and that of those who did change, most were Liberals.

With these declines in class-based political attitudes and partisan identification has gone a striking increase in electoral volatility. The voters, who seemed in the forties and fifties to change their party support only slowly

Table 11.4 Don't Know Percentages in Gallup Polls

Year	Average
1947	11
1948	15
1949	15
1950	9
1951	12
1952	11
1953	12
1954	13
1955	13
1956	16
1957	17
1958	17
1959	16
1960	16
1961	16
1962	17
1963	17.5
1964	17
1965	15.5
1966	15
1967	16.5
1968	21
1969	22.5
1970	17.5
1971 (first six months)	18.5

DATA SOURCE: *Gallup Political Index, 1947–1971* (London: The Gallup Poll).

and infrequently, now shift rapidly back and forth among the parties and "Don't Knows." Not long ago, once a Government had won power, it could count on enjoying wide public support for a period of years. In the emerging pattern, by contrast, a Government barely takes power before its public support begins to slip away and by-election defeats erode its majority. Moreover, changes of opinion among the electorate may be even greater than the shift away from one party indicates. This effect has been brought out by surveys conducted by the Conservative Central Office, which, especially since the mid-sixties, has made an extensive and highly professional use of survey research. Between the 1964 and 1966 general elections, the Conservative vote dropped from 11.6 million to 11 million. This small net change, however, was the result of large movements back and forth between the parties. Apparently, some 3.5 million Conservative voters moved away from the party, while some 2.9 million who had not supported the party in 1964 shifted over to the Conservative column. Overall, some millions of voters had changed parties.

The new volatility of British political opinion is also brought out in other survey data. One measure is the monthly change in the ratio of support for the two parties as shown in the Gallup surveys. When, for instance, the survey for one month shows Conservative support as 35 percent and Labour support as 30 percent and for the next month as 37 percent and 29 percent respectively, the Conservative lead has moved from 5 percent to 8 percent, constituting a change of 3 percent over these two months. In the early postwar years these changes were moderate. But between 1948 and 1970 the yearly average rose from 2 percent to 6 percent.

The raw data themselves indicate that something quite unusual has been happening in British politics. The Gallup monthly surveys measuring support for the parties were begun in 1947. On a graph the curves of support for the two main parties show a new pattern emerging in the sixties. While for the earlier postwar period the curves are relatively flat, for the sixties the slopes become markedly steeper, indicating large shifts of support up and down in short periods of time. Whether the central tendency of support for a party over a longer period of time, such as a year, was up or down, the dispersion of support around that tendency at shorter intervals had clearly increased. A conventional method of measuring such dispersion is to calculate the standard deviation. When this is done for the monthly data for each year, as in Table 11.5, volatility becomes vividly apparent, especially for the Labour party in the late sixties. On the Conservative side volatility showed some slight rise in the sixties, although the main increase took place in 1957 and 1958, when the party was in power, and just before the general election of 1959. Since 1965, on the other hand, Labour support in its up-and-down movements showed a volatility unmatched in the previous generation. Indeed, it was the volatility of the electorate that was responsible for the fact that almost all public opinion polls erred in their forecasts of the winner in 1970. Contrary to previous experience, the campaign did significantly affect voting intentions, and a late swing to the Conservatives just before polling day was missed by nearly all surveys.

Bases of Class Behavior

The most striking aspect of the general election of 1970 was not the Conservative victory in the face of contrary predictions by the polls, but rather the wide, wild swings of voter opinion between the parties in the years before the election—which, moreover, have continued after it. During the campaign, a Labour party agent of a London constituency was asked about this new volatility. "People don't vote the way they used to," he replied. "They don't vote like their fathers. They don't vote as members of a community or a class, but as a matter of individual choice." Normally in the past, in Britain perhaps even more than in other modern polities, a

Table 11.5 Index of Party Volatility Standard Deviations for British Gallup Polls

Year	Labour	Conservative
1947	6.86	4.91
1948	1.30	2.50
1949	2.33	4.07
1950	2.50	1.25
1951	6.02	2.27
1952	4.16	2.45
1953	1.25	1.45
1954	2.34	1.90
1955	0.74	2.24
1956	1.97	2.61
1957	2.36	11.34
1958	1.64	15.85
1959	1.46	6.47
1960	3.44	0.68
1961	1.80	4.72
1962	2.66	3.00
1963	1.81	1.35
1964	3.73	4.10
1965	8.04	6.24
1966	12.59	2.75
1967	14.48	6.39
1968	12.75	7.35
1969	14.90	4.53
1970	8.42	2.96
1971 (first six months)	7.31	7.08

DATA SOURCE: *Gallup Political Index, 1947–1971* (London: The Gallup Poll).

massive array of influences and institutions has corseted the individuality of the voter: family, neighborhood, class, church, pressure groups, parties, and so on. In this way political opinions and party preferences have been stabilized and indeed made heritable, and political leaders have been provided with those cohesive majorities that are necessary for steady and coherent governance.

As modernization proceeds, these old protective influences break up and fall away, leaving the individual voter isolated and unsupported, an atom in the mass electorate. Left to rely upon his own "private stock of reason"—to quote Burke's admonitory phrase—and whirled along by the forces of electronic communication, he will inevitably swing back and forth in his judgment of men, governments, and parties.

A new atomism in British society appears to be producing a new individualism in British politics. Negatively stated, the change appears especially as a decline in class solidarity, affecting both party activists and party voters. Local organization flags as activists fail to maintain old levels of effort and recruitment. Party voters generally draw back from their old allegiances—or, in the case of new voters, fail to develop the deep attachments felt by their fathers—and easily and frequently switch their political preference. While these changes also affect Conservatives, they are especially vivid on the Labour side. Not just the party, but also the trade unions are affected—the whole of what was called "the Movement." Like the party, unions are also faltering in recruitment and losing the loyalty of those who do remain members. Strikes tend to be numerous, small, and locally inspired. The push they give to price rises does at least as much harm to workers generally as to the profit makers, and it certainly does more harm to the unorganized and the poor. It would appear that while the great wave of industrial action in the first and second decades of this century reflected the rise of a united working class, the myriad uncoordinated strikes of the present phase result from its decline and decomposition (see Chapter 10).

Such a development seems natural and logical when we project some of the inherent tendencies of modernization. The concept of class is complex and ambiguous, but in political analysis it has commonly been used to identify certain sorts of social and economic conditions that promote concerted action among a number of people. As we have seen, in Britain two broad groupings of occupations can be identified whose members tend to vote similarly. Occupation has been an excellent indicator of the class to which a person will be assigned by himself and by others and of how he will vote. When we ask, however, what it is about an occupation that has led people to assign it to one class or another, no simple answer appears.

One influential aspect is standard of living. A person's occupation is a good rough index of his income and thus of what he can buy in the way of food, clothing, housing, education, and recreation. In this respect a qualitative change has transformed the standard of living of all occupational groups and classes in Britain, as in other Western countries, as a stage of unprecedented productive power has ushered in the age of affluence. Slums can still be found, and serious destitution afflicts many families. But the massive squalor of working-class London that horrified the reformers of the late nineteenth century, and which could still be found in spots during the interwar years, no longer exists. Moreover, the welfare state has supplemented the rise of affluence by creating a new level of security explicitly guaranteed by the society as a whole. Marked differences in standard of living remain, but the old inequities in material style of life between the working class and the middle class have been blurred and reduced.

During the 1950s, as real income in Britain rose an average of 3 percent a year under a Conservative regime and automobiles, refrigerators, and TV sets were acquired by families of all classes, Labour continued to lose, in four successive elections receiving a steadily declining percentage of the two-party vote. Some observers not unnaturally found in the new levels of consumption the roots of a political *embourgeoisement* that was turning the working class away from the old "cloth-cap" socialism. This view of the new political realities inspired the rise of revisionism under Hugh Gaitskell and, after him, Harold Wilson. The victories of the mid-sixties appeared to vindicate the revisionist analysis.

It may be doubted, however, that a social sentiment as strong as class identification can be greatly affected by a mere change in consumption levels. Another basis of class is often found not on the consumption but the production side of economic relations. In the Marxist view class distinctions are related to the mode of production, the owners of private property being set off from, and opposed to, the nonowners. This foundation for concerted behavior on the part of opposing classes, however, has also been greatly eroded in the collectivist phase of modernization. Ownership has become widely diffused. The control of economic enterprise has shifted into the hands of men who are not owners, but managers, while on lower levels the workers have formed unions and have dealt collectively with management. Thus the sharp distinction between owners and nonowners has been lessened by bureaucratization, and a degree of industrial democracy has moderated the conflict of interests and institutionalized its management.

Already during the early decades of this century in Britain, the rise of organized labor and organized business was marked by these tendencies. Also the huge growth of the public sector has absorbed from the private sector many of the conflicts between levels of a bureaucratized economy. At the same time, technology has further diminished distinctions among the various strata of employees by increasing the proportion of nonmanual to manual workers. In manufacturing alone, for instance, between 1954 and 1964 administrative, technical, and clerical workers rose from 18.4 percent to 23.1 percent of the work force.

A third and more fundamental basis of class distinctions is power: the ability of one person to impose his will upon another person. The concept is broad. It includes the ability to control others that results from shared conceptions of authority, as in the political system, or from other legitimizing beliefs, such as the right of the employer to hire and fire. It also extends to control based on physical force, economic benefits, or psychological identification. Income and property as determinants of class are specific forms of the broad category of power. Income is power over the labor and products of others, and property in the means of production is power to organize the labor utilizing them. Degree of power is a major determinant of the schemes of social evaluation expressed in popular conceptions of class. It is significant that in distinguishing between the two main classes, British respondents draw the line not precisely between manual and nonmanual occupations, but between the nonmanual occupations with and those without supervisory duties.

The possible foundations of a class system are as subtle and numerous as the forms of power. Seen in this light, the elimination of class may seem an endless quest, each new stage of equality being achieved only to reveal a new dimension of domination and subjection. To eliminate private property and equalize incomes would not necessarily eliminate class, because great differences in power might remain. Indeed, under some circumstances these steps might intensify class distinctions and class conflict—if the new polity were founded on dictatorial bureaucratic socialism, for example.

Income, property, and power in their protean forms help account for class-based behavior. They are sometimes referred to as "objective" bases of class, a term that is permissible only if it is recalled that social relationships are never objective in the sense of being purely physical patterns, but always involve meaning. Keeping this in mind, we may identify another aspect of class that is relatively more subjective. This consists in a culturally conditioned mode of perceiving the objective relationships of affluence, ownership, organizational position, and domination and subjection. With respect to this cultural aspect, societies may differ greatly even though they resemble one another in economic structure. Thus although both countries are highly industrialized, the sense of class is much stronger in Britain than in the United States. In Britain a "sense of degree" has long been a powerful ingredient of the social outlook normally passed on to each generation. This difference in the "inner eye" of the Briton means a greater readiness, as compared with an American, to perceive social stratification and to identify with a class. As an influence on behavioral solidarity and conflict the effect is to reinforce other bonds arising from objective factors and to enhance class-based action in economic and political life.

Modernization and Class

Modernization has a bearing on this potent force in British political life because of its patently premodern origins. From one era to another the sense of degree has taken different concrete forms, and the various categories of persons in society have differed in numbers, in functions, and in relations with one another: from the "sundry estates and degrees of men" of old Tory times; to the "ranks, orders, and interests" of the eighteenth century; to the "upper, middle, and lower classes" of Victorian days; down to the occupational hierarchy of contemporary collectivist Britain, where the leading positions of the various bureaucratic sectors constitute not an estate, or governing, class, but "the Establishment." Throughout, however, the ideas of hierarchy and degree and the sentiments of deference and noblesse oblige have powerfully shaped political, economic, and social relations.

The thrust of modernity has been mixed, but on the whole contrary to inequality and class. In their structures of control, industrialization and bureaucratization have often created new objective references for the class system. New hierarchies of capitalist and entrepreneur in the nineteenth century and of technocratic and managerial elites in the twentieth century constitute realities on which the inherited expectations of the Briton can crystallize. On the other hand, modernity has mobilized ever new levels of the populace and has drawn them into political participation. Upbringing is being supplanted by education as a basis for advancement and for judging capacity. Mobility is undermining the family and neighborhood foundations of working-class culture. Above all, voluntarism, with its increasingly democratic and egalitarian tendencies, works against distinctions and identities based on social evaluation. Abstractly, its goal is a single, universal class of equal and independent individuals.

The upshot of modernization, it should be repeated, is to undermine not only the distinctions but also the identities of the class system. The solidarity of the working class on which the Labour movement in its political and economic forms was founded derived both from the objective structures of nineteenth-century capitalism and from the attitudes of premodern traditionalism. The current phases of modernization weaken both the modern and the premodern bases of class. Affluence and bureaucratization, democratic participation through party government and functional representation, and not least the advance of the rational, egalitarian spirit in British political culture have been loosening the bonds of class as both a horizontal and a vertical force of integration. The new volatility of electoral behavior is a natural expression of this new atomism in social structure.

To say that modernity dissolves the hierarchical and corporatistic heritage of medievalism is merely to point again to what deeply alarmed the earliest critics of modernity. Burke feared the tendencies of his time to destroy the organic unities, "the little platoons" and the great "establishments," that helped both to preserve order and to satisfy the human heart. At the start of the nineteenth century Auguste Comte was no less alarmed by the prospect of disintegration, as the increasing division of labor in both the economic and moral spheres threatened, in his eyes, to "snuff out the spirit of togetherness." Later Emile Durkheim saw society becoming a "dust of individuals," while the Fabian Graham Wallas feared the lack of "sufficient cohesive force" in modern society. In the British polity class has been such an integrating force and a principal aspect of "the modernity of tradition." In the course of development, however, modernity may come to overbalance tradition so far that the old solidarities are set on the way to final dissolution.

The Liberal Revival

Along with party decomposition and heightened electoral volatility, certain new forms of political action have suggested possible future patterns of organization and purpose. As attachment to the two major parties flagged in the sixties, new modes of action attracted support. Leading the way was the Liberal party which enjoyed a vigorous but brief revival that elaborated themes that came to be strongly reflected in the new politics of reform of the late sixties and the early seventies.

As tends to happen when a successful party of innovation is confronted by a new challenge, the Liberals, after their great Radical victories before World War I, being faced by the powerful upsurge of socialism, rapidly lost electoral and financial support to the Conservatives. By 1935 the new party dualism of Labour versus Conservatives as well as the new issues of collectivism had been decisively established (see Appendix). During the height of the collectivist period, the Liberal members of the House were reduced to half a dozen, while observers, hard put to explain even such tenuous survival, impatiently awaited the party's final demise. Then quite unexpectedly, beginning in the very late fifties and continuing with increasing strength through the early sixties, the Liberals staged a strong recovery. By 1964 their vote for Parliament had risen to 3 million, four times what it had been in the mid-fifties. At the same time they also made striking gains in local elections, probably quadrupling their representation on local councils of all categories. Moreover, the number of seats won at Westminster and in localities was never proportionate to the strong surge of favor recorded in opinion surveys. At one point in 1962, the Gallup survey showed that with the support of fully 30 percent of the sample the Liberals by a slight margin outpolled both the big parties.

While Liberal strength soon sank back to its previous level, the revival brought forward a distinctive critique of collectivist policy. As Liberals themselves insisted, they were not merely a third party poised between Conservatives and Socialists, but rather, as the representatives of the individualist position, the sole alternative at an opposite pole from the two great adherents of collectivism. Thanks in no small part to Jo Grimond, the politically magnetic and intellectually distinguished head of the party during the revival, this emphasis was embodied in constructive criticism that did much to transform the terms of political discussion in Britain.

The new ideas put forward by the Liberals centered on two serious and virtually inherent deficiencies of the managed economy and welfare state. These have occupied earlier pages of this study, so they need only be briefly mentioned and related to the problem at hand. First, the managed economy, by making national economic efficiency its chief goal, must often downgrade local economic and social values. In 1963, for instance, the so-called Beeching Report, charged with making proposals to reduce the deficits of the British railroad system, recommended that most lines that were not paying their way be closed down. It so happened that the major portion of the railroads of both Scotland and Wales were in this position, the upshot being that when the recommendations were carried into effect, much hardship was suddenly visited on many rural areas in the Celtic fringe. Yet given its terms of reference the report made good sense. In this way what may appear to local eyes as overcentralized and bureaucratic government is less a matter of choice than a natural consequence of the basic goals and structures of the managed economy. Moreover, these situational forces are supplemented by political pressures. Producers groups usually have a national coverage and act through centralized structures that find parallel organizations in central government departments to which the groups have ready access and in which they find similar national viewpoints.

The flaw in the welfare state consists in the dysfunctions of universalism. Modern egalitarianism, as in democratic socialism, leads to schemes for flat-rate benefits, available to all free of means tests (see Chapter 10). Ironically, however, the commitment to universalism may result in many of the most needy being excluded, while benefits go to those not greatly in need. In 1965 the Milner Holland Committee reported that this was the overall effect of the British system of housing subsidies; council tenants of public housing and owner-occupiers received substantial aid even though not poor, while private tenants, who included a far higher percentage of the poor, received no such help. Here again the political factor is important. Benefits directed only to the few poor may be unpopular with the taxpaying majority, while a scheme that spreads benefits to the many not in need is likely to be well-received. As a result, an arrangement intended to tax the majority for the sake of the needy minority becomes one in which the majority tax themselves for their own benefit.

With regard to both deficiencies of British policy, the Liberals took a strong initiative, putting forward their ideas as early as 1962 in a series of well-argued pamphlets on tax reforms, industrial organization, education, consumer protection, social policy, and reform of local and regional government. Their bias toward dispersion of power was reflected in their support fo. copartnership in industry and plant bargaining in industrial labor relations. Their faith in local self-government, an ancient Liberal orthodoxy, was expressed in detailed proposals to strengthen local government and promote devolution. While favoring greater equalization of opportunity in their tax, education, and consumer reports, their housing proposals reflected their concern to get at this aspect of the problem of poverty by a selective approach.

Their revival tells us something important both about the Liberals and about the present tendencies of British politics. One reason the Liberals were espe: lly sensitive to these deficiencies of the welfare state and managed economy was that they had never in the first place fully accepted the collectivist system. Odd as some of their policy proposals had been at times—and as a minor party anxiously looking for supporters they did tend to pick up some freakish allies—they retained a basic allegiance to the political, economic, and especially moral aspects of their nineteenth-century individualism. One of the most striking traits of Liberals, as their attitudes have been revealed in opinion surveys, is their rejection of class. They reject class both as an analytic concept explaining behavior and as a normative concept indicating to the individual where his social allegiance should lie. Moreover, the party enjoys a remarkably even spread of support among all strata, in contrast with the polarization of support for Conservatives and Labour. "In marked contrast to the intimate ties between class and Conservative and Labour support," as Butler and Stokes remark, "support for the Liberals was remarkably unrelated to class self-image and to occupational grade."[4] Like their great Victorian predecessors, individualist in outlook and hostile to class, the Liberals carried these older values into the collectivist age and, as the orthodoxies of that age began to weaken, came into their own. They had endured long enough to become relevant once again—but only for a moment.

The New Politics of Reform

It is a seldom-examined cliché that small third parties are a source of new ideas in a two-party system. In the case of the Liberal revival this did happen. During the sixties the big parties put forward on their own many of the proposals being urged by Liberals, partly in response to the same conditions, but also partly in imitation of the Liberal lead. "The Grimond decade," wrote *The New York Times,* "will be remembered . . . as a time when the Liberals sowed for others to reap; when their efforts in several key areas had enough impact to persuade both Tory and Labour Governments to steal their policies."[5] One fully intentional result was that the Liberal appeal was blurred and weakened in favor of the two main parties.

Also influential in offsetting the Liberal appeal was the development of initiatives often launched by the Liberals by a host of new reform groups outside the two-party system. Such groups, which are sometimes termed promotional or cause groups to distinguish them from the interest-oriented groups that people the structures of functional representation, have occupied a large place in British politics since their first appearance as the earliest movers of nineteenth-century liberalism (see Chapter 9). Yet it is

---

[4]Butler and Stokes, *op. cit.,* p. 79.
[5]January 18, 1967, p. 42.

fair to say that recent years have seen an increase in their numbers and activities, especially a shift to concern with the gaps and the deficiencies of collectivist policy. They include such well-known organizations as the Howard League for Penal Reform, the National Council for Civil Liberties, and the National Society for the Prevention of Cruelty to Children. One of the more notable has been the Child Action Poverty Group. Founded in 1965, it took the Wilson Government severely to task for the fact that the problem of family poverty had actually worsened under Labour's rule. The group's influence was acknowledged when the Government adopted its proposal to help the very poor by increasing family allowances for all families and then "clawing back" a large portion of the sum distributed by taxing those who were better off. The problem of homeless people in the welfare state led to the founding in 1966 of SHELTER by an explosive young New Zealander named Des Wilson. Within three years, it became one of the largest charitable organizations in Britain, raising £2 million and itself providing housing for some 3,000 families. During the sixties there was also a proliferation of small, local voluntary associations. In 1960 the first Association for the Advancement of State Education was set up; by 1966 there were 120. The Councils for Social Service, which had long existed as coordinating bodies for local social-service organizations, showed a vigorous new life. In the early sixties, membership in the National Union of Students, the official and long-established student organization, grew rapidly from 150,000 to nearly 400,000. At the same time advocates of "student power" produced the Radical Students Alliance.

Writing of the new politics in general, one Labour observer recently commented,

> Thousands of such pressure groups or action groups have come into existence: community associations, amenity groups, shop-stewards movements, consumer societies, educational campaigns, organisations to help the old, the homeless, the sick, the poor or under-developed societies, militant communal organisations, student power, noise abatement societies, and so on.[6]

Local self-assertion against central government achieved its sharpest form in the sudden surge of Celtic nationalism. The Scottish National party, championing ultimate independence from Westminster, had only modest success after its founding in 1928, polling less than 1 percent of the total vote in Scotland by 1959. In the next decade, however, membership in the party rose from 2,000 to 135,000; and in the election of 1970 the party won 11.4 percent of the total Scottish vote, although this gave it only one seat in Parliament. The change in outlook and sentiment that accompanied this change in voting behavior is illustrated by the drastic shift in rhetoric

---

[6]Anthony Wedgewood Benn, *The New Politics: a socialist reconnaissar.ce,* Fabian Tract 402 (London, 1970), p. 9.

of the Scottish trade-union movement. From the time of its foundation in 1897, the Scottish T.U.C. had disdained nationalist sentiment and had used the standard rhetoric of all-British working-class solidarity and social-'st centralism. Then abruptly in the sixties Scotland and its problems shifted to the center of the Scottish T.U.C.'s deliberations.

Plaid Cymru, the Welsh Nationalist party, founded in 1925, also grew rapidly in the sixties, by 1970 its membership reaching 40,000 and its vote in the general election 11.5 percent of the total in Wales. It may also be noted that the Cornish Nationalists, known as Mebyon Kernow, or Sons of Cornwall, were represented by a candidate who won 2 percent of the vote in his constituency, while a hotelkeeper championing more local self-government for the Isle of Wight won 2.8 percent of the vote there under the banner of the Vectis Nationalists—Vectis being the Latin name for the island.

Conclusion

After a period of stability, the British polity is changing, perhaps in quite fundamental ways. Already this development has impaired the performance of government. The decline of class and of the complex of traditional sentiments that have been associated with class have had a disintegrating effect in the spheres of both authority and purpose. The solidarity of support for the parties has been weakened. A new volatility deprives Governments of the time and toleration needed to develop new lines of policy and put them into effect. Such a loss of authority weakens party government as a means of social choice and popular control.

The loosening of these traditional bonds of social cohesion also affects the moral coherence of the parties. Vernon Bogdanor has written that the fragmentation of socialist ideology is in part "a reflection of the erosion of the social base of the Labour Party, the manual working class." When the party was formed, this class was

> sufficiently united in its aims to provide a broad and coherent basis for a common policy. But with the weakening of class feeling, the social base of the Labour Party has become eroded. And with the erosion of the social base, the politics became eroded also. The Labour Party thus ceased to provide an agenda for radical change. On the central issues which faced it in office—on devaluation, on the maintenance of military bases East of Suez and on the Common Market—the Labour Party found itself divided. It could be held together only by the tactical skill and the political ambiguity of Harold Wilson.[7]

---

[7]Vernon Bogdanor, "The Labour Party in Opposition, 1951–1964," in Vernon Bogdanor and Robert Skidelsky (eds.), *The Age of Affluence, 1951–1964* (London, 19' () p. 114.

As history produced the parties that flourished in the collectivist age, history may transform them in the future. That ancient and essentially political distinction between classes founded upon domination and subjection will surely persist and, given the technocratic trends of modernity, may become even more marked and significant. Yet modernization has weakened many of the bases of the two-party system, and the new political initiatives of recent years may prefigure a looser, more diffuse, more individualist system for expressing different views of the common good. These neo-Victorian pressure groups must remind one of a time when parties were far less cohesive, monopolistic, and authoritative than they are today.

In content as well as form the new politics brings an echo of the past. The attempt on both the Left and the Right to decentralize and give expression to local and regional aspirations appears to be another individualist phase of the recurring individualist-collectivist cycle in British political development. Along with this turning away from collectivism, the issues of the future may include a new expression of the ideal of equality, which accepts the security brought by the welfare state but qualifies the consequences of its universalism and bureaucracy.

Radically new and postmodern issues might arise. The framework of values developed by the party system over the past 300 years came into existence at the same time as the modern nation-state (see Chapter 9). Moreover, while the national question has at times caused bitter and even violent struggles, the main conflicts of political development have presupposed a "united kingdom" and a sovereign state. Britain's entry into the Common Market, however, raised the question of a new dimension of political controversy and party division. During the long and bitter parliamentary struggle over entry, both parties were split, especially Labour, and the crucial vote was carried by the Government only with bipartisan support. The possibility—distant, but worth noting—is that entry into Europe may impose a center-periphery conflict upon the class division that has for so long been such an important focus of British party conflict. If so, a qualitatively new issue would be introduced, transcending the boundaries that for some 300 years have limited the party battle to the arena defined by the coordinates of equality-inequality and collectivism-individualism.

Epilogue: Northern Ireland

Northern Ireland—or Ulster, as the region has been called since the Middle Ages—is an apt theme to provoke final reflections on British government and politics. It challenges collectivist politics by refusing to conform to the categories of class-based political behavior. It challenges British politics as a severe test of the ability of British leaders and institutions to solve a fundamental problem. For the political scientist Northern Ireland is a challenge to the British political system, because it raises the question whether Ulster should be considered a part of that system for the purposes of political analysis.

Before the United Kingdom government in London imposed "direct rule" in March 1972, the government of Northern Ireland was the most striking example of territorial decentralization in the British political system. Its authority was based on an act of 1920 that gave Ulster wide powers of Home Rule. The act distinguished between "reserved powers," dealing with such questions as defense, treaties, and nearly all taxation, which continued to be matters for the London government, and the remaining powers of government, called the "transferred powers," which included jurisdiction over health, education, welfare, employment, agriculture, commerce, transport, and a small range of taxation. To exercise these transferred powers, a government was set up in Belfast with its administrative center on the outskirts of that city at Stormont Castle, from which was taken the name by which the regime was commonly known.

In the British manner, the Stormont government included a responsible Cabinet and a bicameral legislature, consisting of a House of Commons with fifty-two members and a Senate with twenty-six. Since Ulster was ruled in some fields of policy from London, its six counties were also divided into constituencies of the United Kingdom Parliament, to which twelve members were sent. The Stormont regime, one might say, was an intermediate tier of government between the usual array of local authorities and the central government in London—rather like an American state, except for the crucial fact that London retained the supreme authority to alter or abolish these arrangements.

This exceptional regime was established because the Protestant majority of the North refused to join the Irish Free State—later called the Republic of Ireland, or Éire—which was set up by the overwhelmingly Catholic South of Ireland after a long and violent struggle against British rule. With Protestants outnumbering Catholics about two to one, the Ulster polity divided sharply along religious lines, and the Ulster Unionists, the political arm of the Protestant majority, never had less than forty of the fifty-two seats in the lower house. Moreover, knowing that many or most Catholics wished to see a united Ireland, the Unionists took further steps, such as gerrymandering and limitations on the franchise, to reduce Catholic political power in local government and at Stormont. In the case of Ulster, the result of territorial decentralization of government was not to increase democracy, but to diminish it.

The politics of Ulster departs sharply from the collectivist model that prevails generally in the rest of the United Kingdom. In Northern Ireland voting follows the lines of religious cleavage, and these lines cut across class divisions. Protestants tend to outnumber Catholics in the better-paying and more prestigious occupations, but members of both religious communities can be found in all social and economic strata. As Richard Rose points out, "there are more poor Protestants than there are poor Catholics."[8] If Ulster voters behaved as British voters do, Northern Ireland would be a promising field for socialist politics. But in fact the Northern Ireland affiliate of the Labour party was never able to win more than four of the twenty-two industrial constituencies of the Stormont Parliament. Nor have the more radical efforts of recent years—as symbolized, for instance, by the fiery Bernadette Devlin—been any more successful in building a substantial political following on a working-class appeal. On the contrary, working-class Protestants, like Protestants of the professional and managerial classes, have voted overwhelmingly Unionist in elections to the Stormont Parliament and to the London Parliament, where the eight Unionist M.P.s accept the Conservative whip. Similarly, the Orange Lodges, a social organization of militant Protestants, include members from all classes.

Judging from behavior as well as rhetoric, it is obvious that the religious cleavages of Ulster are important to its political divisions. Yet this religious background provokes almost as many questions as it answers. One problem is that the correlation between religion and political affiliation that prevails in Ulster does not carry over to other parts of the United Kingdom. In various parts of Britain there are substantial numbers of Catholic voters. But in contrast with their coreligionists in Ulster, they fit fairly easily into the collectivist model, tending for the most part to vote Labour (along with millions of Protestants), in accordance with the high percentage of manual workers among them.

It is tempting to say that in Ulster religion is merely an indicator of a deeper cleavage, which centers on nationality. From the 1920s the principal opposition party in the Stormont Parliament has called itself "nationalist" and has aspired to unity with the South. In its constitution Dublin claims to be the legitimate government of the whole island, including Ulster. Certainly, the Catholics of Ulster claim passionately that they are Irish in nationality—and hence, should be under an all-Ireland government. But again there is a difficulty: Ulster Protestants also claim Irish nationality, and not unnaturally, since their ancestors came to Ireland more than three hundred years ago. This claim to a common nationality, it would seem, should be a bond of unity between Catholics and Protestants. And indeed it was during the eighteenth century, when men of both religious

---

[8]Richard Rose, *Governing Without Consensus: An Irish Perspective* (London, 1971).

persuasions resisted the British and many worked and fought together for a united, secular, and republican Ireland. Today, however, the Protestant Irishmen of Ulster say that they are also British in nationality and look to Britain for their security.

The pursuit of security is an important clue to the political behavior of Ulstermen generally. On both sides of the barricades, fear moves people to their depths. We may ask what real reason there can be for such fear. No doubt the Unionists have used their political power in discriminatory ways. Scandalous instances of discrimination in the assignment of public housing have been brought forward by Catholic spokesmen. Belfast's development efforts have favored the industrialized Protestant East over the more rural and Catholic West, and unemployment has been higher among Catholics than Protestants. Yet Catholics in large numbers do enjoy the benefits of subsidized public housing. Ulster has adopted nearly all the social services of the British welfare state—with the help of substantial British financial aid—and Catholics share these on the same terms as others. On their side, Protestants fear the influence of the Catholic Church on any government of a united Ireland, with all this might mean in the form of censorship and church interference with the rights of privacy in such matters as contraception.

Yet even if we grant that there is substance to the fears each side entertains toward the other, the effects must still seem unbelievably out of proportion to the causes. The objective realities are simply inadequate to explain the bitterness and bloodshed of the past few years, not to mention that in previous generations. For this sort of intercommunal rioting and homicide, down to the very patterns of street fighting in the very same streets, has been a recurrent feature of the life of Belfast for a hundred and fifty years. Indeed, this terrible heritage from the past, sustained by myth and legend and renewed each generation by traumatic experience, is a principal key to understanding the tragedy of the present. Every observer of Ulster's passion has emphasized the power of history, and any observer of the TV clips of the rioting can see how that power is perpetuated. From the age when he is first able to throw a stone and utter a curse, the child brought up in this discord acquires a sense of identity as one who attacks and is attacked by Protestants/Catholics. Attitudes that have their genesis in these formative years do not need reasons in order to continue producing their terrible effects. In short, the sheer fact that Ulster Catholics and Ulster Protestants have fought one another so bitterly for so long is a principal explanation of why they continue to fight today.

A background of concrete social interaction can, of course, have a happier consequence when it has followed patterns of harmony and cooperation. Such a historical background has helped give the British system that strong sense of national community that has enabled it to sustain the shocks and discords of modern politics. But Ulster does not belong to this community and the political system founded upon it. Nor does Ulster belong to the community that sustains the polity of Southern Ireland. History that has made nations of both Britain and Éire has made of Ulster a kind of anti-nation with a hopelessly divided regime

Statistical
Appendix

Appendix British General Election Results
(Selected Elections 1832–1895; All Elections 1900–1970)

	Percent Share of Party Vote						M.P.s Elected						
Year	Conservative	Liberal Unionist	Liberal	Irish Nationalist	Labour	Other	Conservative	Liberal Unionist	Liberal	Irish Nationalist	Labour	Other	Unopposed Seats
1832	32.1		67.9				172		473				200
1841	51.0		48.8			0.2	360		295				325
1852	57.4		42.5			0.1	346		286			1	243
1868	40.8		59.2				286		365				199
1874	45.6		49.3	3.5		1.6	345		242	48		4	181
1880	43.8		53.2	2.4		0.6	248		325	56		4	107
1886	37.5	14.0	44.9	3.6			316	79	190	85			223
1895	49.2		45.4	3.9	1.1	0.4	341	70	177	82			185
1900	51.1		45.9	2.5	0.5		334	68	184	82	2		243
1906	43.7		49.0	0.6	5.9	0.8	134	24	399	83	30		114
1910	46.9		43.1	1.9	8.0	0.1	242	31	275	82	40		55
1910	46.4		43.8	2.5	7.1	0.2	240	34	270	84	42		163
1918	38.7		25.6	6.7	23.7	5.3	383		161	80	73	10	107
1922	38.2		29.1		29.5	3.2	345		116		142	12	57
1923	38.1		29.6		30.5	1.8	258		159		191	7	50
1924	48.3		17.6		33.0	1.1	419		40		151	5	32
1929	38.2		23.4		37.1	1.3	260		59		288	8	7
1931	55.2		10.7		32.2	1.7	473		72		64	5	67
1935	53.8		6.4		38.6	1.3	432		21		158	5	40
1945	39.8		9.0		47.8	2.8	213		12		393	22	3
1950	43.5		9.1		46.1	1.3	298		9		315	3	2
1951	48.0		2.5		48.8	0.7	321		6		295	3	4
1955	49.7		2.7		46.4	1.2	344		6		277	3	0

1959	49.4	5.9	43.8	0.9	365	6	258	1	0
1964	43.4	11.2	44.1	0.3	304	9	317		0
1966	41.9	8.5	47.9	1.7	253	12	363	2	0
1970	46.4	7.5	43.1	3.0	330	6	287	6	0

NOTE: Data for the eight elections of the nineteenth century reported in this table were compiled from constituency results published in McCalmont's *Parliamentary Poll Book* for the 1832–1874 elections and Dod's *Parliamentary Companion* for the 1880–1895 elections. Party affiliations were based on the respective author's determinations. Appropriate adjustments were made for multiple-member constituencies. Comparisons with other election data indicate a margin of error of about 5 percent.

These statistics should be interpreted as indicative rather than definitive. Historians have cautioned that the absence of formal political organizations, changes in the mode of election, and local constituency practices preclude the use of election data as a substantive measure of political opinion. The data do offer, however, a useful perspective of party development over a 150-year period.

DATA SOURCES: Frederick H. McCalmont, *The Parliamentary Poll Book of All Elections 1832–1895* (London: 1895); Dod's *Parliamentary Companion 1843, 1852, 1874, 1880, 1886, 1895*; David Butler and Jennie Freeman, *British Political Facts, 1900–1968* (London: 1969).

The Appendix was prepared by Glenn A. Robinson.

Select Bibliography

Basic Factual Information
Annual Abstract of Statistics. Annually revised. London: H.M.S.O.

The Annual Register of World Events. Annually revised. London: H.M.S.O.

Britain: An Official Handbook. Annually revised. London: Her Majesty's Stationery Office (H.M.S.O.).

Butler, David, and Jennie Freeman. *British Political Facts: 1900–1968.* London: Macmillan, 1969.

National Income and Expenditure. Annually revised. London: H.M.S.O.

British Constitutional and Political Development
Amery, L. S. *Thoughts on the Constitution.* 2nd ed. London: Oxford University Press, 1953.

Bagehot, Walter. *The English Constitution.* 1st ed. London: Chapman and Hall, 1867, and subsequent eds.

Birch, A. H. *Representative and Responsible Government.* London: Allen and Unwin, 1964.

Chrimes, S. B. *English Constitutional History.* London: Oxford University Press, 1965.

Feiling, K. G. *History of England from the Coming of the English to 1938.* Oxford: Clarendon Press, 1950.

Guttsman, W. L. *The British Political Elite.* London: Macgibbon and Kee, 1963.

Keir, D. L. *The Constitutional History of Modern Britain.* 7th ed. London: Adam and Charles Black, 1964.

Marsh, D. C. *The Changing Social Structure of England and Wales.* London: Routledge, 1965.

Taylor, A. J. P. *English History 1914–1945.* Oxford: Oxford University Press, 1965.

Cabinet and Prime Minister
Crossman, R. H. S. *The Myths of Cabinet Government.* Cambridge, Mass.: Harvard University Press, 1972.

Daalder, Hans. *Cabinet Reform in Britain 1914–1963.* Stanford, Calif.: Stanford University Press, 1963.

Jennings, Sir William Ivor. *Cabinet Government.* 3rd ed. Cambridge, England: Cambridge University Press, 1959.

King, Anthony, ed. *The Prime Minister.* London: Macmillan, 1969.

Mackintosh, John P. *The British Cabinet.* 2nd ed. London: Stevens, 1968.

Morrison, Herbert. *Government and Parliament.* London: Oxford University Press, 1954.

Walker, P. G. *The Cabinet.* London: Jonathan Cape, 1970.

Civil Service and Administration

Campbell, G. A. *The Civil Service in Britain.* 2nd ed. London: Duckworth, 1965.

Chester, D. N., and F. M. G. Willson. *The Organisation of British Central Government 1914–1964.* London: Allen and Unwin, 1968.

Clarke, J. J. *The Local Government of the United Kingdom.* 15th ed. London: Pitman and Sons, 1956.

Cohen, E. W. *The Growth of the Civil Service 1780–1939.* London: Allen and Unwin, 1941.

Dale, H. E. *The Higher Civil Service.* London: Oxford University Press, 1941.

The Fulton Committee. *Report on the Civil Service.* Vol. 1, Cmnd. 3638. London: H.M.S.O., 1968.

Griffith, J. A. G. *Central Departments and Local Authorities.* Toronto: University of Toronto Press, 1966.

Mackenzie, W. J. M. and J. W. Grove. *Central Administration in Britain.* London: Longmans, Green, 1957.

Report of the Royal Commission on Local Government in England. *(Maud Report.)* Vol. 1, Cmnd. 4040. London: H.M.S.O., 1969.

Public Enterprise and Economic Planning

Beer, S. H. *Treasury Control: the Coordination of Financial and Economic Policy in Britain.* Rev. ed. Oxford: Clarendon Press, 1957.

Brittan, Samuel. *Steering the Economy: the Role of the Treasury.* London: Secker and Warburg, 1969.

Caves, Richard E. et al. *Britain's Economic Prospects.* Washington, D. C.: Brookings Institution, 1968.

Control of Public Expenditure (Plowden Report). Cmnd. 1432. London: H.M.S.O., 1961.

Dow, J. C. R. *The Management of the British Economy 1945–60.* Cambridge, England: Cambridge University Press, 1966.

Eckstein, Harry. *The British Health Service: Its Origins, Structure and Achievements.* Cambridge, Mass.: Harvard University Press, 1959.

Grove, J. W. *Government and Industry in Britain.* London: Longmans, 1962.

Hall, Mary P. *The Social Services of England & Wales.* London: Routledge, 1969.

Shonfield, Andrew. *Modern Capitalism: the Changing Balance of Public and Private Power.* London: Oxford University Press, 1965.

Parliament

Butt, Ronald. *The Power of Parliament.* London: Constable, 1967.

Crick, Bernard. *The Reform of Parliament.* London: Weidenfeld and Nicolson, 1964.

Finer, S. E., H. B. Berrington, and D. Bartholomew. *Backbench Opinion in the House of Commons, 1955–1959.* London: Pergamon Press, 1961.

House of Commons Debates (Hansard). London: H.M.S.O., daily, weekly, and annually.

Jennings, Sir Ivor. *Parliament.* 3rd ed. Cambridge, England: Cambridge University Press, 1957.

May, Sir Thomas Erskine. *Treatise on the Law, Privileges, Proceedings and Usage of Parliament.* 18th ed. London: Butterworth, 1971.

Richards, Peter. *Honorable Members.* 2nd ed. London: Faber, 1964.

Young, Roland. *The British Parliament.* London: Faber, 1962.

Parties, Interest Groups, and Electoral Behavior

Beattie, Alan, ed. *English Party Politics.* 2 vols. 1600–1906 and 1906–1970. London: Weidenfeld, 1970.

Beer, S. H. *British Politics in the Collectivist Age.* Rev. ed. New York: Vintage Books, 1969.

Blank, Stephen. *Government and Industry in Britain.* London: D. C. Heath, forthcoming.

Blondel, Jean. *Voters, Parties and Leaders: The Social Fabric of British Politics.* Harmondsworth, England: Penguin Books, 1963.

Butler, David, and Michael Pinto-Duschinsky. *The British General Election of 1970.* London: Macmillan, 1971.

Butler, David, and Donald Stokes. *Political Change in Britain: Forces Shaping Electoral Choice.* New York: St. Martin's Press, 1969.

Eckstein, Harry. *Pressure Group Politics: the Case of the British Medical Association.* Stanford, Calif.: Stanford University Press, 1960.

Finer, S. E. *Anonymous Empire: A Study of the Lobby in Great Britain.* 2nd ed. London: Pall Mall Press, 1966.

Lieber, Robert J. *British Politics and European Unity: Parties, Elites and Pressure Groups.* Berkeley, Calif.: University of California Press, 1970.

Manzer, R. A. *Teachers and Politics.* Manchester, England: Manchester University Press, 1970.

McKenzie, R. T. *British Political Parties: The Distribution of Power within the Conservative and Labour Parties.* 2nd ed. London: Heinemann, 1963.

———— and A. Silver. *Angels in Marble: Working Class Conservatives in Urban England.* Chicago and London: University of Chicago Press, 1968.

Nordlinger, Eric A. *The Working-Class Tories: Authority, Deference and Stable Democracy.* Berkeley, Calif.: University of California Press, 1967.

Ranney, Austin. *Pathways to Parliament: Candidate Selection in Britain.* Madison, Wisc.: University of Wisconsin Press, 1965.

Rasmussen, J. S. *The Liberal Party: A Study of Retrenchment and Revival.* London: Constable, 1965.

Rose, Richard. *Influencing Voters: A Study of Campaign Rationality.* New York: St. Martin's Press, 1967.

Self, P., and H. Storing. *The State and the Farmer.* Berkeley, Calif.: University of California Press, 1962.

Wootton, G. *The Politics of Influence: British ex-servicemen, Cabinet decisions and cultural change (1917–57).* Cambridge, Mass.: Harvard University Press, 1963.

Academic Journals

The British Journal of Political Science

Government and Opposition

Parliamentary Affairs

The Political Quarterly

Political Studies

Public Administration

Index

Index

Administration, problems of, 48–50

Aereopagitica (Milton), 143, 159

Alford, Robert R., 205

Amery, L. S., 23, 24; on Conservative party policy, 173

Anti-Corn Law League, 11

Armstrong, Sir William, 82n

Association for the Advancement of State Education, 219

Association of British Chambers of Commerce, 186

Attlee, Clement, 31, 52, 84, 96, 140, 147

Attlee government, 175, 190, 197, 198; and rebellious Labourites, 120–121; legislative program, 171–172; and foreign policy, 198

Authority: bipolar, 23–25, 27; conceptions of, 156; of Whigs and Tories, 159–161, 173–174; and functional representation, 170

Backbenchers: role in party government, 116–119; influence, 121–127

Bagehot, Walter, 96

Baldwin, Stanley, 24

"Baldwin Confession," 24–25

Balfour, Arthur, 90, 193

Barber, Anthony, 130

Beattie, Alan, 84n

Beeching Report, 216–217

Benn, Anthony Wedgewood, 219n

Bentham, Jeremy, hypothesis of modernity, 8, 20; applied to welfare state, 15–16; as inspiration for reform, 153

Berrington, Hugh, 166

Bevan, Aneurin, 34, 90; leadership of Labour rebels, 120–121

Bevin, Ernest, 32, 125, 167 advocacy of N.A.T.O., 175

Bismarck, Otto von, 17, 19

Bogdanor, Vernon, on Labour party erosion, 220

Brittan, Samuel, 81n

Brown, George, 72, 77

Bureaucracy: increased scale of, 48–50; social composition of, 51–52; loyalty of, 52–53; Fulton Committee recommendation on, 54–56, 135; expertise, 54–59; and class, 56–57; territorial decentralization, 59–62; functional decentralization, 62–65; control by Treasury, 79

Burke, Edmund, 153, 160, 215; hypothesis of tradition, 8–9, 20, 152; on legislature's role, 143, 148; on political parties, 144; critical of natural rights philosophy, 160

Butler, David, 92, 93, 140, 205n, 206, 208, 218

Butler, R. A., 70, 123–124, 146, 157

Butskellism, as economic management, 70, 146, 175

Butt, Ronald, 101n, 124n; on influence of opposition, 127–128, 129–130

Cabinet government: and party gov-

Cabinet government (*continued*)
ernment, 21–23; sources of power,
27; modern weaknesses, 28–29;
make-up, 29–31; constraints on,
31; authority of Prime Minister, 31–
32; collective responsibility in, 33–
36; role of secretariat, 36–39;
growth of committee system in,
39–43; dominance over House of
Commons, 95–99
Callaghan, James, 77, 126
Cambridge University, and civil serv-
ice, 56, 57
Canning, George, 157
Capitalism, Socialism and Democracy
(Schumpeter), 17
Castle, Barbara, 126
Central Electricity Authority, 123
Central Policy Review Staff (C.P.R.S.)
of Heath government, 43, 80; po-
tential role, 82
Centralization, 59
Chamberlain, Joseph, 24
Chamberlain, Neville, 33, 102, 122,
157
Chamber of Manufacturers of Great
Britain, 163
Child Action Poverty Group, 219
Churchill, Sir Winston, 4, 31, 77, 88,
90, 91, 102, 140, 176, 189
Civil service, *see* Bureaucracy
Class: and age of reform, 12–13; and
civil service, 56–57; and House of
Commons, 91–94; and party, 149–
152; in voting, 204–208; decline in
influence, 208–210; bases, 210–214;
and modernization, 214–215; Liberal rejection of, 218
Closure, 105
Coherence: as criterion of public policy, 26; of cabinet government, 26–
27
Coke, Sir Edward, 87
Collectivism, 16; economic, 7–8; and
economic planning, 66–68; and
mass politics, 137–140; and party,
150–151, 189–196; period of, 166–
169; Conservative version, 173–

175; consensus of, 175–178; and
functional representation, 180–189;
and party government, 189–196;
and party decomposition, 201–204;
and Liberal revival, 216–218; weakening of, 220–221; and Northern
Ireland, 221–225
Committee of Imperial Defence, 37,
39
Common Market, 30, 34, 198; British
attitudes toward, 176, 187, 221
Comte, Auguste, 215
Confederation of British Industry
(C.B.I.), 71, 186–187
Conservative party, 16, 19–20, 62, 65,
189; and economic policy, 70–71,
72, 73; class composition, 92–94,
206–208; revolts in, 122–124; and
Suez crisis, 129–130, 175; and
Heath government, 137–138, 189–
192; and welfare state, 146, 173–
178; history, 156–157, 164–165; as
innovator, 157–158; policy, 189–
192; manifesto and mandate, 199–
200; *see also* Party government;
Tory party
Constant, Benjamin, 20–21
Corn Laws, 10, 11, 13, 146, 158
Councils for Social Service, 219
Crick, Bernard, 115
Cripps, Sir Stafford, 79
Crossman, R. H. S., 28n, 32, 38n, 121;
on loyalty of civil service, 54; views
on party government, 84–85, 126–
127, 198–199

Dalton, Hugh, 32
de Gaulle, Charles, 5, 101, 176
Democracy in America (Tocqueville),
12
de Jouvenel, Bertrand, 4, 8
DeLolme, Jean-Louis, 87
Department of Economic Affairs
(D.E.A.), 68, 72, 75, 77, 79
Derby, Lord Edward Stanley, 146
de Sismondi, Charles, 10n
Devlin, Bernadette, 223

Disraeli, Benjamin, 19, 20, 157, 158; and social reform, 136–137; and extension of franchise, 174
Douglas-Home, Sir Alec, 31, 96
Durant, Henry, 205
Durkheim, Emile, 215

Economic control, Treasury's role in, 77–82
Economic planning, and management, 66–72
Economic policy, failure of, 5–8
Eden, Sir Anthony: Suez policy, 46–47; on socialism, 174
Election results, 1832–1970, 228–229
Elites, political, as factor of stability, 18–19, 21, 139
Engels, Friedrich, 10
Engineering Employers' Federation, 187
Enlightenment, 9, 14
European Common Market, see Common Market
Exclusion Bills, 141, 142

Fabian Society, 17–18, 168, 206; early history, 153–154
Federation of British Industries (F.B.I.), 71, 186, 187
Finer, S. E., 58n, 182
Fisher, Sir Warren, on civil servants, 52
France: Monnet Plan, 71; National Assembly, 89; system of interpellation, 101; Chamber of Deputies, 130
Fraser, Sir Michael, 196
French Revolution: Tocqueville on, 12; effect on Toryism, 157
Fulton, Lord John, committee recommendation on civil service, 54–56, 135
Functional representation: as conception of authority, 170–171; developed by Labour party, 170–172;

Conservative version of, 173; make-up, 180–189

Gaitskell, Hugh, 34, 64n, 70, 146, 176, 195, 213
Germany: Marxism and Social Democratic party, 17; Weimar Republic, 17, absence of elite in, 19
Gladstone, William Ewart, 13, 105, 108, 109, 136, 163, 165
Greater London Council, 60
Grey, Charles, Earl, 12–13, 167
Grimond, Jo, 216, 218
Grove, J. W., 50

Hall, Sir Robert, 35n
Haworth, David, 186n
Healey, Denis, 32
Heath, Edward, 30, 31, 117, 132, 176; and R.P.M. revolt, 124
Heath government, 40–41, 43, 61, 65, 110; domestic proposals of, 137–138; new directions of, 189–192; and party mandate, 200
Herbert, A. P., 91
Herring, E. P., 181
Hitler, Adolf, 4, 33
Hoare, Sir Samuel, 34
Hoare-Laval plan, 34
Hogg, Quintin, 158
House of Commons: unreformed, 10; reform of 1832, 12–13; as seat of authority, 23–24; relations to Cabinet, 29–30; party government in, 85–86, 164–165; power of, 86–87, 115–116; and expressive symbolism, 87; description of, 87–91; class composition, 91–94; decline, 95–99; private business vs. public business, 98–99; policy criticism and control, 99–102; legislative procedure, 102–106; delegated legislation, 106; financial control, 107–109; proposed reforms of, 109–113; role of Opposition, 127–130; inner circle, 130–131

House of Lords: legislative procedure, 104–105; function, 131–134
Howard League for Penal Reform, 219
Hudson, George, 163

Ilbert, Sir Courtenay, 27n
Industrialization: strain of, 9; impact on polity, 9–10, 151; and age of reform, 10–11
Inflation, politics of, 70, 72–75
Interests, proliferation of, 135–140
Ireland: Home Rule for, 96, 165; territorial decentralization for Northern, 221–225
Irish Free State, 222

Jenkins, Roy, 73
Jones, Jack, 184, 194

Kingsley, J. Donald, 51n

Labour party, 20, 62, 153–154, 189; and welfare state, 15–16, 146, 171–172, 190–191; and bureaucracy, 51, 52, 53, 54; economic policy, 68–69, 72, 75; class composition, 92–93, 150–151, 204–207, 220; P.L.P., 117–118, 119, 120, 121; revolts in, 120–121, 125–127; and collectivism, 166–169, 177; and Liberal party, 168; and socialism, 168, 171–173; and functional representation, 170–171; foreign policy, 175, 176; structure, 192–194, 203, 204; National Executive Committee (N.E.C.), 196, 197; manifesto and mandate, 197–199; volatility of support, 208–210, 211; decline, 220; see also Attlee government; Party government; Wilson government
Laski, Harold, 51n, 139
Laval, Pierre, 34
League of Nations, 24

Lederer, Emil, 139
Lever, Harold, 28n
Liberal party, 11, 157, 166; and establishment of welfare state, 16; values, 162–163; radicalization of, 164–166; and Labour party, 168; revival of, 216–218; impact on other parties, 218
Liberty: twofold character of, 14; and hierarchy, 20
Lloyd, Selwyn, 72
Lloyd George, David, 20, 37
Local government, 59–62
Locke, John, 153, 160
London Workingmen's Association, 11
.owell, A. Lawrence, 3, 13

Macaulay, Thomas Babington, 162
MacDonald, J. Ramsay, 32, 38, 193
Mackenzie, W. J. M., 50
Mackintosh, John P., 29n
Macmillan, Harold, 31, 46, 127, 157, 158; economic policy, 70, 71–72; foreign policy, 176
Maitland, F. W., 102
Mandate and manifesto, parties, 197–200
Mandate theory, 24–25
Marxism, effects on German Social Democrats, 17
McIlwain, Charles H., 142
McKenzie, Robert, 207n
Mebyon Kernow (Sons of Cornwall), 220
Middleton, W. L., 130n
Mill, John Stuart, 143, 159
Milner Holland Committee, 217
Milton, John, 143, 159
Model of mass politics, 138–140
Modernity, and party, 140–145
Modernization: and industrialization, 151–152; and parties, 210–211; and class, 214–215; effects of, 220–221
Monnet Plan, 71
Morrison, Herbert, 63, 102; on role of

Parliament, 112–113; on back-benchers, 122
Muggeridge, Malcolm, 4n

Nasser, Gamal Abdel, 46, 175
National Board of Prices and Incomes (N.B.P.I.), 73
National Coal Board, as public corporation, 63–64
National Economic Development Council (N.E.D.C.), 42, 71–72, 171, 188, 189, 190
National Health Service, 107, 170, 172
National Incomes Commission, 71, 72
Nationalism, in Scotland and Wales, 59, 104, 219–220
National Liberal Federation (N.L.F.), radical formation of, 164–166
National Union of Manufacturers, 186
N.A.T.O., 175
Neumann, Sigmund, on rise of parties, 141
Neustadt, Richard E., 47n, 122
Nobel Prizes, table, 58
North Atlantic Treaty Organization, 175
Northern Ireland, and territorial decentralization, 221–225

O'Donovan, Patrick, 4n
The Old Regime and the French Revolution (Tocqueville), 12
Ortega y Gasset, José, 139
Oxford University, and civil service, 56, 57

Paisley, Rev. Ian, 131
Parliament, 85–86; decline of, 95–99; see also House of Commons; House of Lords; Party government
Parliamentary Labour party, role in party government, 117–118, 119, 120–121
Parties: unity in, 96–97; and moder-nity, 140–145; stages of development, 145–148; and values, 155–159; and pressure groups, 149–152; role of intellectuals in, 152–154; policy, 189–192; structure, 192–196; manifesto and mandate, 197–200; decomposition, 202–204
Party government: and Cabinet government, 21–23; and democracy, 84–86; and electoral system, 115–116; organization of, 116–119; party whip, 118–119; discipline, 119–121; and backbenchers, 116–119, 121–127; and revolts, 122–127; as model for analysis, 139–140; in Labour party, 171–172; relevance, 178–179; and collectivism, 189–196
Peacock, Alan T., 61
Peel, Sir Robert, 11, 157, 158
Penty, A. J., 173
Pinto-Duschinsky, Michael, 92, 93
Pitt, William, 14, 157
Plaid Cymru (Welsh Nationalist party), 220
Planned economy, 66–68
Plowden, Lord, 35n
Political conflict, lulls in, 146
Powell, Enoch, 122n
Pressure groups: emergence of, 11; party, class, and, 149–152
Prime Minister: authority of, 28–29, 31–32, 43–47; choice of cabinet, 30
Public Accounts Committee, 111, 112
Public Expenditure Survey Committee, 80
Pulzer, Peter, 204n

Radicals, values of, 162–163, 165–166, 167, 168
Rationalism, 155, 159; as element of modernity, 8
Reform, 9–14, 143; of bureaucracy, 54–56; new politics of, 218–220
Reform Act of 1832, 12–13, 162, 166
Reform Act of 1867, 24, 136, 147
Reform Act of 1884, 164

Resale Price Maintenance Bill, and Conservative revolt, 124, 157
Roosevelt, Franklin Delano, 4
Rose, Richard, 115n, 205, 223
Rudolph, Lloyd, 8n
Rudolph, Susanne, 8n
Ruskin, John, 173

St. Simon, Count Claude Henri de, 153
Salisbury, Robert Cecil, 3d Marquess of, 32, 133, 193
Scanlon, Hugh, 184
Schumpeter, Joseph A., 94, 139, 153; on England, 17–20, 56–57
Scotland, revival of nationalism, 59, 104, 219–220
Scottish National Party, 219
Select Committee on Estimates, 110
Select Committee on Nationalized Industries, 112
Select Committee on Public Expenditure, 110
Select Committee on Statutory Instruments (Scrutininzing Committee), 106
Self-criticism, 4
Shaw, Bernard, on Fabian Society, 18
Shaw, Tom, 84
SHELTER, 219
Shils, Edward, 154n
Shore, Peter, 198
Short Time Committee for the Ten Hour Bill, 11
Silver, Allan, 207n
Smith, Adam, 14, 67; role in reform, 11
Social Democratic Federation, 18
Socialism: German vs. British, 17–18; Labour party, 168, 171–173
Sovereignty: and symbolism, 86–91; and party, 148
Specialization: and control of public sector, 50; and political development, 149
Speer, Albert, 6
Stability: elements of, 12–14; political elites as factor of, 18–19, 21, 139

Stewart, Michael, 32
Stokes, Donald, 140, 205n, 206, 208, 218
Stormont Parliament, 222, 223
Stuart, Charles (Bonnie Prince Charlie), 147
Suez Canal crisis, 46–47, 129–130, 175
Swedish Employers' Federation, 187

Taxation, 108
Technocracy, as new elitism, 139
Timuss, Richard, 198
Tocqueville, Alexis de: on France, 12; on England, 12–14, 19, 94
Tory party, 141, 142, 147; history, 156–159, 165; vs. Whigs, 159–161
Trade associations, 186–189
Trade unions: and economic planning, 68–69, 74–75; reform controversy, 125–127; and functional representation, 182–186; in Labour party structure, 194–195
Trades Union Congress (T.U.C.), 16, 125, 126, 194; origins, 167–168; membership, 182–186; Scottish, 219–220
Treasury, 68, 75–77; and economic control, 77–82
Tudor monarchs, origins of parties under, 156, 159, 160, 161

Ulman, Lloyd, 74n
Ulster, see Northern Ireland
Unions, see Trade unions
United States: party government, 21, 140; cabinet, 47; absence of Socialist party in, 154

Values: and party development, 155–159; Liberal party, 162–163; Radicals, 162–163, 165–166, 167, 168
Vectis Nationalists, 220
Voluntarism, 155, 215; as element of modernity, 8
Voting: and class, 204–208, 210–214;

new volatility in, 208–210; election results, 1832–1970, 228–229

Wales, nationalism in, 59, 104, 220
Walker, Patrick Gordon, 27n, 28n, 33n
Wallas, Graham, 215
Webb, Sidney, 194
Welfare state, 172; founding, 14–21; see also Collectivism
Whig party, 141, 142, 147, 151; and aristocracy in political development, 152, 159–161; secularism, 161
Whitley Commission, 173

Wilson, Des, 219
Wilson, Harold, 31, 32, 96, 132 137, 213; and controversy over trade union reform, 125–126; and foreign policy, 198
Wilson government, 121, 158, 190; problems of, 28, 75, 77, 219; structure of, 39–40, 53, 62, 110–111
Wiseman, Jack, 61
Wootton, Barbara, 69n

Your Personal Guide to the Future Labour Offers YOU, 177

About the Author

Samuel H. Beer, general editor of *Patterns of Government* and author of Part 1, "Modern Political Development," and Part 2, "The British Political System," is Eaton Professor of the Science of Government at Harvard University. He studied at the University of Michigan and Oxford University and won his Ph.D. at Harvard. Chairman of the Department of Government at Harvard from 1954 to 1958, he is the author of *The City of Reason, Treasury Control,* and *British Politics in the Collectivist Age,* which was given the Woodrow Wilson Award as the "best book on politics, government or international affairs published in the United States in 1965." He served as Vice-President of the American Political Science Association in 1964–1965, has held Fulbright and Guggenheim Fellowships, and was Messenger Lecturer at Cornell University in 1969. His principal fields of interest are comparative politics and American federalism, and he has published articles on political parties, economic planning, the British Parliament, the methodology of social science, state government, and American political thought. He has been active in Democratic party politics and recently served as a member of the McGovern-Fraser Commission on Delegate Selection and Party Structure.